KU-784-364

MORE
case studies in reference work

AN LEABHARLANN,
CEARD CHOLÁISTE RÉIGIÚM
LEITIR CEANAINN.

OTHER BOOKS BY DENIS GROGAN

Case studies in reference work
Science and technology: an introduction to the literature

MORE
case studies
in
reference
work

DENIS GROGAN BA FLA

HEAD OF THE DEPARTMENT OF BIBLIOGRAPHICAL STUDIES
COLLEGE OF LIBRARIANSHIP WALES

AN LEABHARLANN,
CEARD CHOLÁISTE RÉIGIÚM
LEITIR CEANAINN.

CLIVE BINGLEY *b* LONDON

FIRST PUBLISHED 1972 BY CLIVE BINGLEY LTD
16 PEMBRIDGE ROAD LONDON W11
SET IN 10 ON 12 POINT LINOTYPE TIMES AND PRINTED IN UK
BY THE CENTRAL PRESS (ABERDEEN) LTD
COPYRIGHT © DENIS JOSEPH GROGAN 1972
ALL RIGHTS RESERVED
0 85157 124 7

contents

introduction

THE ENCOURAGING RECEPTION given to my *Case studies in reference work* (1967) has persuaded me to offer this second collection of case notes on the use of information sources. The sources demonstrated in the earlier collection were limited to general reference works, and this restriction has been relaxed in this work to embrace, for instance, books of quotations, biographical dictionaries, and gazetteers, but specific subject sources as such are not treated. As in *Case studies,* however, this limitation applies only to the sources used and not to the problems discussed in the individual cases, some of which involve very specific subjects indeed. Once again the cases are grouped into chapters for convenience. These groupings are not mutually exclusive categories, nor is it intended to imply that every reference enquiry will be found to fall neatly into one or the other. This is a textbook and the groupings are those that have been found useful for teaching purposes.

The interested reader is invited to consult the introduction to *Case studies* for a brief discussion of the principles followed in the selection and preparation of the cases. Throughout the library profession in recent years there has been great interest in the use of ' the case method ', and there are now well over a dozen published collections of such cases in librarianship. It is worth emphasising, however, that there are several kinds of cases and several methods of using them. One interesting variety, deriving from the method pioneered at the Harvard Business School, is the case presented as a ' situation ' or ' problem ' for which the student is encouraged to suggest a

7

solution (or indeed solutions, for there are often several). The case histories in this and my previous collection derive from a much older tradition, best exemplified in the legal and medical textbooks, and pioneered in librarianship over thirty years ago by Herbert Woodbine in the pages of the *Library Association record,* and by Ranganathan, whose *Reference service* (1940) was the first published collection of case studies in our field. These are *resolved* cases, complete descriptions of particular problems from start to finish, including the ' solution ' arrived at.

This renewed interest in case studies has not been without its misunderstandings. It is not sufficiently realised that the compiler of a collection of cases cannot proceed merely by objective sampling, however scientifically performed. Each case must be subjectively chosen to demonstrate a specific point, and, ideally, to illustrate a particular principle of general application. For instance, it is an observable fact that often when asked for information on a particular subject (such as infra-red cooking, or piano-tuning, or computer graphics, or television announcing), the reference librarian will immediately recall to mind a specific book devoted to the topic. Furthermore, he may be able to locate it right away on the shelves, without benefit of catalogue or bibliography or reference book. I have myself done just this hundreds of times. But there is no profit in describing such an incident in a case study. For one thing, despite the glow that one feels at the time, it is no more reference work than the butcher retrieving for his customer a lamb chop from his cold store, or the railway booking-office clerk producing on request a first-class return ticket to Aberystwyth. To maintain otherwise is to reduce this area of the reference librarian's art to a mere memory skill. But even more importantly, the narration of such an event as a case history *does not teach the student anything about reference method,* for, however frequently it occurs in practice, it does not illustrate any principle that he can apply in a wider context.

These cases then, like those in my earlier book, are hand-picked. They also describe actual problems and actual searches, and are therefore not set up as models to be copied, for this is not a ' how-to-do-it ' book. Its aim is simply to illuminate the reference process by showing how reference sources *have been used* in real situations. Of course I have attempted to eliminate cases that would mislead or confuse the student, for he is surely already aware that reference librarians occasionally behave in illogical, inconsistent, unpredictable, and inexplicable fashion. But as they share this behaviour pattern with practically the whole of the human race, I have thought it superfluous to illustrate it by case histories in a textbook of librarianship.

I must again pay tribute to my own students both postgraduate and undergraduate at the College of Librarianship Wales for their continued tolerance.

Aberystwyth   **D J Grogan**
September 1971

AN LEABHARLANN,
CEARD CHOLÁISTE RÉIGIÚM
LEITIR CEANAINN.

1

periodicals

THE NORMAL REACTION of the reference librarian in a well-stocked library when asked for information on a particular subject is to head for the books on that subject. This is a response no doubt conditioned in librarians (at least subconsciously) by hundreds of years of professional practice amid their carefully classified and catalogued collections. Probably the vast majority of such material-finding requests for ' something on ' a topic are satisfied by recourse to a convenient and appropriate book. Indeed, a good library should be programmed to respond to such approaches automatically by means of its catalogue, its classification scheme, its layout, its shelf-guiding, *without the intervention of the reference librarian.*

Frequently, of course, he will find himself assisting the hesitant or inexperienced or reluctant or merely lazy reader to operate the system. Librarians have always helped their readers and, it is hoped, always will. But he should not deceive himself that by locating books on a shelf in a merely routine fashion he is practising the art (or science) of reference work, except in those cases where he is positively compensating for the deficiencies of the system, or where the reader can give no precise indication of his needs. Real reference work only starts either when it is discovered that the system is not programmed to respond to a particular type of request, as for instance, many enquiries for specific facts which the librarian can unearth only by calling upon his knowledge of reference and bibliographical sources; or, when the system does respond to a particular approach, but does so inadequately.

It is this latter position that confronts the librarian (and his reader) when he discovers that the books on the subject (and those related books which are drawn to his attention by the system, *ie* by the classification scheme or the catalogue entries) do not furnish the required information. Indeed in some instances, particularly if the enquirer needs the most recent information, the librarian will not even trouble to approach the books, but will turn almost instinctively to what in fact is the largest single group of reference material—the periodical literature.

Case 1: When asked some years ago for a book on sauna baths the librarian recalled that he had seen these advertised in the Sunday papers over a period of some months, but he was not quite sure what they were. He tried the most recent dictionary he could think of (*Penguin English dictionary*) where he was gratified to read that a sauna was a 'Finnish type of steam bath'. He was not so fortunate when he attempted to find a book on the subject: there was nothing in the library catalogue, or in *British books in print*, or in BNB. There was nothing in *Subject guide to books in print* either, so he worked his way back through the volumes of *Cumulative book index*, where he soon found a 235-page work by A S Olin *Sauna, the way to health* (1963), sub-titled 'America's first book about the sauna'. Three years further back he found in the CBI volume covering 1960 an earlier work presumably in English but with a Helsinki imprint and a price in Finnish marks, containing 126 pages and entitled *Sauna, the Finnish bath* by H J Viherjuuri. This was the sum total of his findings, however, even though he scanned not only CBI but also the whole of the Library of Congress *Catalog: books: subjects* back to its commencement in 1950.

When reporting this to his reader he had to explain that neither of these books was in the library, and might take some time to obtain. As this was received with less than enthusiasm, he suggested he could perhaps find something in a journal if the reader was prepared to wait a little longer. A rapid check was made of the last six or seven years of the general periodical indexes. There was nothing to be found in *British humanities index* (or its predecessor); the only reference in *Social sciences and humanities index* (and its predecessor) was to a ten-page article in the *Annals of the Association of American Geographers* sub-titled 'a cultural index to settlement'.

11

There were more references in *Readers' guide to periodical litera-ture*, but all were to journals not taken by the library. And then the librarian remembered he had not tried *British technology index:* steam baths could be technological, he supposed. And there at last he found an illustrated article from *Steam and heating engineer* for November 1965: ' Sauna bath: a form of health treatment new to this country '.

[Sauna baths are now widespread in Britain, as the yellow pages of any telephone directory will show, but at the time of writing no book on the subject has yet appeared in BNB. The 1960 book by Viherjuuri, mentioned above, was listed in the *Bookseller* for the last week of February 1969, and appears currently in *British books in print*.]

It is impossible to overstate the importance of periodicals as sources of information. Margaret Hutchins says '. . . almost every question *can* be answered by means of a periodical, if one searches long enough '. Citation studies show that in science and technology some four-fifths of all literature cited is from periodicals. There is evidence, where independent periodicals divisions are set up within libraries, that they are taking over substantial parts of the enquiry work of the general library. Margaret Hutchins goes on to say, however, ' it does not follow that [every question] can *best* be answered that way ', and here lies the source of the librarian's dilemma. He knows that periodicals are more difficult to manipulate than books: he is aware in particular that they are not organised for consultation as are other reference sources like encyclopedias, dictionaries, yearbooks and directories. When, and for what, should he turn to periodicals for information?

There is no really satisfying form of words to describe precisely what a periodical is. The American Library Association definition of ' serial ' (a slightly broader term) serves as well as any: ' a publication issued in successive parts, usually at regular intervals, and, as a rule, intended to be continued indefinitely '. The special role that periodicals play in reference work stems directly from the differences they have with books; this definition serves to point out the first and perhaps the most significant—their currency. Where a book is a once-and-for-all publication, inevitably out-of-date by the time it appears, the periodical has a quarterly or monthly or

12

even weekly chance to come again. The simple technical and economic facts of publishing life give the periodical a major advantage in the speed of its printing and distribution, for its contents are usually brief, are issued unbound, and are in most cases sent direct to waiting subscribers. It is by definition closer to the frontiers of knowledge, and the librarian turns first to periodicals therefore for information too recent for the books.

Case 2: When asked over the telephone for information on space shuttles, the information officer was sufficiently well-informed to be aware that they were a recently much-discussed type of transport in space. He knew that this enquirer, an engineer, would want hard technical data and not mere newspaper discussion. As for trying to trace a book on the subject, that was a course never even contemplated; for if a book had been published (and he felt confident it had not) it could not be sufficiently up-to-date in such a rapidly developing subject field. He turned immediately to his periodical indexes, and specifically to *British technology index*. It took him a moment to find the heading he wanted: the only kind of shuttles that appeared were 'shuttles: looms', and under 'space flight' he was confronted by the command 'see astronautics'. Once he had homed on to 'astronautics: transporters', however, immediately in the current monthly issue he found a reference to a six-page illustrated article, 'Space shuttle' by Kenneth Gatland, in *Spaceflight* for May 1971. Tracking backwards he soon found a couple more from 1970 journals: 'Europe and the space shuttle' in *Flight*, and 'Space shuttle: NASA leads Europe in military two step' in *Science journal*. As a first stage, therefore, he decided to obtain copies of this introductory material for his enquirer, while holding himself available if required to extend the search into the specialised astronautics indexing and abstracting services such as STAR (*Scientific and technical aerospace reports*) and *International aerospace abstracts*.

It is a cliché now to say that books (particularly in science and technology contain only second-hand information, but in many subjects indeed the first book on a subject is only a digest of the periodical articles already published, and for further advances in

13

knowledge the reader has to turn to more recent periodicals. As Collison puts it, ' The extent of knowledge in any field consists . . . of the information given in the books on the subject *plus* the periodical articles that have been published since the latest book was written '.

Case 3: The tutor-librarian in a large college of education library had been asked for advice by a student preparing a project on the peaceful uses of atomic energy. In particular she was interested in the use of nuclear explosives in civil engineering. It did not take much bibliographical searching to find in BNB for 1968 at the class number for civil engineering excavation (624.152)—traced *via* the index entry 'nuclear explosives'—a 335-page work by Edward Teller *The constructive use of nuclear explosives.* Although there was no copy in the college library, a phone call to the local city library soon procured the promise of a copy on library interloan. Meanwhile the tutor-librarian felt obliged to point out that the student should also endeavour to take note of developments in the three or four years since the writing of this book, particularly in a field of such obvious potential for development. He therefore introduced her to the periodical indexes, especially *British technology index.* Under ' nuclear explosives : excavation ' a good half-dozen recent articles were traced in periodicals such as *Journal of nuclear energy, Nuclear energy, Journal of the British Nuclear Energy Society,* but the most recent, by a principal scientific officer from Aldermaston writing in *New scientist* (the only one taken by the college library!), had this to say: ' . . . none of the two dozen or so suggested engineering uses of nuclear explosives have as yet been *demonstrated* to be feasible, economic and safe in practice '.

For any serious searcher using a library there is the major difficulty in most libraries that the key to its collections, the catalogue, does not include periodical articles. He has to rely entirely on bibliographies, which for the librarian (or reader) conducting a literature search for books are supplementary to the catalogue. As we have seen, the first of these bibliographies are the general periodical indexes, of which it has been graphically claimed that they turn piles of waste paper into useful reference tools.

14

The absolute necessity in some subjects, particularly in the fields of science and technology, of access to the very latest information is the explanation for many special libraries spending more on periodicals than on books. In any enquiry, if really up-to-date, first-hand information is essential, then almost invariably periodical articles will be required, but it would be a mistake to assume that the reader (even in science and technology) always requires this. Those textbooks and handbooks and encyclopedias and treatises which expound and survey and summarise and articulate are in many cases just as suitable, frequently more available, and certainly more manageable.

Case 4: The request received in a large college of technology library for details of machines for grading eggs had come by phone from the Department of Mechanical Engineering. In pondering just where to look, the tutor-librarian could see that this was without doubt a very specialised, highly technical enquiry, suggesting a search through periodical indexes such as *British technology index* and *Applied science and technology index,* or the more specialised abstracting tools such as *Engineering index* and *Packaging abstracts,* with perhaps even a patent search to follow. But then the thought came to him that grading eggs was by no means a new problem; it must be covered in the basic works on the topic of weights and measures. It did not take him long to locate what was obviously the standard work on the subject, a three-volume treatise by T J Metcalfe *Weighing machines* (1969-), described in its preface as ' a full exposition of the theory and practice of visible weighing machine construction . . . Endeavour has been to include all basic patterns of weighing machines currently produced for use for trade '. He found that the whole of chapter 12 in the first volume was devoted to egg-grading machines—seven pages of text and two folding diagrams.

It would also be a mistake to suppose that the periodical's only function is to update the book, or, to put it another way, to take for granted that all the information in the periodical articles eventually gets incorporated into the books. In reference work periodicals are called upon very frequently for those topics which are not recent, but which are too small, or too trivial, or too local, or too transient, or too specialised ever to justify treatment at length in book form. There are countless thousands of these, usually subjects which are of interest only to a limited number (such as formation aerobatics, or wheelchair games, or the printing of banknotes) or subjects on which there is simply not very much to say (such as the manufacture of lead pencils, or the design of telephone kiosks, or the history of the zip fastener). Nevertheless, librarians know that readers will continue to ask after these things, and that more often than not periodical articles will supply the information needed.

Case 5: When it was announced from Buckingham Palace in October 1965 that the Prince of Wales, then aged sixteen, was to spend a term at an Australian school there was a flurry of interest in this institution so suddenly thrust into the limelight. The name was new to most people in Britain, and even the reference librarian, asked on the phone for ' anything on Geelong College ', knew no more than he had, providentially, read in his *Times* while commuting to work that morning.

He found an extensive section devoted to education in the *Official year book of the Commonwealth of Australia* and a briefer account in the Europa volume on the *Far East and Australia: a survey and directory,* but neither mentioned any school by name or referred to the existence of a directory of Australian schools. The ten-volume *Australian encyclopaedia* listed by Walford might well have been a good source to try, but the library did not possess a copy.

Not in a particularly hopeful frame of mind he turned to his general periodical indexes, scanning in turn the last few years of *British humanities index/Subject index to periodicals, Readers' guide to periodical literature,* and *International index.* The first two proved to be of no assistance, but a solitary entry in the last led him to a four-page spread, in the *Illustrated London news* of 11th November 1961, with well over a dozen photographs of this ' great Australian school '.

Case 6: The request received one evening in a public reference library about crowd safety in football grounds came from a young boy. A moment's discussion revealed that he had chosen to write a report on this topic as a school task. The librarian felt confident that it would not prove too difficult to produce a sufficient amount of information of the right level to satisfy this very modest request.

Ten minutes later his confidence had begun to ebb when after looking through the football books on his shelves and the lending library shelves, and a search of BNB back to 1950, he was still empty-handed. Even on the subject of football grounds in general he had traced virtually nothing. His next port of call, therefore, was the periodical indexes. Starting with a ten-year check of *British humanities index,* his only find was made at the very outset in the latest quarterly issue, traced without undue effort under 'football grounds: safety': an article from the *Sunday times* for 10th January 1971, entitled 'Football safety: a history of neglect '. To try to increase his meagre catch he next tried the H W Wilson indexes, in the hope of some comparative information from the US. Referred from ' football stadiums ' to ' stadiums ', he found lots of general articles but his specific haul was disappointing. Neither *Social sciences and humanities index* nor *Readers' guide to periodical literature* had anything on safety questions, other than a couple of references on the scarcely vital topic of splinter-free seating.

The location in a newspaper of the solitary reference so far traced reminded him to check the *Index to the Times.* This led very quickly (under ' football (assn.): grounds ') to a report in the issue for 31st July 1970 about the approval of a Football Association plan requiring grounds to issue a safety certificate, covering facilities and installations, including terracing, floodlighting and seating. Mention was made of ' last year's Lang report on crowd behaviour and control '.

Although perhaps not specifically on safety, this report clearly had some relevance and so the librarian attempted to trace it. ' Last year ' meant 1969, so BNB was consulted, under Lang as the presumed author, and under subject. Achieving no success, he tried the 1968 and 1970 volumes and then *Whitaker's Cumulative book list* for good measure, but to no avail. Pausing for a moment to contemplate, the thought struck him that this could be an official report, perhaps even a government report with Lang as chairman. And so it proved: an examination of the annual *Government publications* for 1969 revealed the Ministry of Housing and Local Government *Report of the working party on crowd behaviour at football matches,* chairman John Lang. Although only twenty pages, this was judged clearly worth acquiring and so an urgent order was despatched to HMSO, while in the meantime the two newspaper articles were produced for the young enquirer.

Case 7: The librarian in a college library in the Midlands had never heard of Alun Hoddinott, about whom one of his readers was asking, but after a few moments' discussion he had established that he was a contemporary Welsh composer and musician. His entry in *Who's who,* describing him as Professor of Music at the University College of South Wales, extended to 38 lines, including a list of his compositions, but this was not enough for the enquirer who said she wanted something 'more personal', to help her in writing a programme note. Surmising that a brief, popular account would probably serve the turn, the librarian decided not to plunge into the musical literature at once, but first to try the general periodical indexes. Commencing with *British humanities index* he discovered he was in luck, for he soon traced an article on Hoddinott written by Edward Greenfield in the *Guardian* for 27th February 1969, entitled 'Master of the Principality's music'. Although not retaining any newspapers permanently, the library did maintain a three-year file of the *Guardian,* among others. When she saw the article, the reader's reaction was 'This will do fine'.

A minor difficulty in practice is to pick out for checking in the periodical indexes just those topics on which no books have been written. This is really impossible to accomplish every time, particularly with new subjects such as (at the time of writing) the use of state forests for recreation, genetic counselling, electronic video-recording cassettes for the domestic market, the open university, or with older subjects showing a recent spurt in interest such as (again at the time of writing) player-pianos, voting by referendum, local radio, concrete verse. It is a not uncommon experience in the case of topics such as these for the very first book to appear literally while the librarian is conducting his search. More chastening, and of course even more frequent, is the case where the first book is published perhaps just within a week or a month after the search is concluded.

Case 8: Some years ago a librarian of a public commercial and technical library was asked for information on industrial espionage. Public interest in this topic was still dormant at that time and the librarian had to ask the reader one or two questions to clear his mind before beginning the search. The enquirer was in fact a free-lance journalist preparing an article on the growing problem of, for instance, employees selling a company's secrets to a rival firm.

A check of the library catalogue and of BNB showed, as expected, that a whole book on the topic was unlikely, so the librarian plunged right into the periodical indexes. *British humanities index* referred him from 'espionage' to 'spying', where under 'spying, industrial' he soon located articles from the *Times, Guardian, Observer* and *Sunday times,* of various dates in 1965 and 1966. But he was interested to note that although he checked back a further ten years no earlier articles were traced, confirming his impression that this was a topic of quite recent interest, at least in Britain. He had no success with *Social sciences and humanities index* (or its predecessor *International index*), but *Readers' guide to periodical literature* under 'spies, industrial' furnished him over a ten-year period with over twenty references to US journals such as *Time, Newsweek, Readers' digest, Business week.*

And then shortly after the reader had gone contentedly on his way two books were published within a month of each other: Peter Hamilton *Espionage and subversion in an industrial society* (August 1967), and Ronald Payne *Private spies* (August 1967). In the bibliography appended to the former of these the first sentence read : ' The author has been able to discover no previous works of reference bearing directly on the subjects of this book, and he has already pointed out in the Acknowledgements that much of his information has come from press sources '. The second book, a more popular account of what the author described as ' an alarming phenomenon —industrial espionage, the fastest growing business of modern times ', quoted examples ranging from ' The $100,000,000 case ' to the instance of ' employees disclosing to another firm the names of male customers confidentially supplied by the firm with toupées '.

What many enquirers do find it difficult to believe is the surprisingly large number of subjects of very far from minor interest and concern that do not seem to have had a book written about them.

Case 9: When asked in a busy city lending library for a book on the manufacture of bells the readers' adviser made confidently for the catalogue. There were, it is true, a handful of works on bells listed there, but they were almost all on bell-ringing. This was also the case with *British books in print* and *Subject guide to books in print*. A careful check through BNB brought to light an occasional pamphlet on the bells of a particular church or region, or of a specific founder, but there was no solid work on the actual making of bells. To trace quickly the books on a specific subject prior to BNB the librarian had always found invaluable the *Subject index of the London Library*. Although providing bibliographical access to over half a million titles, the four volumes can be checked in a moment; but here again was the same story—dozens of books on bells, apparently nothing specific on bell manufacture.

Appreciative by now of just what a specialist topic he had been set to look for, he went across to the reference library to scan the periodical indexes, warning his reader as he went that a book to read by his fireside seemed a forlorn hope. It did not take more than a few minutes with *British technology index* to locate under the heading 'bells: casting' a short illustrated article by C J Evans 'From foundry to cathedral' in *Tin uses* for 1970 (not available in the library, as it happened), together with a whole series of articles in what was obviously the prime source of technical information on the subject, the *Foundry trade journal*—of which a file was available for the enquirer to peruse.

It is said that with experience the reference librarian sometimes will develop a sixth sense which tells him that there is a book (and one book only) on artificial cricket pitches (Reginald Wesley *Artificial cricket pitches* (1955), traced *via* BNB or CBI), or on building stone walls without mortar (Frederick Rainsford-Hannay *Dry stone walling* (1957), traced *via* BNB, CBI or Library of Congress *Catalog: books: subjects*), or on coal-hole covers (Aescalapius Junior, *Opercula (London coal plates)* (1929, reprinted 1965), traced *via* BNB under 'coal plates: cast iron: artistic metalwork'); but that the book on building ice-skating rinks, or on the history of pole-vaulting, or on traffic lights has yet to be written. To tell the truth, apart from those instances where up-to-the-minute data is essential, there is no difference at first sight between those queries best answered from books and those for which a periodical article will serve. Standard practice is to try the library catalogue and the bibliographies of books first, unless there is a particularly obvious reason for starting with the periodical indexes. One such reason would be an enquiry, perhaps historical, which can only be satisfactorily answered from sources contemporary with the event, normally more easily traced in periodical form.

Case 10: A phone call received in a large city reference library simply asked what the opinion of the Victorians was about Atlantis, the fabulous island that vanished beneath the waters of the Atlantic. Although the librarian was dying to ask why his caller required to know this, he curbed his curiosity and turned to the encyclopedias. *Britannica* had a brief though informative article on this ' legendary island in the Atlantic ocean ', tracing literary references as far back as Plato's *Timaeus* and to the Egyptian belief in its existence as a powerful kingdom 9,000 years earlier. Nearer to our own time, ' Even in the 17th and 18th centuries the credibility of the legend was seriously debated, and sometimes admitted, even by Montaigne, Buffon and Voltaire '. But there was no mention of the 19th century.

In the hope of contemporary articles in the journals of the Victorian era the librarian consulted *Poole's index to periodical literature,* where he soon traced perhaps a dozen possibles. Concentrating his attention on British journals, he selected for his enquirer's attention four likely titles: ' The lost Atlantis: examination of the legend ' (in *Royal Historical Society transactions*); ' Lost Atlantis and the Challenger soundings ' and ' Search for the lost Atlantis ' (both in *Nature*); ' The lost Atlantis: not a myth ' (in *Journal of science*). He was of course not helped in his selection by *Poole's* practice of indicating only the first page of a citation, thus obviating any hint as to length. *Poole's* other idiosyncrasy, the omission of dates, he was able to circumvent by means of the ' Chronological conspectus ', where he learned that the dates of the four articles were, respectively, 1886, 1876 (or 1877), 1882 (or 1883), and 1879.

An additional related advantage over the book that is bestowed by the periodical's currency is its uniquely favourable position to reflect the *changes* in contemporary life and thought. Periodicals are invaluable for a continuing as opposed to a static survey of public opinion. Used imaginatively, they have a special value in recreating a mood or an atmosphere. Leafing through the bound volumes of a journal is a well-tried method for getting the 'feel' of a period: immersion in the early issues of the *Motor* or *Autocar*, for instance, gives a reader the unmistakable flavour of what motoring was like in the first decade of the century. Less well known is the similar use of the general periodical indexes, *without* following up the references, to gauge trends over a span of years.

Case 11: A student approached the enquiry desk in a college library with an open book in his hand. He showed the librarian a brief passage, asking him to read it. From the title page the librarian saw that it was an American work by M L Ernst and A U Schwartz *Privacy: the right to be left alone* (1962). The page that he had been shown stated that the origins of this right ' do not lurk in the gloom of the far past, for if we go to England we shall not find it. It is odd that the British, who really fasten themselves in behind walls and gates and hedges and live quite impregnably, have no rubric privacy, but so it is.' The enquiry posed by the reader stemmed from his feeling that the scene had changed considerably in Britain in the ten years or so since the publication of this book, with the citizenry now far more vigilant against infringements of the right to privacy. What he required specifically was a brief outline of this growth of this awareness in recent years.

The librarians knew that this development in public opinion would of course be reflected and indeed documented in the periodical press of the previous decade; he felt equally sure that this reader would not wish to work his way through the literature merely to gauge the trend. The chances were remote that a routine search of the general periodical indexes would reveal a summary of the movement of public opinion that was both brief and up-to-date. He decided therefore that they would indeed check through the periodical indexes together, not with the intention of locating articles on the topic to read, but in the hope of obtaining an overview of the changes in public attitudes over a period as reflected in the approach and distribution of articles published on the subject over the period under scrutiny.

Taking 1962 as the starting point (the date of the Ernst and

Schwartz volume) they first of all worked backwards to see if indeed it was the case that the British had not in the past paid much attention to the right of privacy. Certainly, the Library Association *Subject index to periodicals* bore this out, for the only article in the ten years prior to 1962 was a 23-page paper by A J Ayer in the 1959 *Proceedings of the British Academy* entitled quite simply ' Privacy '. The librarian knew enough of the work of Professor Ayer and of the British Academy to surmise that this paper would be a learned philosophical essay.

Moving forward through *British humanities index* from 1962, on the other hand, they discovered an outburst of interest in 1962 with no fewer than fourteen articles. Closer examination revealed that no less than twelve of them (including contributions by Brigitte Bardot, Paul Getty, and Adam Faith) were from what was obviously a special issue of *Twentieth century* for Spring 1962, extending to well over a hundred pages. Other articles during this and the following year, such as ' The protection of privacy ' (thirteen pages in *Modern law review*) and 'A right to privacy?' (twelve pages in *Juridical review*) were a clear indication that the legal profession was beginning to show concern.

The dwindling of entries in the *Index* over the succeeding years seemed to indicate a lull in interest, but when the topic began to figure again, the librarian noted that the articles were now appearing in the much more widely circulating weeklies such as *New statesman, New society,* and *Spectator;* secondly that from 1969 onwards many articles with titles such as ' When they've got your number ' began to appear under a separate heading ' computers and privacy ', adding a new dimension to the problem. Then among the 1970 references was noticed one entitled ' Government will set up committee to consider right of privacy '. Finally, and rather ominously, the last to be traced, in the *Economist* for 1971, had the title 'Is 1984 here?'

It cannot be assumed that all the people who know most about their subjects will write books on them. There are many scholars and scientists who have built world-wide reputations on the papers they have published in the learned journals, but who have not produced a ' book ' in the conventional sense. There are many other famous figures among the ranks of businessmen, politicians, men of action, for instance, who are simply not men of letters: surprising though it may seem to the librarian struggling in a sea of books written by all kinds of people, there are those who would no more think of writing a book than of entering a monastery. But a fair proportion of them have been willing to string sufficient words together to make a paper in a journal, or to give an interview which then appears as a periodical article.

Case 12: When asked for information about John Ford's views on film-making, the librarian in a major research library did not antici-pate much difficulty. Ford he knew as one of the world's major directors, renowned particularly for his contribution to the film 'western'. He was slightly concerned to discover in the library catalogue no books by Ford, although there were one or two *about* him. The quickest way he could think of to check on this was to look up his entry in *Who's who,* where invariably provision is made for a section headed 'Publications'. Thirty one lines were found about John Ford (real name Sean O'Feeney), described as the director of more than eighty films, but no publications were listed. The British Museum *Catalogue of printed books to 1955* and its *Ten year supplement, 1956-1965* gives his real name in its Irish form, Sean O'Fearna, but the only entry was a 'see' reference to *An index to the films of John Ford.* The Library of Congress *Catalog of books/National union catalogue* was only slightly more helpful, listing a 176-page Danish work published at Copenhagen in 1968 by the Danish Film Museum, and a 1967 book by Peter Bogdano-vich, *John Ford.*

Clearly the great man was not one for rushing into print, and so the librarian's thoughts turned to periodicals, working his way back in turn through the last few years of *Social sciences and humanities index, Readers' guide to periodical literature* and *British humanities index.* With the first of these he had no luck at all; in the second he traced articles *about* Ford but not *by* him; but in the third he struck gold at last with the report of an interview in the *Listener* for 12th February 1970: 'John Ford talks to Philip Jenkinson'. Encouraged by his success, he continued his search back through the predecessor of BHI, the Library Association *Subject index to periodicals.* A minor hazard encountered *en route* was the presence of many articles about John Ford, the seventeenth century dramatist. The BM *Catalogue* and the LC *Catalog* distinguished the two, by adding the word 'dramatist' or dates of birth and death, but here both men were confusingly subsumed under one heading, 'Ford, John'. Eventually, however, he found in the 1951 volume another reference: Lindsay Anderson 'The quiet man', described as '[Interview with Ford]', published in the journal *Sequence*.

As the reader still seemed to require more, the librarian suggested that an examination of the references *on* Ford might be profitable. Together they looked at the latest of them, the Bogdanovich 1967 title, which turned out to be a very useful, well-illustrated small paperback. They were interested to read that Ford 'genuinely does not like to be interviewed and becomes bored discussing his films'; they agreed that the author had brought off quite a *coup* by managing to fill 73 pages of his little book with 'an edited version of an interview with Mr Ford recorded at his home in Bel Air, California, over a period of seven days in the Summer and Fall of 1966'.

The brief bibliography at the end included two further references to items in periodicals that looked promising: an interview (probably in French) in *Cahiers du cinéma,* no 183 for 1966, and 'Ford on Ford: report of a UCLA symposium' in the June-July 1964 issue of *Films in review.*

[The January-March 1971 issue of *British humanities index* contains a reference to a recent interview by Joseph McBride in *Sight and sound,* commencing with the words, 'Knowing John Ford's fabled disdain for interviewers . . .' The text contains the claim by Ford that 'This is positively the last interview I am going to give . . . everybody asks the same questions, all you people, and I'm sick and tired of trying to answer them, because I don't know the answers'.]

A further common type of enquiry pointing in the direction of a periodical article for its solution is the request demanding no more than a brief summary, because another of the significant differences between the book and the periodical is the not inconsiderable advantage of brevity characteristic of the average periodical article. It is not unusual to find such summaries are also more readable than an account in a book, and so they are found of value both for the scholar in search of a condensed treatment of a topic unfamiliar to him and for the man in the street looking for popularisation. It should never be forgotten that the periodical (in the form of a

' magazine ') is more familiar to the great majority of the public than the hard-back book. Students in particular, often hard-pressed for time, are discovering in increasing numbers the advantages of the periodical article.

Case 13: When the young enquirer in a busy public library asked about Jensen's work on race differences, the librarian remembered that a major controversy had erupted on this topic some months ago. He seemed to recall that Jensen was a Harvard psychologist, but a few moments discussion made it clear that the enquirer was not a psychologist, and did not want Jensen's original paper, merely an ' outline '.

Hopefully, the librarian tried *Social sciences and humanities index* under ' Jensen ', but by the time he had gone back five years without success he knew he would have to try elsewhere. Although he was certain Jensen was American, he considered *British humanities index* worth looking at. Once again a five-year check proved fruitless, although because the author section appears in the annual cumulation only of course, and not in the quarterly issues, he had author access only as far as 1969. Almost as an afterthought he turned to the main section, arranged by subject: perhaps he would find Jensen entered as a subject, not as an author. And so it proved. The 1969 volume revealed an article in the *Spectator* for 9th August entitled ' The Jensen bomb ', which gave a very brief summary of the conclusions of Dr Arthur Jensen of the University of California (*not* Harvard): ' On average the IQ of the American negro is fifteen points lower than that of the American white . . . intelligence is about 75 per cent heredity and 25 per cent environment '.

An outline was what the reader had specifically asked for, but less than one whole page of the *Spectator* was too sketchy even for him, and so the librarian set about supplementing it. Confined as it is to US periodicals published in the US yet of a general, non-technical and popular character, the *Readers' guide to periodical literature* was the obvious choice. Immediately the latest annual volume brought to light not only two articles *by* Dr Jensen, but ten articles *about* him: though a number were in journals not taken by the library, the librarian was soon able to produce a good half-dozen from the *Saturday review, New York times magazine,* and *Newsweek*

with titles such as ' IQ: God given or man made '; ' Jensenism ';
' Race and intelligence '.

[The obvious specialist indexing service, *Education index,* would
not have produced such a satisfactory outcome in this instance,
where what the reader required was a layman's summary. It would
however have located what seems to be Jensen's original 157-page
paper, ' How much can we boost IQ and scholastic achievement ',
spread over two issues of the *Harvard educational review,* together
with a round dozen of papers in this and other specialist journals
about Jensen's views.]

Even after the information in a periodical has been digested in
book form it frequently happens that the original article still needs
to be consulted for more background or detail. It must be remembered that it is the periodical that is the *primary* source in such
cases: the book is secondary, based largely, if not entirely, on the
periodical literature.

Case 14: A letter received in a large city reference library expressed
great interest in the ships of the defeated Spanish Armada that had
been wrecked on the coasts of Ireland, and asked the librarian to
suggest the best source of information on the topic. To weigh up
the size of the problem the librarian turned first to what he knew
was the most substantial recent study, Garrett Mattingly *The defeat
of the Spanish Armada* (1959), where he read through ten pages of
chapter 31, headed ' The long road home . . . around Ireland to
Spanish ports '. He learned that the commander, the Duke of
Medina Sidonia, had emphasised in the sailing orders issued to all
ships that in their flight back to Corunna ' Ireland must be given a
wide berth " for fear of the harm that may happen to you upon
that coast " '. Unfortunately, the already battered fleet ran into
nothing but storms from the worst possible quarter, the south-west,
and many ships were forced to seek Ireland. Mattingly wrote mov-
ingly: ' They came in without charts or pilots, often without
anchors, in ships so crippled as to be barely seaworthy and with
crews so weakened by privation and disease they could barely work
them, and split themselves on rocks, or wedged themselves on reefs,
or were torn from insecure anchorages by sudden squalls and dashed

27

against cliffs '. The notes to the chapter estimated the number of ships wrecked in Ireland as one galleass, ten galleons and greatships, two hulks (and possibly four more, for ' no one has ever made a real search for records concerning these four ships '), and a handful of small craft. Reference was made to a ' useful guide ' in the shape of a 23-page article by William Spotswood Green ' The wrecks of the Spanish Armada on the coast of Ireland ' in the *Geographical journal* for 1906.

Published the year after Mattingly was Michael Lewis *The Spanish Armada,* a handsome volume in the ' British battles ' series. The section of text headed ' Dispersal and disaster: Ireland ' covered nine pages, including a map of Ireland showing the sites where twelve named and five unknown ships were wrecked. Lewis strongly disagreed with Mattingly's low figure of losses, claiming the figure should be at least twenty-five ships and perhaps several more. He appealed for confirmation to the source quoted by Mattingly, ' the invaluable work of W Spotswood Green, Inspector of Irish Fisheries in the early years of this century '.

It was clear to the librarian that this article written in a periodical over sixty years previously was still the key reference, praised equally despite their differences by the two learned authors (the former was Professor of European history at Columbia University, the latter Professor of history at the Royal Naval College, Greenwich, and both had previously published extensively on the Spanish Armada). This was further confirmed by the most recent major book on the Armada, Alexander McKee *From merciless invaders* (1963). The author devoted two full chapters to the Irish wrecks including a map showing twenty-six wreck sites, and his note on sources commended the useful documentation of Green's article.

Upon examination, the Green paper turned out to be a most thorough account, read before the Royal Geographical Society, illustrated with seven photographs and a detailed map showing the sites of all the wrecks, upon which the maps by Lewis and McKee had clearly been based. It was obviously an attempt at a comprehensive study; indeed the author assumed that ' every detail that can be found out as to the wrecks is worthy of record '. His success may be measured from the discussion which followed, to which the three greatest living authorities on the subject contributed: Martin Hume expressed his gratitude for this ' extremely interesting and learned paper '; Professor Laughton thought that ' further comment

on the paper is almost unnecessary '; and Julian Corbett described it
as an ' admirably exhaustive paper '.

What these cases have not yet demonstrated is that looking up
subjects in an index is not always as simple as it sounds. There is
for example the immediate problem of which index to turn to first.
Even confined as we are for the purposes of this chapter to the
general (*ie*, multidisciplinary) indexes, we would produce different
answers in different libraries. Perhaps the only general counsel
worth giving is to search first through those tools which index titles
more likely to be located in one's own library. More positive advice
can be offered on the problem of the order in which a set of indexes
should be searched: unless the enquiry provides a clear indication
of date it is wisest to begin with the most recent issues and search
backwards. This ensures that the latest material is brought to light
first; it is not uncommon to unearth review articles and bibliographies in this way which most usefully survey all that has gone
before.

Case 15: A student in a college of commerce came to the librarian
for help with her project on the reclaiming of derelict industrial land.
She appeared to know very little about the subject, although her
enthusiasm was evident. Knowing that there was ample material on
the topic (many articles in periodicals as well as at least half-a-
dozen titles in BNB since 1956) the librarian could see that his first
task was to show her how to search for and digest this material in
an efficient and painless manner. Starting with the most recent issues
of *British technology index,* they worked their way backwards in the
hope of finding an up-to-date and brief but expert survey of the
state of the art which could serve as a starting point. They were in
luck, for in the October 1970 issue of the *Journal of the Institution
of Municipal Engineers* was a four-page illustrated article by J R
Oxenham, leading British authority on the topic and author of the
standard work in the field. Entitled ' Land reclamation ', this article
was found (when borrowed from the local public library) to be ideal
for the purpose, an authoritative yet simple account of the position
to date, with references appended.

2

A question that is impossible to answer is how far back should you check in the indexes. As one aspect of the more general problem of when to call a halt to a search, it can only be considered in relation to the topic of the enquiry.

Case 16: The topic, given as 'the use of computers to classify fingerprints', was simple enough, and presented no search problems so far as subject was concerned. It was only when the reference librarian had checked the last five years of *British technology index* to no avail that he knew he was faced with a specific search decision as to whether he should continue further with that particular index, or try the more recent years of, say, *British humanities index*. Obviously the subject was of fairly recent origin; his hunch was that it was within the last three or four years. Though he had no concrete evidence for this, he regarded himself as fairly well-informed and was well aware that among experienced reference librarians such apparently instinctive feelings are often based on subconscious knowledge—and sometimes are borne out in due course by the facts. He decided to limit his search to five years.

It had struck him at the outset that the topic partook of two quite distinct and well-established subject fields: computers (part of technology), and criminology (part of social sciences). Having searched his major index in the first field (BTI) he now turned to *Social sciences and humanities index*. Once more a five-year search revealed nothing.

Moving on to a five-year check of the more general indexes he was more fortunate: *Readers' guide to periodical literature* brought to light an article 'Computer encoding of fingerprints' in *Science news* for 25th May 1968; *British humanities index* also produced one article by C Northcote Parkinson from the *Illustrated London news* of 4th June 1966 'Digital computer . . . or all that is unprintable'. And then the last source he tried, *Applied science and technology index,* supplied a further reference from *Machine design* for 29th May 1969 entitled 'Computer reads finger prints with only one minor trouble'.

With these three references the reader was more than content, and the librarian felt he could regard the case as closed. But as he turned away he reflected on two aspects of the search: the first, most gratifying from his point of view, was the vindication of his decision to limit the search to the last five years. Indeed, as he discovered when he checked, there are *no* earlier references to be found in any of the sources he had consulted. The second aspect was the realisation in this instance of the limitations of mere titles of articles as indicators of content, for in addition to the articles he had singled out from those under the heading ' fingerprints ' there had been a number which could have been relevant, although their titles did not put beyond doubt their connection with computers, *eg,* ' Report on police checks: a fingerprint bank for nation?', 'Automating fingerprint identification', ' Hardware will automatically read, classify, and sort fingerprints '.

There is a huge literature on alphabetical subject indexing which it would be inappropriate to discuss here, for the problems are general to the whole question of the subject approach to information, and not particular to periodical subject indexes, but a brief indication of three common difficulties will be useful. Firstly, the choice of what to look under in the index may give pause for thought. It is not uncommon for the librarian to find himself with quite an adequately clear idea of what he is looking for, but to be unsure what term it will be entered under in an index.

Case 17: An elderly reader in a busy medium-sized public reference library one afternoon expressed his interest in what he called bat radar for the blind. The librarian had to ask for further elucidation of the topic, for although he knew what a bat was, and radar, and the blind, he never before encountered them in the same context. Fortunately, the enquirer was able to help by explaining in more detail what he wanted. He had heard in conversation of a new invention which permitted the blind to ' see ' in the way that a bat can ' see ' in the dark, that is to say by a kind of natural radar, making use of very high-pitched signals transmitted by the bat and picked up again as they echo back from objects in its path.

Although now quite clear as to what he was looking for, the librarian was still faced with the problem of how to approach his catalogue and the bibliographies. Taking the most obvious line first, he looked up ' bat ', ' radar ' and ' blind ' in the card catalogue: entries were found under all, but none of them combined the three in the shape of a book.

31

Turning therefore to the general periodical indexes, he had tried the last ten years of *British humanities index/Subject index to periodicals* to no avail before reflecting that he would probably have done better to start with *British technology index*. And so it turned out: in the 1967 volume he quickly found the heading he wanted, ' blind people: ultrasonic guidance aids ', and an appropriately brief article in *Engineering* for 14th July 1967, ' Electronics to the aid of the blind '. Checking further back produced more articles, *eg*, ' Sonic aid for blind people ' (in *Industrial electronics* for May 1965); ' Ultransonic sensing probe as a mobility aid for the blind ' (in *Ultrasonics* for April-June 1964); ' Ultrasonic radar guides the blind ' (in *Design and components in engineering* for April 1963). While the reader was looking at the first two of these (the remaining two journals were not taken by the library, although the librarian had checked their availability in the National Lending Library *Current periodicals received* and offered to obtain them if required), the librarian, now armed with further keywords to search under such as ' sonic ', ' ultrasonic ', ' sensing ', turned to his bibliographies. In CBI under ' blind, apparatus for ' he located the four-volumed proceedings of a 1962 international congress on technology and blindness, which seemed a likely source, although probably in need of updating. More helpfully in BNB under ' sensory devices: blind people ' he found the 489-page *Proceedings of the international conference on sensory devices for the blind* (1967). For this assistance the enquirer was almost embarrassingly grateful: though he did not wish at the time to pursue the topic further he made a careful note of all the references traced.

[Had the 1967 conference been followed up (as perhaps the enquirer did later) the *Proceedings* would have been found to contain a whole series of papers on the topic of interest, *eg,* ' Some acoustical differences between bats and man '; ' Ultrasonic spectacles for the blind '; ' Travel-path sounder '.]

As there are often several names for the same subject, the searcher needs his wits about him to ensure he does not miss any relevant citations. Although he can expect a good index to link together such synonyms by means of ' see ' references, he must always be prepared to be adaptable.

Case 18: A young enquirer in a public library one evening was in search of information on sand yachts to help him with a project on transport he was working on at school. The librarian was fairly sure the library had no book on the subject, as a look through the catalogue soon confirmed, but when she discovered neither BNB (back to 1950), nor CBI (back to 1933) had anything to suggest either, she knew she must try the periodical indexes. She had no reason to suppose that this was an instance of a topic too recent for the books —on the contrary she felt certain she had herself seen photographs of sand yachts when she was a child. The absence of a book probably meant no more than that sand yachts as a subject were neither sufficiently important nor sufficiently widespread to justify a whole book about them. As recency therefore was not an issue in this case she could have started her search in the indexes at any point in time, but as she had to begin somewhere she decided to work her way through *British technology index* from its beginning in 1962. This proved a false start, for she found nothing at all under ' sand ' or under 'yachts ', and she had the same luck with a search of *Applied science and technology index*. She felt it unlikely that sand yachts would be within the scope of either *British humanities index* or *Social sciences and humanities index,* but when she checked just in case, although her feelings about the former were vindicated, in the latter under ' sand yachts ' she found indexed a brief article from *Illustrated London news* for 1962, ' Sand yachting in Lancashire '. She could not help remarking that this was a British journal, listed by *British humanities index* as one of those indexed.

Encouraged by this success she made for the companion indexing service to *Social sciences and humanities,* namely *Readers' guide to periodical literature.* The first item she struck was a reference under ' sand sailboats ' directing her to '*see* land sailboats '. There she found a couple of articles, ' Sailing the seas of sand ' from *Business week,* and ' Boat you sail on sand ' from *Popular science.* Following this heading through in later volumes she was amused to find herself directed back again in the 1967-68 volume by an instruction ' land sailboats *see* sand yachts '. This path led to a further article ' Dry land fleet sails the Sahara ' in the *National geographic magazine.*

Of the four references thus turned up only the first and last were in the library, but as both were clear and well-illustrated the librarian judged them suited to their purpose. The delighted reaction of her young enquirer left her in no doubt.

More disturbing is the reverse situation, often encountered with new or out-of-the-way topics where there is no well-known or generally accepted term to describe the subject. This can call for the exercise of considerable ingenuity on the part of the librarian.

Case 19: The reference librarian of a busy medium-sized borough library had to get his enquirer to explain further when he was asked for ' anything on space selling '. He did not entirely follow the explanation of the term (which turned out to be the enquirer's occupation!), but he gathered that it involved the selling of advertising space in a newspaper to potential advertisers. The librarian had no idea that such a job existed, but he turned to the library catalogue and the bibliographies to see what he could unearth. The first thing that he discovered was that it was pointless looking under either ' space ' or ' selling ', since both terms led to a vast array of other headings in both the catalogue and the bibliographies like BNB, CBI, and *Subject guide to books in print,* and yet under neither term did the precise combination ' space selling ' appear.

Clearly he was faced with a difficult problem. Of course, librarians are frequently asked for information on the most specialised and even extraordinary occupations, from arctic exploring to zoo keeping, but in most cases these jobs have quite precise and particular descriptions, as for example, saggar maker's bottom knocker. But the phrase used to describe this vocation was the reverse of this, being made up of two quite vague and generalised terms. In search of further information, and perhaps inspiration, he looked up the expression in *Webster's third,* where not without a degree of persistence, he found as the twelfth of the thirteen meanings of ' space ' that it was a synonym for ' linage ', which in its turn was defined, *inter alia,* as ' the amount of space occupied (as by advertising matter in a newspaper or periodical) '. By way of illustration, the phrase given was ' sell space for a newspaper '.

This helped to clear his mind on the matter, but was of little help in suggesting search terms to use in the bibliographies and indexes. He tried hard to think of a specialised indexing or abstracting service for advertising which might have been a starting point. Certainly his library did not subscribe to one, and neither Walford nor Winchell had any titles to suggest. The most likely multidisciplinary index to try was the H W Wilson *Business periodicals index,* but it took more than a few moments effort among the dozens of pages under ' advertising ' in each volume to light upon the right heading—' advertising, soliciting of '. So far as references were concerned he was home and dry, with a wide selection of articles such as ' Seven sins of some space reps '; ' Newspaper ad selling '; ' Media rep should link publisher and client '.

Less happily for the enquirer, all the articles were in US journals, which meant firstly that only a limited number were immediately available for consultation, and secondly, that their relevance to his own British context was less than he had hoped. Surer now of his ground, the librarian turned to the modest collection of books on advertising on his shelves. Searching through them with his enquirer he almost immediately encountered in a standard British text, N T Sandbrook and L Livesey *Lane's Advertising administration* (fourth edition 1968), an eleven-page chapter headed ' Space selling ', which the reader seized upon. Continuing the search meanwhile, the librarian next came upon M P Davis *Handbook for media representatives* (1967). In the preface he read a quotation from a 1963 speech: ' I challenge anyone to find a more specialized activity than selling space or time in advertising media . . . What is missing, however, is a book for media salesmen '. The Introduction expounded further: 'As yet . . . no book has been written for media representatives. Books on different aspects of advertising are available in abundance, but all are written from the viewpoint of advertiser or agency, rather than the specialist contribution of the media representative.'

Obviously, this was just what the enquirer was looking for, but as he contentedly studied its pages, the librarian began to contemplate why he had not traced the work in his preliminary search of his card catalogue and of BNB. He checked that it was indeed included in BNB, but he noted that it had been classified merely under ' advertising: general works ' at 659.1, a placing followed by his own library. He knew already that it was not indexed under either ' space ' or ' selling ', and now learned that it was not indexed under ' media ' or ' representative ' either. Clearly, he had stumbled across yet another instance of one of the classic indexing problems.

Secondly, this difficulty of selecting the right 'approach term' is given an extra dimension where the subject sought for is composite in that it cannot be expressed in a simple word or phrase. Examples of such subjects are advertising by nationalised industries in Great Britain, or industrial involvement in university research. The added problem here for the researcher is one of component order; again the structure of references in the index by linking together these terms should guide him to the correct entry point, but it is as well for him always to be prepared to meet the indexer half way.

Case 20: Although the request for 'anything on building ships out of concrete' was undoubtedly technical, it was clear, precise and quite understandable (even if a trifle surprising) to a layman. The technical librarian guessed that this was a fairly recent development, and his enquirer confirmed this, so his first thought was to try the periodical indexes: perhaps the most appropriate sources would have been the abstracting services (as listed by Walford) to be found in the *Journal of the British Ship Research Association* and in the *Institute of Marine Engineers transactions,* but neither of these were available. He turned first, therefore, to the bound volumes and monthly parts of the last five years of *Applied science and technology index,* and uncertain whether to look under 'concrete' or 'ships' he plumped for the latter, checking 'shipbuilding', 'ships', and adjacent headings. Many dozens of entries he found, but none on concrete ships. Trying under 'concrete' produced no better result among the hundreds of entries. From adjacent headings like 'concrete bridges', 'concrete dams', 'concrete pipes', 'see' references were given to 'bridges, concrete', 'dams, concrete', 'pipes, concrete', but no headings bearing even faintly on ships could be found. Casting around for alternative approach terms, the librarian came up with 'boats'. There had been no cross-reference to 'boats' under 'ships', but he judged it worth a try. Immediately he discovered the entry term 'boats, concrete', with a citation for a three-page illustrated article, complete with bibliography, in the *American concrete institute journal* for 1969, entitled 'Ferro-concrete boats'. A glance under the same heading in earlier volumes revealed two more articles.

The British counterpart to *Applied science and technology index* is of course *British technology index.* Not least among its differences, however, is its sophisticated (and some would say difficult) subject-heading system. Fortunately, this is briefly explained in the introduction to the annual volumes (ASTI lacks any such account), and so the librarian had some familiarity with its construction. He was well aware, as J R Sharp emphasises, that in using conventional alphabetical indexes 'the principles and rules of formulation of headings must be understood by both indexer and searcher so that precise and consistent specification is always achieved by both'. Without hesitation, therefore, he looked under 'ships: concrete' (*ie*, 'thing: material' rather than under 'concrete: ships'), only to find that the heading was not used. Then he remembered that '*Index* users often discover pertinent material under a term narrower in meaning than that which they consulted first as approach term' (Introduction). He knew also that the 'related heading' references indicate such alternative approaches by referring from more or less general terms. Under 'ships', for instance, he found listed over a dozen of these related headings, such as 'tugs', 'dredgers', 'yachts'. To have checked them all would have been insupportably tedious, so picking on the most promising, he looked up 'boats' where he at once found an article 'Concrete boatbuilding' in the *Concrete quarterly* for 1969. He noticed that the actual heading was 'boats: hulls; concrete', and recalling again the words of the introduction about inversion references (' The routine instruction is simply to note the sub-heading terms and then look them up in the main sequence'), he decided to check under 'hulls'. Here again he found a three-page article, with references, from *Concrete* for February 1970. Under 'concrete' as expected he found an array of 'see' references to the headings he had already scanned, but one of them was new, 'fishing: vessels; concrete reinforced'. This in due course produced four or five more articles in *Fishing news international*.

By this stage he had become aware that the subject was not as novel as had at first been surmised, so he thought it just worth checking the bibliographies for the last few years. In BNB for 1969 he found G W Jackson and W M Sutherland *Concrete boatbuilding: its technique and its future,* a 106-page book by two specialists from New Zealand, where this technique had become very popular. Although the very first example, a rowing boat, still in existence, dates from 1848, the jacket claims 'This is the world's first book on thin shell-ferro cement boatbuilding'. In spite of this boast the librarian did find on checking CBI an even earlier work published in Canada in 1968: J W Samson and Geoff Wellens *How to build a ferrocement boat*.

Thirdly, a stage beyond this is reached when it becomes necessary to search for combinations of subjects, that is to say, to be able to select simultaneously several topics. As Urquhart has explained, '. . . the problems are becoming more and more complex: as the scientist seeks to know more and more about less and less, he ceases to be interested primarily in the inter-relationships of two subjects —he is mainly interested in the relationship of two subjects only when a third factor is present'.

It is at this point that the conventional alphabetico-specific index becomes inadequate, for to ensure retrieval in all such cases by one-place reference to the system would mean a prohibitively large number of entries. Here it is that the more flexible post-coordinate indexes have their great contribution to offer, for the *ad hoc* co-ordination of the topics in the required combination need not be made until the time of the actual search.

Case 21: When faced with a request for information on the microbial corrosion of metals it did not take the librarian in a college of technology long to grasp that in his search he would need to ensure the co-ordination of three concepts: microbes, corrosion, and metals. Knowing his collection well enough to be sure he had no books on the subject in stock, he did not trouble to consult the catalogue (although this would have been an interesting exercise of search tactics in the circumstances). He turned first to the index he thought would be most productive on account of its sophisticated classificatory method of indexing—*British technology index*. He was sufficiently familiar with its basic rules of component order for headings (in this case 'thing: action: agent') to know that he should look under 'metals: corrosion: microbes' rather than under 'corrosion: metals' or even under 'microbes' to find what he wanted. When he was unable to trace such a heading under 'metals' he looked at the related headings' only to find dozens and dozens of metals listed from aluminium to zirconium. Looking up some of these he noticed that they did appear with the sub-heading 'corrosion' (as 'zinc: corrosion'), but he soon realised he could not possibly check every metal in every one of the many BTI volumes and monthly parts.

Modifying his search strategy, therefore, he looked under 'corrosion'. As he expected he found a whole array of 'see' references for the various metals, eg, 'corrosion: copper. *See* copper: corrosion'. By this tactic he had narrowed down the headings he would have to search to those in which two of his three concepts were present, ie, metals and corrosion. But for his taste there were still too many to check, so he looked under the third concept 'microbes'. This term appeared not to be used, although 'microbiology' was. Related headings were given as 'bacteria', 'bacteriology', 'micro-organism'. These in their turn were looked up and at last in the 1970 volume under 'bacteriology' was found a series of 'see' references to, firstly, 'copper: corrosion: water: bacteria', and secondly to similar headings under 'nickel' and 'zinc'.

Clearly, this remarkable index had justified the claim in its introduction to be 'primarily a reference tool for tracing articles on highly specific subjects'. But as this introduction also states that the *Index* is a guide to the contents of the British technical journals, the librarian was momentarily taken aback to see that the four articles cited under the headings he had so painstakingly tracked down were all in French! The journal in which they appeared was indeed British, in the sense that it was published in Oxford, but its Latin title, *Electrochimica acta,* did provide the explanation: this was obviously one of the increasing number of international multilingual journals.

As he expected, his engineering enquirer did not know French, and so the search continued through the earlier volumes of BTI. Three or four unsuitable papers on mild steel and aluminium came to light, and then in the 1966 volume was found a four-page paper with references and illustrations from *Anti-corrosion methods and materials* entitled 'Microbial corrosion of metals'. Despite its age, this was the one that the reader said he wanted to see, so the wheels were set in motion to obtain a photocopy for him.

It used to be thought that to place overmuch reliance on indexes that give merely the unsupported titles of articles on the subject sought was a course fraught with danger. Yet while it remains true that the title of an article may mislead as to its content, and some indexing services make a feature of 'enriching' the plain titles given by authors, there is now evidence to show that titles do serve reasonably well as indicators of an article's content, particularly if the user keeps his wits about him.

The user of periodical indexes can also be hindered by difficulties of a less intellectual order, which may nevertheless be equally frustrating. Indexes issued weekly, monthly or even quarterly can be a burden unless regularly cumulated—here the H W Wilson titles furnish splendid models. Inevitably too, indexes are always late, for no one has yet devised a means of eliminating the delay between the publication of an article in a journal and the appearance of entries for it in the periodical indexes. Selective indexing, where an indexing service only chooses to cover some of the articles in the journals it claims to index, can be particularly annoying when, as is often the case, the criteria of selection are not specified, or even worse, when it is not made clear that selection is being used at all.

Case 22: The visitor to a small country reference library wanted to find something out about people who study the future. The librarian's first thoughts were of fortune-tellers and prophets, but wisely he questioned his enquirer further, when it emerged that the men he was interested in were those who make a profession of assessing what the future holds in order to enable governments and industry and commerce and others the better to prepare.

The librarian could not immediately think of a reference book to try for this one, and he was fairly certain that the small general stock of his library did not hold a book on the topic—as the catalogue confirmed when he checked it. It seemed to him that a periodical article was the most likely source, so he went to the *British humanities index,* looking under 'future, the'. In the 1968 volume his attention was thus drawn to the related heading 'politics, international: 1968-2000', which in due course revealed in the *Listener* for 20th June an article 'Scenarios of the future [*The year 2000,* by Herman Kahn and Anthony Wiener]'. This looked as if it might be a review of a book—a suspicion reinforced by a glance at the 1968 BNB, which showed the work to be a 460-page American volume subtitled '*a framework for speculation on the next thirty-three years*'. The only other reference traced in a ten-year search through

BHI was in the *Times* for 3rd June 1967: 'American "think-tanks" study the future'.

Unfortunately neither the *Listener* nor the *Times* were available, and so while the reader was making out an interlibrary loan form for the Kahn and Wiener book, the librarian quickly flipped through the issues of those few journals that were retained. One of these, *New society,* had its indexes in the boxes with the loose weekly parts: though he knew that this was one of the journals indexed by *British humanities index,* he scanned them just the same. Not to his entire surprise he found that the 1969 index directed him to a 3-page article entitled 'Professional futurist' in the *New society* issue for 12th June 1969. From the recently published *Mankind 2000* edited by Robert Jungk and Johann Galtung, it took the form of a detailed account of this new professional discipline, written by Edward Cornish, President of the World Future Society, Washington, DC. This delighted the enquirer, who promptly changed his mind about applying for the book. The librarian too was fascinated to read that 'The growth of the literature is shown by the appearance of Erich Jantsch's *Technological forecasting in perspective,* whose bibliography lists 413 titles . . .'

[This new profession seems now to have emerged further into the public consciousness, for the January-March 1971 issue of BHI lists two articles under 'futurologist' and three under 'futurology'—one in the *Listener* and the remainder in the *Observer*.]

(*See also* case 18.)

Although there is not a great deal the individual librarian or information officer can do about it, there is one serious obstacle in the path of bibliographical control of periodical articles of which he should be aware. This is the intriguing spectacle of 'scattering', *ie,* the fact that articles on any one subject are distributed in periodicals not primarily covering that subject. This is mainly a problem for the indexing services themselves, but the librarian should always be on the alert for articles on his topic in what at first sight may seem unpromising journals or in indexes that might not immediately spring to mind.

Case 23: A college librarian was approached for help by an electronics engineering student in search of information on the topic he had chosen for an extended essay—recent advances in weather forecasting. The library was not large and materials specifically on the topic of weather were sparse. In a large research library the obvious specialised sources to go to immediately would have been *Meteorological and geophysical abstracts,* published by the American Meteorological Society, or the restricted-circulation monthly issued by the library of the Meteorological Office, *Bibliography of literature received,* but in this case neither of these services was available. All that the library had in book form were some volumes of the Meteorological Office *Tables of temperature, relative humidity and precipitation for the world,* and a handful of general books on weather and climate such as L P Smith *Weather studies* (1966), and E S Gates *Meteorology and climatology for sixth forms and beyond* (third edition 1965). The detail they went into on forecasting was not adequate for this enquiry, and in any case none was sufficiently up-to-date. The library did subscribe to *Weather,* the attractive little monthly published by the Royal Meteorological Society, and so the student was set to look through the issues of the last couple of years while the librarian turned to his periodical indexes.

Here, without any difficulty, he found in *British technology index* over the previous few years references to a large selection of appropriate articles with titles such as ' Recent developments in weather forecasting ', ' Forecasting the weather by computer ', and ' Weather forecasting in the satellite and computer age '. Some of these were located in general science journals taken by the library such as *Endeavour, Science journal, Advancement of science,* and *New scientist,* but what struck the librarian most forcibly was the wide subject spread of the other titles, *eg, Agriculture, Applied statistics, Chemistry in Britain, Computer journal, Dock and harbour authority, Institution of Civil Engineers proceedings, Motor boat, etc.*

Paradoxically, the one meteorological journal possessed by the library proved no assistance at all, for the student found only two references to forecasting in the 1970 index to *Weather* and only two in the 1969 index, none of them relevant.

Because a thorough search through a run of indexes can be very time-consuming, a few moments spent on preliminary investigation will often suggest valuable modifications of search strategy. A quick glance at the encyclopedia or dictionary, for instance, could furnish alternative keywords to search under in the indexes, or could provide inclusive dates which would allow the search to be more precisely directed. The enquirer can often help in such cases: almost invariably he knows more about the topic of his query than he has stated. While much of this will not be relevant to the search, any clue as to date or period certainly is; the enquirer may not volunteer such information simply because he is unaware of its significance in terms of a search through a set of indexes shelved in date order.

Case 24: A student in a large university library asked for help in tracing a reference she had been given: Rose Macaulay *Against Basic English*. A few brief questions soon elicited that this was the full extent of her information about what she was looking for, as she had been given the author and title orally and simply told to read it as an account very critical of Basic English. She had of course tried to find it in the library catalogue before seeking help. First of all, however, the librarian felt obliged to double-check this, because it was a very large catalogue and he knew the readers often had difficulties with the hundreds of cards for authors with surnames prefixed ' Mac '. Next he tried the British Museum *General catalogue* and its *Ten-year supplement* to 1965, where he found dozens of entries for books by this most versatile writer, but not the work sought for. This immediately alerted him to the possibility that it was a periodical article rather than a separately published book or pamphlet, so he turned to the periodical indexes. But where to start? The BM *General catalogue* showed that Rose Macaulay had been writing books since 1907, and he quailed at the thought of a trek through perhaps hundreds of individual annual volumes. In the hope of a clue that might allow him to limit the dates of his search he looked up the articles on Basic English in the *Encylopaedia Britannica* and in *Chambers's encyclopaedia*. From the latter he learned of the invention in 1930 of this system of 850 English words, planned as an international secondary language, but in the former he read, significantly as it turned out, that ' . . . it was not until Winston Churchill . . . with the support of Franklin D Roosevelt put forward the argument for Basic English in 1943, that the general public became interested in its future '.

Starting therefore with the indexing services for the years around 1943 he drew a blank with *Linguistic bibliography* but struck oil immediately afterwards with the *Annual bibliography of English language and literature* for 1943-4 (not published however till 1956) which located the article in *American mercury* 173 1944 58-60 and the delighted reader set off to find the volume in the stacks. Within ten minutes she was back: ' I still can't find it ' was her story. Patiently the librarian returned with her, but as he took down the two volumes for 1944 he noticed they were numbered 58 and 59—and of course the citation had given the volume as 173. Checking further he was unable to find the article at the cited pages (58-60) in either volume, or in the indexes bound into each. Clearly the *Annual bibliography of English language and literature* had got it wrong!

Back with the periodical indexes he began again, this time with the 1943-46 cumulation of the H W Wilson *International index,* forerunner of the *Social sciences and humanities index.* Here the article was located in the January 1944 issue of the *Cornhill;* this time the librarian went with his reader to the shelves, but he need not have troubled, for there she found quite easily the five-page article, a powerful attack on ' the notion of foreigners being deliberately taught to speak English wrong ' and particularly on the way ' Mr Churchill accoladed it at Harvard '. Clearly this reader was content, but the librarian, a conscientious man, thought he should try to lay the bibliographical ghost raised by the *Annual bibliography.* One source he had not tried (because it did not include author entries in 1944) was the Library Association *Subject index;* but it was but the work of a moment to find the Rose Macaulay article indexed under its subject. Imagine his surprise, however, when he saw that it was not the *Cornhill* (a long-established London Journal) that was cited, but *Atlantic monthly* (an equally illustrious and venerable American journal, published in Boston). Following up the reference, he found in the April 1944 issue the identical article to the one published three months earlier in the *Cornhill,* but with no indication at all that it was a reprint. And then he noticed the volume and page numbers of the article: 173 and 58—identical with the incorrect *American mercury* citation. Light began to dawn when he also realised that both *Atlantic monthly* and *American mercury* had the same initials. Referring back to the *Annual bibliography* he confirmed the truth of his suspicions: the compilers had cited the wrong abbreviation, AM, which according to their own key at the beginning of their volume stood for *American mercury*. This same key showed that the abbreviation they should have used was AMO.

(*See also* cases 27, 28, 31.)

This last case is of course an example of an author enquiry. Not all periodical indexes provide for this approach, *eg, Applied science and technology index, Business periodicals index,* and *British technology index* have never had author entries (now in BTI from 1972). *British humanities index* does not include author entries in its quarterly issues but furnishes a separate author section in its annual cumulations. *Poole's index* lacked such an approach for well over a hundred years until a separate author index was supplied in 1970.

Case 25: ' I am trying to trace all the poems written by this man ' was the approach made in a large city reference library by a reader holding a small yellow paperback in his hand. The librarian saw that the book was the Vista Books Pocket Poets 1963 edition of the selected poems of Dannie Abse, whom he knew from television as a Welsh-Jewish poet, novelist and doctor. Reference was made inside to what were presumably three other selections of his poetry, *Walking under water* (1952), *Tenants of the house* (1957) and *Poems: Golders Green* (1962). The first step obviously was to trace other collections published in book form. The library catalogue had two of the three listed, together with the more recent *Selected poems* (1970).

To these the British Museum *General catalogue* (including the *Ten-year supplement* to 1965) added *After every green thing* (1949), and *British books in print* supplied two further titles which might have been poems or might not: *Demo* (1969) and *A small desperation* (1968). BNB confirmed that the latter at least was a book of poems, but had no entry for the former. Cross-checking with the *Cumulative book list* (always a good precaution) soon solved this problem, clearly indicating that *Demo* was a book of poetry. *Cumulative book index* (checked back to 1938) had nothing to offer that had not already been unearthed, so eight volumes seemed to be the grand total.

It now remained to locate those poems published in periodicals that had not yet found their way into the collections. Since 1961 the

Library Association *Subject index to periodicals/British humanities index* has provided a separate author section in its annual cumulation, but a check of this for poems by Dannie Abse revealed not one. The *International index/Social sciences and humanities index* on the other hand includes author entries in one sequence with the subject entries: a scanning of these produced well over a dozen poems, not only in the American journals such as *Kenyon review, New Yorker,* and *Sewannee review,* but also in in the British *New statesman, Encounter,* and *Spectator,* which nominally are indexed by *British humanities index.*

This seemed an appropriate query to check in the American *Index to little magazines,* which retrospectively to 1943 covered some 49 periodicals not indexed in *Social sciences and humanities index* or in *Readers' guide to periodical literature;* over half-a-dozen likely references were traced in journals such as *Arts in society, Chelsea, Beloit poetry journal, Poetry book magazine.* At this point the librarian felt he could leave the reader to check all these references for himself to see which had been included in the collections and which not.

[The librarian should have known that *British humanities index* ' excludes fiction, poetry and other pure literature ' (Walford).]

One advantage there is in conducting an author search, or indeed any search where the approach term is a personal name, for in the great majority of cases there is obviously no doubt as to what to look under in the indexes. This advantage is shared with other enquiries where the topic of interest has a name, as for example places, buildings, institutions.

Case 26: ' I am doing a piece on the Pentagon. Can you find me some background material on the actual building, with lots of illustrations?' was the urgent phone call from the local television company. Promising to ring back within the hour, the assistant in the big city library started the search with *Encyclopedia Americana,* where she was disappointed to find no more than a mention. *Collier's encyclopedia* was more helpful, describing it as ' the largest office structure in the world ', containing 92 acres of usable space, and of course housing the US Department of Defense HQ at Washington. Accompanying the article was a striking aerial view of this huge five-sided block, and the date of completion was given as the early 1940's.

More certain now as to what she was looking for the assistant made for her library catalogue. She was not overly surprised to find nothing at all. She was a little more disconcerted to find the same in all the British bibliographies she consulted (BNB, British Museum *Subject index, British books in print*) and in the *British humanities index/Subject index to periodicals* back to the 1940's. She turned therefore to the US bibliographies, although she knew there might be less chance of locating in a hurry copies of any items found. *Subject guide to books in print* had nothing to suggest, but both CBI and the Library of Congress *Catalog: books: subjects* turned up what seemed the ideal source: Gene Gurney *The Pentagon* (1944), a work of 146 pages with 'special photography by Harold Wise'. As expected, however, there was no copy of this American work available locally, but she made a note of it in case her enquirer was prepared to wait till one could be obtained for him.

The US periodical indexes were the next in line. A check of *Readers' guide* was immediately successful. Out of the dozen or more articles listed the assistant first selected those described as illustrated and then looked up those of them that were available in the library. When the time came for her to call back her enquirer she had available illustrated articles from *Life* (' Guide to the Pentagon '), the microfilm edition of *New York times magazine* (' Close-ups of the Pentagon '), and two or three other articles without illustrations. She had also found through *International index* a one-page British illustrated article in *Illustrated London News* and a reference to what she guessed would be a lavishly illustrated thirteen-page French article in *France illustration*.

(*See also* cases 5, 7, 10, 12, 13.)

Books have nothing to compare with such special features of periodicals as letters to the editor, book reviews, obituary notices, news items, and in the case of professional journals for instance, notices and announcements. Advertisements in books are rare now, yet they are the economic life-blood of many journals and newspapers. These are mainly of current interest, of course, but reference librarians are prone to forget that for the average journal the great bulk

47

of its use by readers is while it is still current, *ie,* long before it is indexed. It is true that these are relatively minor features, often ignored as such by the indexing services, but their uniqueness can sometimes give them special value in reference work.

Case 27: A phone request from an unidentified caller asked if the library had a copy of the observations made by the Institution of Municipal Engineers on the proposals of the Royal Commission on Local Government in England. When the library catalogue failed to reveal any document answering this description the librarian took the enquirer's phone number and promised to call back.

As a first step he decided to confirm just what Royal Commission's proposals he was dealing with. With the aid of Keesing's contemporary archives (remembering to look under ' United Kingdom: local government ') he soon identified them as those embodied in the report published on 11th June 1969, known after its chairman (Lord Redcliffe-Maud) as the Maud report.

This was the date to start with then. *British humanities index* for 1969 and succeeding years (under ' local government: Great Britain ') listed dozens of articles on Maud, some incorporating observations of professional groups, but not including the Institution of Municipal Engineers. But perhaps the Institution had a periodical of its own? A glance at David Woodworth *Guide to current British journals* revealed the existence of the monthly *Journal of the Institution of Municipal Engineers;* though it was (perhaps obviously) not indexed in *British humanities index,* the entry in Woodworth showed that it was indeed covered by *British technology index.* Yet a close check of BTI from 1969 to date merely demonstrated the absence of a heading ' local government '. Was this simply a result of the indexing policy of BTI to exclude the non-technological content of what were primarily technological journals? There was only one way to find out—a page-by-page search of the journal itself. Starting with the June 1969 number, the librarian found he had not far to go, for in the January 1970 issue appeared four pages headed ' Comments on the general framework of authorities and functions proposed by the Royal Commission on Local Government in England ', with a note to say that they had been submitted to the Secretary of State on 1st December 1969.

One of these features unique to periodicals is of particular interest to librarians: the book reviews. Perhaps it is for this reason that there are published at least two very useful cumulative periodical indexes solely devoted to the reviews of books in periodicals and newspapers. The older of these, the monthly *Book review digest,* founded in 1905, as its title implies is more than a mere index, including as it does a descriptive note and 'excerpts from as many reviews as are necessary to reflect the balance of critical opinion '. The quarterly *Book review index* on the other hand, a comparative newcomer, started in 1965 and although covering many more journals (230 compared with the 80 indexed by BRD) gives no more than the bare citation for the review. Narrower in subject scope but covering 700 journals in its quarterly issues is the *Index to book reviews in the humanities.* Universal in subject scope but limited to one periodical is the recently available cumulated index to one of the major book reviewing journals in English: the computer-produced index to the *New York Times book review* covers the 73 years of its existence since 1896.

Case 28: When a letter asking about *The jewel in the crown* by Paul Scott was received by a city librarian he passed it at once to the readers' adviser in the central lending library. The enquiry was perfectly straightforward: the reader simply wanted to know the titles of the other two books in the trilogy. F M Gardner *Sequels* (fifth edition 1967) has been compiled to answer just such queries; on finding no entry for Paul Scott the readers' adviser was brought up short. She did not know the book herself, but her catalogue told her it was a novel published in 1966. It also told her that Paul Scott was the author of at least five other novels, although all of them were out on loan at the time. *British books in print* indicated that he had written at least eight books in addition to *The jewel in the crown.*

Clearly the first priority was to find something out about it. Neither the book nor its author figured in *Reader's adviser*—perhaps because he was either too new or too obscure. In the hope of locating a book review she checked the 1966 volumes of *Book review index* and *Book review digest.* As expected, the *Index* produced more citations (fourteen in all), but the *Digest* was more informative. Six citations were found in the latter (all of them also listed in the former, with the inexplicable omission of the review in the

New statesman, even though it is listed as one of the journals indexed) including a 20-line quotation from the *New Yorker* and a shorter extract from the *Times literary supplement.* The introductory annotation, also taken from the TLS, outlined the story, set in British India during World War II—but nowhere was there a mention of the trilogy or a sequel. A not unreasonable hypothesis, therefore, was that this was the first of the sequence.

Leaving the book reviews for a moment, the librarian took down the latest volume of *Cumulated fiction index* covering 1960 to 1969. She had avoided this before, as it is arranged by subject, without author or title indexes; but now she had a subject, and under ' India: 1939-45 ' she found P Scott *Day of the scorpion* listed with *Jewel in the crown.* Back with *Book review index* she soon located the former in the 1968 volume, with this annotation: ' This novel continues " the story of the twilight of British rule in India [begun in *The jewel in the crown . . .*] " '.

One up and one to play, she checked through BRD right up to the latest monthly issue, to no avail. BNB she also combed likewise, from the date of publication of *The jewel in the crown* in 1966, but all she found were reprints of earlier novels. She even consulted the list of forthcoming books published each spring and autumn in the *Bookseller,* but without success. She was forced to conclude that her letter of reply would have to confess that the third volume of the trilogy could not be traced.

The full exploitation of the resources of the periodical literature is a major concern of all librarians. The size of the role that periodicals play in reference work is in direct proportion to the extent of their bibliographical control, for periodicals without indexes remain closed books, as the young William Frederick Poole observed in the library of Yale University in the 1840's. It is hoped that the cases so far described will have demonstrated the essential function here of the general periodical indexes, each covering a wide range of subject disciplines. Many would regard them as the most useful group of reference tools in the library, after the great general encyclopedias. But it is wise to recognise their limitations. They index, for instance, no more than a tiny minority of periodical titles published: *British humanities index* covers 380, and *Social sciences and humanities index* rather less at 200, with an overlap of some 30 titles. *British technology index* covers 360 and *Applied science and technology index* 240 of the estimated 30,000 current periodicals in science and technology. And of the titles that they do scan we have seen that they do not always index the full contents of each number. Compare this with the coverage of book literature by *British national bibliography*, or *Cumulative book index*, or particularly *Books in English*.

It would of course be an elementary error of reasoning to go on from this and argue that BTI and ASTI and the rest are inadequate as indexes to the periodical literature because they are not exhaustive. An index (which is literally the Latin word for ' forefinger ') is no more than a signpost; like a finger-post at a road junction it can not be called inadequate *for its purpose* merely because it indicates no more than the distance and direction of the nearest town. The stated aim of such services is not to control the whole flood of the periodical literature but to function within libraries as the keys to those journals which the libraries might reasonably be expected to hold. Indeed, the titles for indexing by ASTI and other H W Wilson indexes are chosen by the subscribers themselves.

Case 29: 'Have you got anything on earholes?' was the startling query posed in the technical section of a busy town library. Wisely the librarian repeated the question, and it soon became clear that what the enquirer was interested in was ' air halls '. As the librarian had no idea what these were, he again wisely asked his questioner for help, which was immediately forthcoming: 'They are buildings made of rubber or plastic that you blow up with a pump '.

The library catalogue had nothing to offer, and neither had the *British national bibliography* of the previous ten years. Clearly books on the subject were not plentiful, perhaps even lacking altogether. The library was not large, having only a modest collection of a hundred or so technical journals, but they had been chosen with care, full regard being paid to whether or not they were covered by the indexing services. It was to the latest volume of *British technology index,* obviously the indispensable key to these titles, that the librarian next turned. The appropriate search terms to use was clearly going to be a problem, so initially he tried under every heading he could think of. He drew blanks with ' air halls ', ' halls ', ' buildings ', ' rubber ', or ' plastic ', but after a little to-and-fro-ing he alighted on 'air inflated structures *see* structures, air inflated'. This led him directly to a five-page illustrated article in the July 1970 issue of *Science journal* beginning 'Inflatable structures are still very much a technique of the future'. Three references appeared at the end: a Goodyear company research report of 1960, a monograph published in Berlin in 1962, and the *Proceedings of the 1st international colloquium on pneumatic structures* (Stuttgart, 1967). None of these the library had, the librarian guessed they would be difficult to obtain, and he surmised that they would not be the sort of thing this particular reader wanted anyway. Leaving him contentedly perusing the *Science journal* article, he therefore continued the search back through BTI, tracing some 20 other articles, a good half of which he was able to produce immediately for his enquirer.

One great strength of indexes of this kind is a direct function of their selective approach—their multidisciplinary coverage. For an exhaustive search within a particular subject field the research worker has other sources to turn to, as will be described later. We have seen in the phenomenon of scattering how articles on one subject are to be found distributed through journals primarily devoted to quite other subjects. There are an increasing number of subjects of concern now that straddle disciplines, *eg,* conservation of the environment, the problems of old age. Similarly, there are more and more instances where it is not possible precisely to locate a subject within one particular field, especially if it is a new subject. The interdisciplinary, mission-oriented approach is increasingly needed.

Case 30: The information officer in a large university library knew almost instinctively that there were no books on artificial ski slopes among the many hundreds published on skiing, so he did not even trouble to check. Recent periodical articles on the subject were what was wanted, he was sure. Discussion with his enquirer had confirmed what he was already aware of—that such slopes made of plastics had already been successfully tested and put into use. Clearly *Plastics abstracts* and similar services would soon bring to light any relevant articles. Before embarking on the search, however, he thought he would just check the last few years of the much broader-based *British technology index* and *Applied science and technology index*.

This fortunate afterthought soon revealed that plastic slopes were not the only substitute for real mountains and real snow: one five-page illustrated article in the *Concrete quarterly* described a 'Precast ski resort'; another in *Materials protection* furnished an account of 'Weathering steel used in ski slide'; yet another in *ASHRAE journal* (of the American Society of Heating, Refrigerating, and Air-conditioning Engineers) was entitled 'Artificial snow-making aids nature'.

What can be a decided handicap in some enquiries is the lack of adequate retrospective indexing services before the 20th century. In the general field, with the shining exception of Poole, there is virtually no source to tap for 19th century periodical literature as a whole, and for earlier centuries we do not even have the consolation of Poole. This is surprising when we remember that the periodical has been with us now for over three hundred years, and serious retrospective use is impossible without indexes. Where the search is confined to a specific field, the enquirer may be lucky enough to light upon an *ad hoc* retrospective bibliography devoted to periodical articles, or at least including them, *eg,* the eleven-volume *Index to art periodicals* (1962), compiled by the Ryerson Library, the Art Institute of Chicago; *Index Kewensis* (1893-), which indexes the earliest descriptions of flowering plants; *Index of archaeological papers, 1665-1910* (1907-14) covering 94 journals. Less fortunate searchers have to make shift as they can.

Case 31: A phone call received in a city reference library was from the drama critic of the local evening paper, interested in the contemporary reception of *Trelawny of the 'Wells'*. The assistant taking the call knew no more than that it was a play (which he might have guessed anyway from the enquirer's identity); not wishing to reveal his ignorance he made a careful note of the title, the caller's name and number, and promised to ring back.

W R Benet *The reader's encyclopedia* put him on the right track at once by informing him that the work was an 1898 comedy by

Arthur Wing Pinero; the *New Cambridge bibliography of English literature* (1969) added further that the first production was at the Court theatre (in London) on 20th January 1898, a date that fell conveniently within the period covered by the H W Wilson attempt to index retrospectively beyond *International index* and *Readers' guide to periodical literature*. Somewhat disappointingly there were no more than two references in this *Nineteenth century readers' guide to periodical literature,* only one of which related to the first production: 'Presentation at the Court' in the *Athenaeum* for 29th January 1898. The second, '*Trelawny of the "Wells"* at the Lyceum' in the *Critic* for January 1899 clearly referred to a later production at another theatre.

Poole's index had only one reference, to the *Saturday review,* 85 (decoded *via* the 'Chronological conspectus' as one of the volumes for 1898), but the assistant was intrigued to note the name of the author, G B Shaw.

As this seemed to be the total haul from the general periodical indexes, the assistant, guided by Walford and Winchell, turned confidently to the theatrical indexes and bibliographies. These he found in plenty, but each title he examined (or noted) either excluded contemporary reviews of individual plays (*eg,* B M Baker *Theatre and allied arts: a guide to books; Player's library: the catalogue of the British Drama League;* New York Public Library *Catalog of the theatre and drama collections*); or, while including reviews, did not go back as far as 1898 (*eg, Cumulated dramatic index, 1909-1949;* J M Salem *A guide to critical reviews,* which commences with the 1909-10 season; Irving Adelman and Rita Dworkin *Modern drama: a checklist of critical literature on 20th century plays*). Apart therefore from the two citations in the *Athenaeum* and the *Saturday review,* the most he could do for his enquirer was to indicate to him likely titles of journals and newspapers, contemporary with the first production, which he could search for reviews.

The value in this context as guides to further sources of information of the great unabridged dictionaries which feature fully-referenced quotations has often been demonstrated. It frequently happens that these references are to periodicals and newspapers as well as to books, a point which the alert librarian can often recall to his advantage.

Case 32: In a large university library a member of the lecturing staff approached the librarian: ' I have been trying to find a description of the " dark day " '. When the librarian enquired further, he explained that it was a day sometime during the 18th century when the whole sky grew unnaturally dark, causing great alarm. Trying the encyclopaedias first in the hope of a jumping-off point, the librarian found no mention in *Britannica, Chambers's, Everyman's,* or *Collier's,* but in *Americana* he read that it was ' the name given in the United States to May 19, 1780, when the light of the sun was obscured without any apparent cause . . . the sun rose with the normal brightness until about 9 o'clock in the morning, when darkness gradually settled down over a large area of New England '.

There were, however, no bibliographical references, which the reader found disappointing. ' I was really looking for a contemporary account ', he said. The librarian surmised that the most likely source would be the New England newspapers and periodicals of the day: the former he knew would be very difficult of access, and the latter would be largely unindexed, coming as they did before the commencing date of Poole's *Index* in 1802. He then thought to try the great dictionaries: *Webster's third* had no entry (although the earlier edition—which he always consulted with the third as a matter of course—had a brief sentence), but *Funk and Wagnalls* had a short account. Though neither the OED nor the *Shorter Oxford* listed the expression at all, Mathews *Dictionary of Americanisms* seemed a likely source to try. Here the entry followed *Webster's* almost word for word, but as expected there was a quotation, dated 1806, referring to ' Mass. Hist. Soc. Coll. I.95 Dr Tenney's Letter on the Dark Day, May 19, 1780 '. Since periodicals are not included in the bibliography in volume two, recourse was had to the British Museum *General catalogue of printed books: periodical publications* in order to expand this abbreviated reference to the first volume (1792) of *Massachusetts historical society collections.* When eventually obtained, this turned out to be a three-page letter ' written by a gentleman of literary character' from Exeter (presumably Exeter, New Hampshire). As soon as he had chance to examine it, the enquirer showed great enthusiasm and offered profuse thanks, for not only was this a contemporary account, it was also by an eye-witness.

Case 33: Sensibly enough (as he had never heard the term before) at the start of a search on 'nature printing' the librarian looked up the dictionaries. *The Concise Oxford* define it as a 'method of producing print of leaves etc by pressing them on prepared plate'. *Webster's third* gave more detail: 'a process in which an object (as a leaf or a piece of lace) is pressed into a plane surface (as of soft metal) to make either a direct printing surface or a matrix'. This was clear enough, but disappointingly there was no further clue to aid the hunt—no date, no name, no quotation, no derivation. The librarian continued the search in the conventional manner, but twenty minutes later he returned with empty hands. There was no mention of the term in *Encyclopaedia Britannica,* or in *Chambers's, Americana, Collier's, Everyman's.* No book on the subject could be traced, either in the library catalogue or the bibliographies (BNB and Library of Congress *Catalog: books: subjects*) back to 1950. The term did not appear in the British Museum *Subject index,* the *British humanities index*/Library Association *Subject index to periodicals* or the *British technology index* which were searched back for thirty years, and there appeared to be no book in print on the topic (*British books in print* and *Subject guide to books in print*).

So he turned back to the dictionaries, where he found that the earliest quotation (1855) in the OED article was from 'Bradbury in *Proc. Roy. Inst. Gt. Brit.* II. 106.' This he discovered to be a 13-page information-packed article by Henry Bradbury tracing the art back at least 250 years, and referring to the work of Auer at the Imperial Printing Office in Vienna where the process had recently been perfected. The article was illustrated by three actual nature-printed plates.

[In 1967 appeared *Typographia naturalis: a history of nature printing* by Roderick Cave and Geoffrey Wakeman, a fifty-page, privately-printed account, in which we read 'there has been no detailed study of nature printing published in England for over 100 years'. Had the librarian been shrewd enough to suspect this venerable history at the outset he could have saved himself a lot of trouble by going first to *Poole's index,* which would have drawn his attention to two articles by Bradbury in the *Journal of the Franklin Institute* for 1856 (or 1857—it is not always possible precisely to calculate the date from *Poole's* 'Chronological conspectus').]

Paradoxically, however, there is a sense in which it is true to say that periodicals are better served by their bibliographies than are books: this is the closeness of their indexing. A volume of the *Economic history review* amounting to perhaps 650 pages will have a couple of dozen subject entries and an equivalent number of author entries in *British humanities index*. A similar-sized composite volume such as E E LeClair and H K Sneider *Economic anthropology: readings in theory and analysis* (1968) will be listed once in BNB in the main classified sequence and be entered four times (two author entries, one title, one subject) in the index. In practical terms this means it is often simpler for the reference librarian to search periodical literature indexes for some topic too minor to justify a full-scale book, even though he knows he could probably locate similar information *within* a book on the subject if he were prepared to search through the books on his shelves.

Case 34: Following reports of train derailments attributed to the use of continuous welded track a number of enquiries were received by a public technical library from what seemed to be interested amateurs concerned about just how in fact engineers overcome the problems of expansion in hot weather and contraction in cold weather (provided for in normal track of course by expansion joints between the rails). For such amateurs suitable and up-to-date information was quickly furnished in the form of periodical articles traced through *British technology index* and *Applied science and technology index, eg,* ' British railways' problems with welded track ' (in *Engineering*), ' Some recent facets on continuous-welded track practice in Britain ' (in *Railway gazette*). For those keen to pursue the topic further *Engineering index* (' transdisciplinary index to the world's engineering developments ') provided more technical information, *eg,* ' Equipment for reducing the incidence of pull-aparts in winter and kick-outs in summer in continuous welded rail ' (in *Railway age*).

The overwhelming majority of enquirers for ' something on ' a subject want literally that, and nothing more. Of course the ' something ' has to be precisely ' on ' the subject, and it has to be matched to the reader's requirements as to level, form and amount. There are obviously dangers of trivialisation here: the enquirer asking for 'something on' the Protestant ethic, or the influence of television on politics, or mimicry among insects, or how to run a parish magazine, may sincerely expect to solve his information need by reading a three-page article from a journal. Perhaps it is too much to ask to expect the librarian single-handed to withstand pressures of this kind, fostered by the media. On the other hand, if these are genuine needs, it may be the case that part of the librarian's role is to relay some of these seemingly impossible demands to the primary producers of information—the authors and publishers. Clearly librarians must be aware of these dangers. In all cases they should strive for quality in what they provide: where there is a choice of material their aim should be to furnish the ' best ' information or the ' best ' references. This again is where the general periodical indexes score, for as we have seen they are doubly selective, firstly in the titles they choose to scan, and secondly, in the items from those titles that they choose to index. And whilst their selection is by no means immune from criticism, it is encouraging to remember that the criteria of selection are probably those any experienced reference librarian would use—after all, most of the best-known general indexes from Poole onwards have been compiled by and for librarians.

There is, however, a substantial minority of requests for what amounts to virtually *everything* on a subject. A common example is the need for a university student commencing research work for a higher degree to discover all that has been done before, simply because it is a requirement that his thesis should show evidence of original work. A similar instance in industry is the ' novelty search ' necessary before applying for a patent to ensure that your invention has not been anticipated by someone else. In practice, of course, the phenomenon of scattering ensures that a 100 percent complete search is rarely achieved, but the theoretical aim is complete coverage. It is to cater for this kind of exhaustive approach that in many specific subject fields, particularly within science and technology, special periodical indexing services are published, such as the huge *Index medicus* or the *Bibliography of agriculture*. In many cases the citations include a summary of the content of the article: this of course makes them abstracting services also. Some are available in non-book format, for instance on cards, as for example, *Engineering index,* and an increasing number are making use of mechanical aids to enable them to cope with the swelling tide of publications. Some have moved either partly or entirely to a total computerised system, and a few are available to subscribers in the form of magnetic tape for manipulation on their own computers, as for instance *Chemical abstracts*. Commonly international in scope, many of them cover the literature of their subject outside the periodicals as well, *eg,* in research reports, patents, conference proceedings. The vastly increased manipulative power over data that the computer brings has also stimulated a revival of interest in rotated indexes and citation indexes, as exemplified in *Chemical titles* and in *Genetics citation index*. As specifically *subject* sources all of these are beyond the scope of this chapter, but the principles of their use (and many of their limitations) are similar to those of the general periodical indexes.

Mention of the computer reminds us of the increasing role that the machine is bound to play in periodical indexing—an obvious field for the application of electronic data processing. Most applications so far have been seen in specialised indexing and abstracting services, of which perhaps the best known is MEDLARS, based on the monthly *Index medicus,* but we now have examples of quite extensive computerisation in a few of the great multidisciplinary indexes, *eg, British technology index.* One major example of the application of mechanisation (optical scanning, computers, and electronic typesetting) to the problems of retrospective indexing is seen in the *ERIC 70 year cumulated index to popular periodicals* (1971) which in 22 volumes cumulates into one alphabet the 28 existing cumulations of the H W Wilson *Readers' guide to periodical literature* from 1900 to 1969.

One further way in which modern technology has placed reference librarians in its debt is by enabling catalogue card entries for periodical articles to be reproduced several to the page in book form by photolitho offset. We now have generally available a number of previously unpublished special indexes, compiled originally for their own readers by major research libraries, *eg, Index to periodical articles, 1950-1964, in the library of the Royal Institute of International Affairs* (1964) which in its two volumes reproduces 31,500 cards; and the nine-volume *Articles in Irish periodicals* (1970) from the National Library of Ireland, which covers titles from about 1800 up to the end of 1969. Librarians cannot but applaud the extension of bibliographical control that such enterprise makes possible; it was an American librarian who said that ‘periodicals without an index are almost as worthless as a door without a knob’. And, he might have added, equally frustrating.

The severest difficulty by far in exploiting fully the contents of periodicals is that so many are not indexed by *any* of these services, general or special. We read, for example, that the New York Public Library receives approximately 25,000 periodicals a year, of which less than one-fifth are indexed in any published work. Obviously, periodicals are not purchased solely for reference use: we have already noted that most titles receive most of their use while they are still current. Nevertheless, librarians know that the demand for back numbers more than justifies their retention, often permanently. They also know that without keys to their contents in the form of indexes many back files remain closed books. For lack of anything better they are often forced back on to the individual indexes to their contents published by the periodicals themselves. These vary tremendously. Perhaps most responsible journals with material of lasting value in their pages do attempt an annual index, which often contains more information and is more thorough in coverage than the general and special indexes. But many produce inadequate indexes, covering only part of the journal’s contents, and some are very idiosyncratic, to say the least. And of course, thousands of periodicals do not even attempt to publish an index, leaving the searcher no alternative but to scan the contents list, or even the issues themselves, page by page. By way of contrast, the librarian finds a godsend those cumulated indexes of journals like *Engineer* (1856-1959) or *National geographic* (1899-1946 and 1947-1963).

Case 35: Information about a new soundproof paint was required urgently by the head of a building department in a large college of technology. As the query had come by phone, and through a secretary, it was not possible to seek a lead by interrogating the enquirer direct. Neither was it open to the college librarian to turn to the obvious specialised abstracting service (as listed by Walford) *Review of current literature on paint, colour, varnish and allied industries*. In any case (he consoled himself) if the topic was indeed very recent, it would not have had time to be picked up by an abstracting service; and still less of course would it be found in the books.

Periodicals, therefore, were obviously the best bet, and so first the librarian searched back through *British technology index* and *Applied science and technology index*. References to paint there were in their dozens, as also to soundproofing, but none combined the two concepts. As this was not an enquiry where the librarian felt he could report back empty-handed, he decided to scan the actual literature, to search page-by-page the appropriate journals. Of the four or five journals on the topic that his library subscribed to, the most likely seemed to be the monthly *Paint technology*, and so he made a start with that. Paying particular attention to the regular feature 'New coatings' in each issue, steadily he worked his way back. His reward came when in the April 1970 number he read: 'A British patent (1,108,044) describes a soundproofing paint in which sound is reflected because of the presence of metallic lead pigments. Certainly, here is an area that could be of great interest to the paint industry for the soundproofing of hotels, motels, schools, hospitals and industrial buildings in general where sound is a major problem.'

Consulting the enquirer (this time in person), the college librarian was reassured to learn that he was on the right track. A copy of the patent specification was ordered from the Patent Office Sale Branch, and in due course was supplied to the head of department's expressed satisfaction.

(*See also* case 27.)

It is worthy of note, however, that many journals (and newspapers) maintain home-made and unpublished indexes at their offices. Primarily for the use of their own staffs, they are in emergencies useful sources to remember, for editors are often willing to help with a serious enquiry by post or telephone, functioning on occasion as a *de facto* information service. Outstanding in this respect are some of the trade journals, making up probably one of the largest single categories of periodical, and yet at the same time the type least known to the general public. Titles like *Painting and decorating journal, Jeweller and watchmaker, Pottery gazette, Tobacco, Cabinet maker* have been functioning as organs of their particular trade for a century—vital exchanges for a huge variety of essential trade information. Much of this is ephemeral, of course (although of great value while still current), but many of the trades covered are so highly specialised that there may be very few books on the subject. In such cases the file of the appropriate trade journal may embody the greater part of the total published literature, *eg, Buttons, Pram retailer, Brushes.* Typically, they do not publish indexes to their contents.

Although it is clear in a bibliographical control sense that the periodical indexes have the same relation to periodical articles that bibliographies have to books, this only holds good to a limited extent, for in one direction their function goes beyond the merely bibliographical, whereas in another it falls short. This has been referred to earlier in this chapter, but to explain further : in searching for books the librarian finds that the library catalogue (which indicates what books the library itself possesses) and the published bibliographies (which also list books held by the library) complement one another. On the other hand, since periodical articles are rarely given catalogue entries, except in special libraries, the published indexes play the dual role of catalogues of a library's contents and bibliographies indicating what else has been published.

What periodical indexes are not designed to do is answer queries purely bibliographic, that is to say, about periodicals themselves, such as the price, or the publisher, or the date of commencement. As with books such enquiries are common, but in addition the librarian finds himself challenged by a whole host of specialised queries peculiar to periodicals, such as those demanding circulation figures, advertising rates, frequency, press deadline, or political affiliation. Although this information *about* the periodicals is rarely so much in demand as information *from* the periodicals, there is available a separate range of bibliographical tools designed specifically for this purpose. What many of these are, in point of fact, are trade *directories* rather than bibliographies in the usual sense, and they give directory-type information, such as names and addresses, telephone numbers, statistics, *etc.* Like many similar works their aim is to provide *current* information, and to this end they are often annuals : the *Newspaper press directory* for instance has been appearing each year since 1846. As a rule they cover a defined geographical area, usually a country, but within this area they aim to be comprehensive.

Case 36: The young man at the reference library enquiry desk one evening wanted to see what he described as the *Air traffic con-*

troller's journal. It took the librarian no more than a minute to ascertain that it was not in the library, but before turning his enquirer away empty-handed he asked 'Are you sure that's what it's called?' The young man admitted that he was not absolutely certain, but what he was positive about was the existence of a journal for air traffic controllers.

BUCOP (or to be more precise, the *Supplement to 1960*) knew of a *Journal of air traffic control,* a publication of the (US) Air Traffic Control Association, of Arlington, Va, but the enquirer asserted that the title he was seeking was definitely British. A very thorough check of BUCOP (and its various supplementary publications) to 1970, of David Woodworth *Guide to current British journals* (1970), of *Current serials received by the NLL* (1967), of *Periodical publications in the National Reference Library of Science and Invention* (1969), failed to locate a reference to the elusive title (although both the NLL and the NRLSI had sets of the American journal).

The librarian could find nothing likely in the 'Index to class publications' in *Willing's press guide* under the headings 'air force' or 'transport' (there was no heading 'flying'), but he was more successful with the 'classified index' of the *Newspaper press directory* (which despite its title lists many thousands of periodicals that are not newspapers). Under the heading 'aeronautics, space research' he found listed the *Journal of the Guild of Air Traffic Control Officers.* Turning from the index to the main alphabetical sequence in search of the usual details about this journal, he discovered he could not find it. He tried under 'journal', 'guild', 'air . . .', to no avail. He even looked it up in the other index, the 'ABC index'—without success. Obviously, this was an oversight on the part of the compilers, but it did raise doubts as to whether the journal was still extant. He was encouraged to find a location for it in BUCOP, indicating that the Ministry of Aviation Library had a set from volume one (1955/57), but the date on the BUCOP volume was 1962. Was the journal still current? He checked again under the newly-discovered title in Woodworth and the NLL and NRLSI, to no avail.

Leaving the bibliographies entirely, the librarian tried to track down the Guild of Air Traffic Controllers. This proved a simple task, for it was listed with an address in Buckinghamshire in *Directory of British associations* (third edition 1971-2). Significantly, the address comprised the whole of the information provided, despite the fact that entries for other organisations made a feature of listing their publications. Suspecting the worst, all the librarian could do was advise his young enquirer to write to the Guild.

Among the lists of current periodicals there is discernible a small group of works that approach closer to the bibliography than to these trade lists. Often compiled by librarians for librarians, they are usually selective, even evaluative. They are designed to facilitate the subject approach; indeed they are often arranged in subject order. In some cases their coverage is international.

Case 37: When asked over the phone if he knew of any magazines about war games the librarian wisely enquired further before putting down the receiver. He was aware (although only dimly) that there were different kinds of war games : in this instance, as his enquirer explained, his interest was in table-top battles fought with model soldiers, rather than the very high-powered and often computer-assisted simulations used in training military commanders in strategy. The librarian felt sure that the library did not subscribe to any such journals (and a check of the current list of periodicals soon confirmed this), and so he consulted his bibliographies.

His first point of attack was David Woodworth *Guide to current British journals,* but after three or four minutes he had to think again, for he came upon a blank wall with every approach he tried —'games', 'war', 'toys', 'soldiers', 'models', 'hobbies', 'sports', *etc.* Extending the field of battle beyond the shores of Britain he made next for *Ulrich's international periodicals directory* (thirteenth edition, 1969-70). He was aghast to find 35 columns of titles devoted to 'sports and games', but manfully he began to scan them. Half-way through he glimpsed a ray of light in the form of a reference 'Miniature warfare, see Hobbies—general'. This led to seven more columns of titles, but specifically to the monthly journal *Miniature warfare,* published since 1968 in London. Surprised at its absence from Woodworth, the librarian half-suspected its demise; he was reassured by the 1971 *Willing's press guide* and the 1971 *Newspaper press directory* of its current good health (although he did note that these two excellent directories gave different addresses for the publisher).

64

Back at *Ulrich's*, conscientiously completing his search, he discovered one further possible title, a bi-monthly published at Albany, NY, since 1967, *Strategy and tactics: a journal of American wargaming*. Before calling his enquirer back with the details of these titles, the librarian thought to look at one or two of the books on this topic. Picking on two of D F Featherstone's many works on the subject, *War games* (1962) and *Battles with model soldiers* (1970) he learned of *Wargamers newsletter*, published at Southampton, described as ' the magazine of the hobby)', and of *War games digest*, a quarterly published alternately in California and Southampton. Try as he would, however, he was not able to trace any further information about these titles, both being conspicuous by their absence from all the available directories, bibliographies, and union lists, British (*Willing's*, NPD, Woodworth, BUCOP and its supplements to 1970) and American (*Ayer, Standard periodical directory, Union list of serials* and *New serial titles*).

Case 38: An enquiry combining the subject approach with the directory-type was the request in a small public library from a businessman wishing to advertise some unspecified goods or services in as many police journals as possible. For the experienced librarian this was obviously a simple problem; pausing merely to confirm that the enquirer was interested in British titles only, he made first for David Woodworth *Guide to current British journals*. Conveniently arranged by UDC, this gave him immediately five titles: *Police College magazine, Police journal, Police review, Police world, The warren*. More significantly, it also showed that each of them included advertising pages, although it did not indicate advertising rates and gave the circulation in only one case.

In search of more details of this kind, the librarian turned next to the *Newpaper press directory*. Here for each of the titles he found such vital data for the prospective advertiser as the cost of a full-page advertisement, the type area of a page, the method of printing, the audited circulation, and the address for advertisements where this was different from the editorial or publishing address.

Before leaving NPD the librarian checked the ' Classified index ' under ' police ', where he found three further titles: *Clearway,* the twice-yearly journal of the Traffic and Transportation Department of the Metropolitan Police at New Scotland Yard; *The job,* a free fortnightly; and *Police,* the monthly journal of the Police Federation.

Finally, just to be sure, he tried *Willing's press guide,* where under ' police and prison service ' in the ' Index to class publications ' he did find one more title not listed by Woodworth or NPD —the famous *Police gazette,* published daily by the Criminal Record Office at New Scotland Yard. The direct descendant of *Hue and cry,* which first appeared in 1790, this was a surprising item to find listed, for as *Willing's* noted, it is ' issued to the police only '.

One bibliographical attribute of periodicals of particular concern to librarians is whether they are indexed or not. As is only too well-known each periodical is a law unto itself here, but a useful guide for the librarian is the *TPI list: a check list on the title pages and indexes of . . . periodicals* (1961). Some bibliographies of periodicals also indicate the availability of indexes, *eg, Ulrich's,* and Woodworth, and there are one or two works which list in particular cumulative indexes, *eg* D C Haskell *Check list of cumulative indexes to individual periodicals in the New York Public Library* (1942), now in sore need of updating; concentrating on trade and technical journals is the Special Libraries Association *Guide to special issues and indexes of periodicals* (1962). A feature of *Ulrich's,* Woodworth, and a number of other bibliographies, which is probably even more useful to the librarian, is an indication of which periodicals are abstracted or indexed by which services. The projected five-volume work *Indexed periodicals* edited by J V Marconi (1970-) is the first example of a bibliographical tool specifically designed to furnish this kind of information, to the librarian particularly valuable when he is considering a title for adding to his library.

Even the straightforward bibliographical problems of identification and verification can be greater with periodicals than with books. Frequent changes of name, brief life span, and complicated numbering and pagination are not hazards normally encountered by the librarian dealing only with modern books. As has been written elsewhere on the bibliographical idiosyncrasies of periodicals, ' . . . the student should school himself never to show surprise at any aberration of titling, numbering, dating, frequency, format, pagination, or publisher '. One American librarian with long experience of working with periodicals has spoken thus for his colleagues throughout the world: 'It would be impossible to list all the irregularities offered by the [periodicals] publishing industry. In most cases it would be similarly impossible to find explanation for them. The nuisances, however, which they cause to libraries cannot be discounted.'

But the scholars and scientists and others who write and read the articles are far from blameless. Their methods of work and their systems of communication within their disciplines sometimes add to the confusion. In particular, as David Grenfell has plainly stated, ' The most frequent cause of trouble is that authors of articles in periodicals frequently cite references in other periodicals incorrectly '.

Case 39: ' I have been trying to lay my hands on the *Social science review* for 1965 ' was the problem presented at the counter in a large university library. A trifle resignedly, since he knew that the library had a very extensive collection of journals in the field of the social sciences, the librarian checked—only to find somewhat to his surprise that this was one title not held by the library. He was even more surprised to find that the only journals with this title known to BUCOP (and its various supplements) were one published in New York from 1865 to 1866 and located at the Bodleian only and another with a life span from 1862 to 1866 with no place of publication given, and therefore presumably London. Woodworth, *Willing's* and the *Newspaper press directory* had no knowledge of the periodical at all.

Having silently observed this obviously fruitless search, the reader volunteered the information that it was an American title. Turning therefore to the US tools, in the *Standard periodical directory* the librarian found *Social science quarterly, Social science record,* and *Social science reporter,* all currently appearing, but the reader was adamant that the one he wanted was called *Social science review.* The *Union list of serials,* like BUCOP, included two long extinct journals of that name, the first, a New York publication, running from 1887-1901, the second being the 1862-66 London publication already noted. *New serial titles* came nearer the mark with a *Social science review* of Queen's College, Flushing, NY, Social Science Division, but as this was described as 'v. 1-2 No. 2, 1960?-Spring 1962? ' and the only (incomplete) set was located at the Library of Congress, the librarian felt confident in dismissing it from his consideration. In similar fashion he dismissed *Shakai Kagaku Kenkyu* and *Sahoe Kwahak,* both with the added title *Social science review,* but published at Niigata and Seoul and presumably in Japanese and Korean respectively. When *Ulrich's* proved no help either, the librarian was faced with reporting his failure to the reader.

Taking a positive line, however (since the reader had seemed so sure about what he wanted), the librarian asked where he had obtained the reference. This was quickly forthcoming in the shape of a footnote on page 147 of the 1970 *World year book of education,* entitled *Education in cities,* as follows: 'Basil Bernstein "A socio-linguistic approach to social learning " in J Gould (*ed*) *Social science review* (New York: Pelican, 1965) '.

Of course to the librarian's bibliographically more sophisticated eye this was obviously a book, not a journal; he felt in his heart that the end of the road was now near. Surprisingly, he could not trace the work in the library catalogue, or—more disturbingly—in either *Cumulative book index* or the *National union catalog* for 1965. What he did find in both was the first issue of an annual edited by Julius Gould, *Penguin survey of the social sciences.* This title he knew the library possessed and was able to go straight to it without consulting the catalogue. With no mean sense of achievement he quickly located within its pages the required article by Bernstein.

We have seen (case 24) an instance of how the universal practice of abbreviating the titles of periodicals can add a further contingency that the bibliographer of books does not have to contend with. Yet precise, accurate and unmistakable citation, if anything, is even more important with periodical references than with books, especially if requesting a loan or photocopy at a distance. Some libraries indeed have a rule never to forward to another library a reader's request for an article in a periodical without first checking the citation.

As bibliographies of *books* the value of the printed author catalogues of the great national libraries (and the national union catalogues that are sometimes based upon them) is well known. Works like the British Museum *General catalogue* and the *National union catalog* of the United States are the nearest approaches we have to universal bibliographies. Even more so with *periodicals* do the holdings lists of major libraries and the union lists of titles in a particular geographical area serve as the major retrospective bibliographies, turned to first when attempting to identify an individual title. That they are primarily finding lists, designed to locate particular titles in specific libraries, is but a secondary consideration in such cases: in British libraries, for instance, the *Union list of serials* (and *New serial titles* which supplements it) is so frequently consulted because it is, in Collison's words, 'the most complete of all the bibliographies of periodicals throughout the world'. So comprehensive is its coverage, so scholarly its compilation, so accurate its citations, and so convenient its form, that the fact that the library locations for its 400,000 titles are all confined to the United States and Canada is of little consequence.

Case 40: The assistant on duty in the periodicals reading room of a large university of technology was surprised to learn as a result of a reader's enquiry that the library did not take a journal called *Engineering design*. Following standard library practice in such instances, she checked the bibliographies for details, turning first to the *World list of scientific periodicals*. She could find no entry either in the main set (the volume containing E being published in 1963), or in the supplementary list in the *British union-catalogue of periodicals incorporating World list of periodicals: New periodical titles 1960-1968*. A check of the huge *Union list of serials* and its cumulated supplements in the form of *New serial titles*, encompassing something like 400,000 titles, proved equally fruitless. Neither could she trace the title in any of the current trade lists (*Willing's, Ayer, Newspaper press directory, Standard periodical directory*), or in bibliographies of current journals such as *Ulrich's international periodicals directory* or David Woodworth *Guide to current British journals*. And the holdings lists of the National Lending Library *Current serials received* and *Periodical publications in the National Reference Library of Science and Invention* showed that the title was not known in these two major collections either.

By now the assistant had come to doubt the existence of *Engineering design* so she back-tracked in search of alternatives. In the *World list* she found *Engineering designer* (London, 1955-) and in *New periodical titles* another possibility called *Engineering design abstracts* (Enfield, 1964-66), while *New serial titles* added *Engine design and applications* (London, 1964-). Further checking failed to reveal any more similar titles but did challenge the *World list* starting date of 1955 for *Engineering designer: Ulrich's, Willing's* and the *Newspaper press directory* all agreed that it began in 1950. Unfortunately the enquirer did not seem happy with any of these alternatives, departing from the reading room still convinced that *Engineering design* was the journal he wanted.

But of course the primary aim of ULS and BUCOP and the hundreds of lesser titles included in compilations such as R S Freitag *Union lists of serials: a bibliography* (1964) is to locate specific titles both current and retrospective in individual libraries. For the reference librarian one of the most frustrating ways in which periodicals differ from books is in their general unavailability. There are probably over 150,000 books in print in Britain at the moment. Up and down the country there must be many libraries each with a large proportion of these titles in stock. When we turn to periodicals and newspapers we find that according to the *Newspaper press directory* 6,388 are published in the British Isles currently. The number of libraries with even half of these probably does not run into double figures; indeed it has been said that no library in the world possesses more than half the serials in existence. These considerations have led to the location of wanted titles growing into a significantly large part of the reference librarian's task. The problem is aggravated by two further features of periodicals. Firstly, if they are to be retained for any length of time they demand shelf-space and special physical treatment (binding, tying, boxing, *etc*), and so even in the age of the microform many smaller libraries (particularly public libraries) discard after one, two, or three years, preferring to rely on borrowing, even though the discarded titles may be covered by the periodical indexes on the library shelves. Secondly, many (perhaps most) periodical files in libraries are incomplete to some degree. What all this adds up to for the reference librarian is that with periodicals there is a higher likelihood than with books of *not* possessing a reference traced in the bibliographies and indexes, and this is true even in the largest libraries. Location, therefore, remains an integral part of the ' personal assistance given by the librarian to individual readers in pursuit of information ' that we call reference work; whether this entails actually borrowing the desired periodical, obtaining a photocopy, or merely directing the enquirer to the appropriate library.

Case 41: A telex message from a manufacturing firm to a city technical library asked for the loan or photocopy of an article ' Cutting the cost of rust prevention' from the journal *Motorship,* volume 41 (January 1956), pages 20 to 22. The message went on to quote the library's own call number for the item, which had obviously been taken from its published list of periodical holdings. However, when the set of the journal was examined, it was found that the run had not yet reached volume 41. Neither could the article be traced in the 1956 volume, or in the two or three volumes on either side.

Before reporting his failure the librarian thought he should do what he could to check the reference. Trying the *British union-catalogue of periodicals* he immediately lighted upon a possible source of the confusion: two quite separate journals entitled *Motor ship* and *Motorship.* The former was a London publication, which had begun in April 1920. This was the journal held in the library, and if the librarian had been sufficiently alert he would have observed that the title was different when he looked at it on his shelves. *Motorship,* on the other hand, published in New York, seemed likely to be the title required by the reader. This suspicion was reinforced by its date of commencement, given in BUCOP as April 1916: volume 41 *would* therefore correspond to 1956. But the librarian required more positive confirmation than that, so he consulted *Engineering index* for the years around 1956. He was rewarded by finding the entry for the requested article, citing quite clearly the journal *Motorship* and not *Motor ship.* Turning once more to BUCOP, he studied the locations given; two he could eliminate as their sets came to an end prior to 1956, but he made a note of the other four.

He then composed a reply for the telex operator to send, as follows: ' Regret our periodical is *Motor ship* (London). Your reference, which has been checked in *Engineering index,* is to *Motorship* (New York). BUCOP gives four locations: Glasgow Royal Technical College, Liverpool University, Institute of Marine Engineers, Kings College, Newcastle.'

This previous case also shows how the holdings lists of individual collections can be used as location tools. As has been mentioned, the lists from the larger libraries act as major retrospective bibliographies in their own right, but they (and the similar lists of current titles) are invaluable in supplementing the union lists in locating particular titles in specific libraries.

This is perhaps the most appropriate place to discuss a controversial question that is being given increased attention of late: the absence from our libraries of certain periodicals not because they have been discarded but because they have never been acquired. One reason given is that 'Librarians are eminently respectable; many of the magazines that tell us a great deal about our century do not seem to be respectable'. By way of illustration, the same writer claims that a full set of *Playboy*, 'which nowadays is quoted by the clergy almost as often as Genesis' is held by only two libraries in the US. This may be a spectacular example, but it remains true that it is remarkably difficult to pursue the serious study of the literature of certain aspects of our mass culture (*eg, Gambling illustrated, Romeo, Goal, Weight watchers magazine*), or of the various sub-cultures (*eg, Watchtower, Penthouse, British naturism*), or of the dissident and particularly the so-called 'underground' press (*Red mole, Seed, Berkeley barb, Women in liberation, Oz,* and many others), simply because of general lack of access, both bibliographical and physical. It is interesting to note that an attempt is now being made 'with the commendation of the American Library Association' to publish retrospectively on microfilm specifically for librarians over two hundred underground newspapers.

Case 42: When asked by a bearded young man at the enquiry desk in a university library 'Where can I see *Action*?' it took the librarian more than a moment to focus her thoughts sufficiently to determine from her enquirer that he was trying to trace the whereabouts of a political newspaper called *Action* published in the 1930's by Sir Oswald Mosley, leader of the British Fascist movement. She knew that newspapers after 1799 were not included in the obvious location tool, the *British union-catalogue of periodicals* (or for that matter, after 1820 in the corresponding American work, the *Union list of serials*). The only major retrospective bibliographies of newspapers she could recall were the British Museum

Catalogue of printed books: supplement: newspapers (1905) which only went up to 1900, and the *Times tercentenary handlist of English and Welsh newspapers* . . . which had been published in 1920, still too early for this particular query, and in any case was mainly based on the BM holdings.

She turned first therefore to the British Museum *General catalogue of printed books to 1955,* which despite its title does include periodicals and some newspapers. Though there were two *Actions* listed neither matched the enquirer's specifications. This was a discouraging start: if the BM had no copy the chances of any other library preserving a set were slim. She thought she would set aside the location problem for a moment, and try to find out something about the newspaper itself. It was not mentioned in the lists of publications in Sir Oswald's entries in *Who's who, International year book and statesman's who's who* or *International who's who,* nor in the various references to him in *Burke's peerage* or *Debrett.* As his own 531-page autobiography *My life* (1968) was 'compiled almost entirely from memory', not surprisingly it lacked any lists of sources, but the index did lead to four brief mentions of *Action,* 'the paper supporting the New Party' founded by Mosley, which had apparently collapsed amid the general disintegration of the Party at the 1931 General Election.

So it had really existed! But how to locate an extant copy? At this stage the librarian turned to a colleague for advice. 'Have you tried BUCOP?' was his immediate suggestion. She tactfully pointed out that BUCOP excluded newspapers. 'Ah, yes!' he replied, 'but even BUCOP makes an exception for decidedly out-of-the-way items; in any case it is often very difficult to decide what is a newspaper and what isn't. I would look if I were you'. And sure enough, there among the six periodicals called *Action* was one sub-titled 'the new weekly of the new movement', which had run its brief span from October to December 1931. The location symbols indicated a full set at Cambridge University Library, and (despite the BM *Catalogue*) also at the British Museum.

And there, with the reader quite content, the matter might have rested, had not the librarian out of curiosity checked also in the *Union list of serials.* Here she found entries for no less than ten periodicals entitled *Action,* one of which (located in the New York Public Library and Princeton University Library) was obviously the Mosley paper. But then she noticed one of the other entries, a journal of 1936-40 with the note ' Superseded by *Union,* incorporating *Action*). This called to mind a brief mention she had noticed in *My life* which had puzzled her at the time, referring to *Action* in 1938, seven years after its supposed demise, as a journal supporting British Union. She turned immediately to volume five, which covers the letter U. Under ' *Union,* incorporating *Action* ' she found the imprint ' London, No. 1, F14 1948+'. But three pages before this in a quite separate and unconnected entry with a different set of location symbols she discovered ' *Union.* (Sir Oswald Mosley) London. No. 1, F14 1948+'. The coincidence of the dates was too great: these were obviously the same journal. It therefore followed that this journal's predecessor, the *Action* of 1936-40, was almost certainly a second journal of Mosley's, a revival perhaps of the first, with the same name, although bibliographically quite separate. BUCOP confirmed that this *Action* too, sub-titled ' for king and people ', could be seen at Cambridge and the BM.

One difficulty that compilers of union lists face is defining precisely what they have included. As we have seen, the dividing line between a periodical and a newspaper is not always clear; there has been endless debate on the differences (if any) between periodicals and serials; and some union lists include annuals and others do not. It pays the librarian to study very closely the scope notes appended to such works, and not always to assume that because a certain title does not appear in a particular union list (or library catalogue) it is not available in the libraries covered.

Indispensable as they are for work with periodicals, union lists are primarily only location tools; as bibliographical reference works they commonly exhibit two weaknesses: they rarely give sufficient details about the titles they list and they do not permit access by subject. The unofficial *Subject index to New serial titles 1950-1965* is a worthy if limited attempt to eliminate the latter weakness, but is not entirely successful. To supplement the union lists in bibliographical and subject enquiries the librarian as we have seen turns to directories like *Willing's* and the *Standard periodicals directory* or to bibliographies like Woodworth and *Ulrich's*.

Just as with bibliographies of books, it would be foolish to think that the value to a library of the lists and indexes and abstracts of periodicals depends on how many of the periodicals covered are held in stock. The increasing sophistication of the location tools for periodicals, together with the spread of telex and cheap and rapid photocopying has revolutionised the interlibrary loan system, for periodical articles especially. Indeed, to take full advantage of such facilities, there is paradoxically *more* need in the smaller libraries to ensure that they have the bibliographical tools that serve as keys to stores of riches locked up in the periodical collections of their larger neighbours. It must also be remembered that a number of readers come to libraries in search of references only, in the first instance. It may be some time later, and in some other place, that they require to see the cited articles.

Although lists of periodicals confined to specific subjects are outside the scope of this chapter, it should be noted that they do exist, in their hundreds, comprising all the categories we have noticed among the general lists, namely directories, *eg, Directory of Canadian scientific and technical periodicals* (second edition 1962); selective bibliographies, *eg,* C D Harris *An annotated world list of selected current geographical serials in English* (1960); union lists, *eg, Union lists of periodicals in music in the libraries of the University of London* (1969); and holdings lists, *eg,* Yale University Library *Checklist of Southeast Asian serials* (1968). A further category rarely encountered in the general field is the list of titles scanned by a particular indexing or abstracting service, *eg,* Biological Abstracts *Serial list.*

Conveniently considered at this point are the newspapers. Their function of course is unique and as repositories of much information completely unavailable elsewhere they are irreplaceable. They are the sources *par excellence* of information on current affairs and people of the day, and a substantial minority of the enquiries in all types of library stems from the news of the moment: this is why textbooks for reference librarians stress the value of scanning at least one major newspaper from masthead to colophon each day. For the historian the newspapers are unrivalled as mirrors of contemporary opinion, and many is the learned contribution to historical studies based almost entirely on newspaper reports. Too much should not be made of the differences between newspapers and periodicals as reference sources, however, for in many enquiries they are consulted for information in similar fashion.

It is when the reference librarian needs to seek information within the pages of newspapers that he meets his major bibliographical problem: there is no indexing service to do for newspapers what, for instance, the *British humanities index* or the *Social sciences and humanities index* does for periodicals, although the former does index a very small number of national newspapers on a selective basis. And as for publishing indexes to their own contents, the newspapers in Britain and the US that make the effort can be counted literally on the fingers of one hand. Three of these (*Index to the Glasgow Herald, Wall Street journal: index, Index of the Christian Science Monitor* are comparatively rarely met with; fortunately the remaining two are the keys to what are arguably the major newspapers in their respective countries, the *Index to the Times* and the *New York Times index*. It has often been pointed out, moreover, that these indexes can be made to serve as partial indexes to other newspapers by pinpointing the date of a particular item of news, assuming of course that the other newspapers have covered the story at about the same time.

Case 43: When asked by the local newspaper for ' something on *son et lumière* in Britain ' the reference library assistant thought as she put the phone down that she had better clear her own mind on the topic first, for she had no more than a vague idea that it was something to do with flood-lighting buildings. However, to run to earth even a basic definition took her several minutes, for the term was not to be found in any of the most likely recent dictionaries—*Webster's third* (1961), the *Shorter Oxford* with the 'Addenda' brought up to date in 1955, the fifth edition of the *Concise Oxford* (1964). Neither were the usually reliable French-English dictionaries, including J E Mansion (1934), *Cassell's* (eighth edition 1968), and *Harrap's shorter* (revised edition 1967). She knew the term would be too recent for the OED and Littré, so she omitted these from the search and concentrated on some of the less likely but more recent titles. Her persistence was rewarded in Paul Robert *Dictionnaire alphabétique et anthologique de la langue française* (1967) with ' où un monument est illuminé tandis que se fait entendre une évocation sonore, musicale . . . de son histoire '. A further definition appeared in the useful thirty-page supplement to *Chambers's twentieth century dictionary* (1965): ' a dramatic spectacle presented after dark, involving lighting effects on natural features of the country or a chosen building and an appropriate theme illustrated by spoken words and by music '.

All that the *British national bibliography* revealed on this topic was a twenty-page pamphlet published at Tunbridge Wells in 1969, almost certainly to accompany a particular display: Martyn Hepworth *Son et lumière: the story of the town from 1606 to the present day*. The *Cumulative book index* (checked back to 1933) had not a single title on the topic, and when neither *British books in print* nor the American *Books in print* produced anything at all the assistant concluded, probably correctly, that the subject was too recent for a book. Turning therefore to the periodical indexes, she found after a thorough search of both *British technology index* and *British humanities index* just one solitary reference ' Getting history taped ' in the *Daily telegraph* colour supplement for 12th June 1970. This reminder that BHI indexes selectively the ' posh ' newspapers like the *Guardian* and the *Observer* immediately suggested to the assistant that the *Index to the Times* might be worth investigation. This brainwave paid immediate dividends, for a five-year check produced eight references (some illustrated) to *son et lumière* at, for instance, Blenheim Palace, the Tower of London, and Hampton Court.

(*See also* cases 6, 7, 8.)

It must not be forgotten too that their currency allows periodical and particularly newspaper indexes to serve as reference works in their own right—almost as ends in themselves. Outstanding is the *New York Times index*: its very full entries, often with short summaries, frequently render unnecessary the consultation of the actual newspaper files. And illustrations and maps are occasionally included! Even the less informative entries of the *Index to the Times* can be used to assess trends over a period in a manner similar to that illustrated above (case 11) with the general periodical indexes.

Case 44: When asked by an obvious student enquirer for information on colour television the reference librarian was of course obliged to enquire further, to ascertain for instance whether her interest was in the technical side of the question, or the commercial aspects, or what? As it turned out after a few moments' dialogue, the reader, in the course of preparing a report on the history of colour television in Britain, was looking first for an outline survey to enable her to plan her work programme.

Information on the topic of course was plentiful, but the task of selecting articles or chapters from books to match exactly the reader's needs at this stage could have been very difficult. Happily, the librarian had the thought of scanning the *Index to the Times* over the last few years to see if the entries would provide a sufficiently coherent bird's eye view. In this case his luck was in, for the panorama of entries stretching back to the early 1950's were found to give a surprisingly vivid outline history of the subject, ranging from the early BBC experimental broadcasts through the long years of conflict over differing technical systems (plentifully sprinkled with questions in Parliament) to the culmination of the first transmissions in 1967. Emphasis then shifted to, for instance, surveys of public reaction and sales figures of TV sets.

With all this the student seemed well pleased, although she did ask why the entries appeared under 'television' in the early 1950's and late 1960's, and under 'broadcasting' (with a 'see' reference from 'television') from October 1955 to December 1966. This enquiry the librarian was not able to answer.

As all the cases so far in this chapter have indicated, the sort of enquiries that periodicals are most frequently used to answer are the 'material-finding' or 'something-on-a-subject' type. That is not to say that they are not useful for 'fact-finding' enquiries, but merely to suggest that they are less convenient for such searches than an encyclopedia or a yearbook. This is perhaps not quite so true of newspapers, particularly the indexed newspapers: it is claimed, for instance, that each annual edition of the *New York Times index* 'brings you over *half a million* facts . . . helps you find needed facts quickly . . . pinpoints names, dates, numbers '.

Case 45: ' Picasso's *La famille* was sold last year, I believe. Can you tell me who bought it and for how much? ' was obviously a ' fact-finding ' enquiry. Perhaps the best source to consult would have been one of the specific annual tools such as *Art prices current* or *Art-price annual* or the ' *Connoisseur* ' art sales annual; in point of fact the young librarian turned to the *Index to the Times* for the previous year, 1968. Although 'Picasso, Mr P' appeared several times in the volumes, none of the references related to the sale of this particular work.

Turning therefore to the *New York Times index*—its 24 parts for 1968 very conveniently cumulated into one volume—the librarian looked up Picasso again. She was directed by a 'see also' reference to 'art—sales', where very quickly (without the need to consult the actual newspaper) she gleaned the facts that the drawing was sold in June for $21,600 to a certain R Burton.

[This news item was in fact in the London *Times* also and in the *Index*, but under 'Burton, Mr R.' The accompanying entries made it clear that this was indeed Richard Burton, the famous Welsh actor.]

If periodicals are looked upon as supplements to the books, newspapers can be regarded as supplements to the current affairs yearbooks such as *World almanac* and *Statesman's year-book*.

Case 46: When asked for information on the Runnymede Trust the librarian's first inclination was to consult G W Keeling *Trusts and foundations* (1953), the only reference book on the subject with an entry in Walford. Invaluable as this work is, however, it is in sore need of updating; suspecting the Runnymede Trust to be a recent foundation, the librarian was not surprised to find no entry for it. He realised that his problem was more serious when he found it was not listed in the National Council of Social Services *Directory of grant-making trusts* (1968) (which is noted but not described by Walford), or in the 1971-72 edition of *Directory of British associations*.

Perhaps the newspapers could help? He began to work his way back through the volumes of the *Index to the Times*, where he soon found references to the activities of the Trust, mainly reports and studies on immigrants and race relations. Finally, he located an account of the formation of the Trust, in the issue for 1st November 1968. This included a photograph of the first director, Mr Dipak Nandy, an Indian, and described the Trust as an information centre on race relations, to which anyone can turn for facts and statistics on race matters. Four of the trustees were named, but not the 'three charitable trusts' said to be backing the venture. According to Mr Nandy, 'It owes its name to twin lines of thought . . . human rights and Magna Carta; and J F Kennedy and civil rights.'

It must be admitted that newspapers have long been neglected in some libraries. Problems of binding their awkward size, and then storing their unwieldy bulk, and finally combating deterioration of their cheap newsprint were left in the main to the larger reference and research libraries, with smaller libraries preserving only their local newspapers. The ready availability of microfilm editions and the wider dispersal of microfilm readers over the last twenty-five years has radically altered the picture, and users are now getting to expect a back run of at least the *Times* (with *Index*) for consultation in their library. With files of other papers, however, even though thousands of titles have now been microfilmed, lack of indexing is still a major handicap. Some libraries maintain at least partial indexes to their newspaper files, selecting items according to their own subject interests perhaps. Frequently encountered in public libraries are indexes to the local papers. And as mentioned above with periodicals, many newspapers have devised their own internal systems for indexing their contents for the benefit of their own editorial staff, and in moderation are willing to answer enquiries from librarians, and in some cases permit safeguarded access to their records.

For some years there has been talk of the assistance that electronic data processing could bring in solving this problem, but little positive has so far emerged. One example is the *New York Times obituaries index* (1969) locating the 350,000 death listings published since 1858, and the parent *Index* itself has been computer-produced since 1968. Another instance on a wider base is the University of Saskatchewan project to index fifteen Canadian newspapers back to 1840. Where modern technology has made a noticeable contribution, however, although still on a small scale, is in the use of photo-litho-offset printing methods to make 'home-made' newspaper indexes more widely available, *eg*, the three-volume *Index of obituaries in Boston newspapers, 1704-1800* (1967), compiled by the Boston Athenaeum.

One further method used by many libraries to increase access to the vast stores of unindexed information locked in the files of newspapers is to maintain a cuttings file by regularly clipping items of interest from the current press, particularly the local newspapers. Perhaps very few libraries clip the total contents of the newspapers they thus scan; very commonly selection is based on some pre-arranged plan, *eg,* the local obituaries, reviews of local theatrical productions, matters concerning the activities of the local authority; or, perhaps, items may be selected if they fit into predetermined subject categories, *eg,* athletics, banking and insurance, ecclesiastical, law, science, *etc.* Some libraries, particularly in specialised fields, find it worth-while to subscribe to one or more commercial press-cuttings agencies.

In recent years modern technology has furnished us with a further extension of the information services of the *Times* newspaper in the shape of Xerographic facsimiles of the volumes of the actual cuttings books originally compiled by the *Times* Intelligence Department from as far back in some cases as 1901.

The infinite variety of bibliographical problems that have been described above as arising from periodicals are also common with newspapers.

Case 47: At the enquiry desk of a midlands city library an elderly gentleman explained confidentially that he was on the verge of retirement. He was seeking to buy a house in the Wimborne area and wished to know the name and address of the local newspaper where advertisements for such houses might appear. In the main 'Alphabetical list' in *Willing's press guide* the librarian could find nothing under Wimborne; before consulting the supplementary list 'English counties (index to newspapers)', he first confirmed from J G Bartholomew *Gazetteer of the British Isles* (ninth edition 1963) that Wimborne was indeed in the county of Dorset, as he had thought. Under 'Dorsetshire' he found five newspapers listed, none of them either published at Wimborne or with Wimborne in their titles.

The much larger *Newspaper press directory* he found more helpfully arranged, with useful background information on each specific town listed alphabetically in the section 'English provincial newspapers.' Regrettably, the name of Wimborne was missing. The supplementary 'County index' listed four Dorsetshire newspapers.

In the circumstances, he felt the best he could do was suggest from these lists the name of the Dorsetshire newspaper most likely to be circulating in the Wimborne area. It was only when he glanced at a map that he noticed how far Wimborne was from the main towns of Dorset and how close to the border with Hampshire; it was not beyond the bounds of possibility that the best paper for this reader's purposes would be a Hampshire publication, from Bournemouth perhaps. Back with the *Newspaper press directory* the librarian was rewarded with the discovery among the Hampshire newspapers of one published every Thursday with the title *Ringwood, Fordingbridge, Ferndown, and Wimborne journal.*

One of the more tiresome problems can be the simple physical difficulty of locating a file of the newspaper that is required. BUCOP includes newspapers up to 1799, and the *Union list of serials* includes English and foreign (*ie,* non-US) titles to 1821, but for the later period Britain has nothing to match the excellent *American newspapers, 1821-1936* (1937) edited by Winifred Gregory under the auspices of the Bibliographical Society of America, which covers 37,000 titles, not merely holdings in libraries, but also in newspaper offices, county courthouses, and private collections—nearly 5,700 depositories in all. By way of contrast, the bibliographical tools in Britain guide the searcher towards the great central repository of the British Museum Newspaper Library at Colindale, for in the absence of a union list the major retrospective bibliography of nineteenth century newspapers is the BM *Catalogue of printed books: supplement: newspapers . . . 1801-1900* (1905) listing 75,000 titles, and the *Times tercentenary handlist of English and Welsh newspapers, magazines and reviews* (1920) is based largely on the BM collections. Such union lists as do exist to supplement these titles are nearly all local in coverage, for example, J P S Ferguson *Scottish newspapers held in Scottish libraries* (1956) and R E G Smith *Newspapers first published before 1900 in Lancashire, Cheshire and the Isle of Man: a union list of holdings in libraries and newspaper offices within that area* (1964).

The ephemeral nature of the newspaper, added to the purely physical difficulties of preservation and storage, leaves it susceptible to one particular hazard—the complete loss of all extant copies of particular issues. Even the 'Thunderer', the mighty *Times* itself, is not exempt.

Case 48: What turned out to be a long-drawn-out search began with a simple-sounding request for the 1816 volume of the *St James's chronicle*. As the library, a large city reference library, did not possess this journal at all the librarian instinctively reached for BUCOP, only to find that the title was not listed. He had better luck with the *Union list of serials,* where the entry read: ' St James's chronicle; or, Whitehall and general evening post. London. 1761-1866.' Broken or incomplete runs (none of them including 1816) were located in about 15 American and Canadian libraries. Its London imprint made its absence from BUCOP even more puzzling: even if it were regarded as a newspaper these are included up to 1799, and surely there must be a set somewhere in Britain.

The BM *General catalogue* was the next port of call; remembering that entries are arranged in the *Periodicals publications* volumes under place of publication, he speedily found the title listed (although with a different sub-title: ' the British evening post'). The brief annotation, however, read ' Imperfect, wanting the years 1816-18 '. As was perhaps to be expected, since it is largely based on the BM holdings the Times *Tercentenary handlist of English and Welsh newspapers, magazines & reviews* also had the ominous note ' Imperfect, many years missing ': no location was given, indicating that the only file traced was at the BM.

Perhaps not likely, therefore, but nevertheless possible was the location of the missing years in a library other than the BM. Walford was examined for possible union lists or holdings lists, but the librarian found that practically all of the seven or eight likely titles were confined either to English provincial newspaper files, *eg,* G E Laughton and L R Stephen *Yorkshire newspapers: a bibliography, with locations* (1960). or to locations of English newspaper files in American libraries, *eg,* R S Crane and F B Kaye *A census of British newspapers and periodicals, 1620-1800* (1927). Two works did look as if they might be worth consulting, one a library catalogue, the other a union list: R T Milford and D M Sutherland *A catalogue of English newspapers and periodicals in the Bodleian Library, 1622-1800* (1936); and an American compilation which quite uniquely gave locations in British and Canadian as well as US libraries and newspaper offices, W S Ward *Index and finding list of serials published in the British Isles, 1789-1832* (1953). The former had an entry for the journal, with detailed holdings; the detail did not extend beyond 1800, however, apart from the mere indication that some numbers after 1800 were in Bodley. The compiler of the letter explained in his foreword his own frustrations in searching for newspapers and periodicals of this period, and went on to say that his list was specifically geared to complement ULS and BUCOP. The entry for *Saint James' chronicle* [sic] indicated that the Guildhall Library (London) had a complete file covering 1789-1827 and Oxford Public Library's file was complete from 1806 to 1823.

Supplementing the newspapers as both disseminators and repositories of news are the digest services, perhaps best represented in libraries by the British *Keesing's contemporary archives* and the American *Facts on file,* both weeklies. The latter, indeed, proclaims as its slogan ' How to read 77 newspapers in 30 minutes '. Services classifying and summarising news are not uncommon: what gives these two their special role in libraries and elsewhere is their loose-leaf format and the care taken to index, currently and cumulatively, the weekly or monthly parts.

Case 49: ' Has China got a space programme? ' was the simple question posed in a one-man industrial information unit. The information officer did not know off-hand, but he felt sure the latest *Statesman's year book* would say. He was disappointed to find no more than twelve pages on China and even more downcast to find nothing about space in any of the most likely sections such as ' Defence ', ' Industry ', ' Communications ', 'Aviation '.

Finding the current *Whitaker's almanack* even less informative, he took down the latest *Keesing's contemporary archives* loose-leaf binder. In its system of coloured indexes under ' China: space research ' he soon tracked down a summary of an item from the *Peking review* about the launching of China's second earth satellite weighing 221 kilograms on 3rd March 1971. Following *Keesing's* practice a reference was given to a previous report on the same topic. In the form of a five-paragraph digest from the *Peking review,* the *Times,* and the *International herald tribune,* this earlier report described how China became the fourth nation in space with a 173 kilogram satellite placed in orbit on 24th April 1970, circling the earth every 114 minutes and broadcasting to the world the music of 'The east is red'. The report included a long note on Dr Tsien Hsue-shen, head of the Chinese space programme and a former US Army Air Corps colonel.

As this case shows, much of the information the digests contain is taken (with attribution) from the newspapers. Obviously, therefore, this information is less immediately 'current': where the digests score again is in their indexes, which are certainly many weeks (if not months) ahead of the two-monthly *Index to the Times*, if not so far in advance of the two-weekly *New York Times index*.

Case 50: The visitor to a medium-sized public reference library one quiet morning was a clergyman who explained that he was about to visit Belgium for a conference. He was particularly interested in the long-standing and troublesome language conflicts there, about which he seemed well-informed. What he required from the librarian was a brief account of the latest position, with particular emphasis on any new developments.

Facts on file was immediately consulted, for as a 'weekly world news digest' it had assisted the librarian in many similar current affairs enquiries previously. Without much difficulty he located through the cumulative index under 'Belgium' a five-paragraph report dated 18th February 1970, beginning 'Premier Gaston Eyskens submitted a plan to Parliament Feb. 18 proposing a constitutional amendment aimed at ending the friction between Belgium's three principal language groups . . .'

Showing this to his enquirer, the librarian suggested that fuller reports could probably be found in the major newspapers of this date. He offered to search and produce them, but was told that the *Facts on file* summary would suffice very well.

[Such a report was indeed in the *Times* at least, and could have been traced through the *Index*. However, the volume covering the issues for February 1970 was not published until October, several months after the appearance, fully indexed, of the digest in *Facts on file*.]

In this particularly intractable area it is worth recalling the words of an American historian who has made a special study of the value of newspaper collections in the historical field: 'Despite all the guides, one must continue to use the talents of a Sherlock Holmes, the doggedness of a Dr Watson, and the wiles of a James Bond to achieve anything remotely resembling completeness in this field'.

2

phrase books

MAN'S PERENNIAL FASCINATION with language and its use ensures that many of the enquiries put to reference librarians have to do with words. Dictionaries are of course the obvious sources to turn to for aid, but, as the student will have discovered, they understandably concentrate on individual words. A sizeable proportion of enquiries are about words grouped into phrases, and for these the librarian employs a further battery of reference aids.

Probably the most typical of all enquiries that librarians are faced with in this area are those asking about quotations, and the best known category of phrase books are the dictionaries of quotations. Writers have often speculated on the reasons for man's delight in repeating the words of others, for there is no doubt, as Bernard Darwin says in his introduction to the *Oxford dictionary of quotations,* that 'Quotation brings to many people one of the intensest joys of living'. In his *Quotemanship* (1967) Paul F Boller has categorised 22 distinct varieties of quotations currently used, although, as so often, it is Montaigne who has explained this urge most succinctly: 'I quote others only in order the better to express myself'.

Readers bring their quotation problems to the library in search of one of three things: verification, information, or inspiration. Enquirers in search of *verification* normally have a particular quotation, often half-remembered, sometimes on the tip of the tongue, and they require the librarian's help to complete the phrase or to trace its exact wording. As a starting point for his search the librarian invariably has a word or two of the original quotation, and the

87

major quotation dictionaries take pains specifically to provide for this approach to their contents: John Bartlett *Familiar quotations,* for instance, has a computer-compiled keyword index of 117,000 entries for its 20,421 quotations, and in the *Oxford dictionary of quotations* the index makes up one third of the bulk of the book.

Case 51: ' Can you look up for me what it is that is the hobgoblin of small minds? ' was the enquiry received by phone from its design office by an industrial library in the engineering field. Like many such special libraries, it was used to coping with non-engineering enquiries of this kind, and had available for this purpose in its quick reference section half-a-dozen phrase books and quotation dictionaries. The very first that the library assistant consulted, Bartlett *Familiar quotations,* led from the index entry under ' hob-goblin ' to the full quotation by Ralph Waldo Emerson: 'A foolish consistency is the hobgoblin of little minds ', which appeared in his ' *Essays: First Series* [1841]. Self-Reliance '. Aware that it is always a good plan to double-check quotations, the assistant also tried the *Oxford dictionary of quotations,* which confirmed Bartlett, but did add a more specific bibliographical reference to page 24 of volume one of the Bohn edition of Emerson's works.

Case 52: A wife who had just bought a present for her husband called into a reference library in the North of England one after-noon. ' I want to write something on the card ', she said, ' and I thought that perhaps that old saying about all the world being queer except thee and me would amuse him. Can you find it for me? ' It was not in the *Oxford dictionary of quotations,* or in Stevenson, *Hoyt's,* or *Benham's.* The librarian did find it however, in Bartlett and the *Penguin dictionary of quotations,* but with with differing attributions. The former credited to an unidentified Quaker, ' speaking to his wife ', and the latter to Robert Owen (1771-1858), ' when ending his partnership with William Allen '. The full quotation, which the reader copied down on her card, was 'All the world is queer save thee and me, and even thou art a little queer '.

In choosing the keyword to look under first the searcher in a hurry can find himself torn between the most important word, which may be a common term with hundreds of entries in the indexes to be searched, and other less common words, which being less important in the context of the quotation may not have been indexed at all! To be quite sure he has not missed anything, however, the wise librarian will check under all possible keywords.

Case 53: A clergyman (perhaps writing next Sunday's sermon) asked for assistance in tracking down a passage he remembered in his reading which compared man's life span with the flight of a swallow (or was it a sparrow?) through a building. After a preliminary unsuccessful glance at what he thought might be a useful source in *Brewer's dictionary of phrase and fable,* the librarian commenced searching the dictionaries of quotations: making use of the well-tried device of looking first under the least common word, he concentrated on swallow (and sparrow). Bartlett, Stevenson, *Benham's* and *Hoyt's* provided no clues, but he found what he wanted (in two different translations from the original Latin) in the ODQ and the *Penguin dictionary of quotations.* The latter gave the full quotation, from the Venerable Bede (673-735) *History of the English church and people,* as: 'When we compare the present life of man with that time of which we have no knowledge, it seems to me like the swift flight of a lone sparrow through the banqueting-hall where you sit in the winter months . . . The sparrow flies swiftly in through one door of the hall, and out through another . . . Similarly, man appears on earth for a little while, but we know nothing of what went on before this life and what follows.'

There are some quotation books lacking indexes of keywords where this approach is not possible, for instance, F P Adams *FPA book of quotations,* H L Mencken *A new dictionary of quotations,* but since these are usually arranged by subject they prove very useful, together with other subject-ordered sources like Stevenson *Book of quotations,* in those cases where not even a single word of the original has been correctly remembered, merely the general sense. The subject approach can also prove useful in those cases where the keywords remembered are so vague or general as to preclude for practical purposes an attack *via* the indexes.

Case 54: The librarian's assistance was called upon by a reader looking for the exact wording of the quotation about the price that we have to pay for freedom—being continually on the alert. The index entries under 'Freedom' in Bartlett, ODQ and Stevenson revealed nothing that might be relevant, but turning to the eight columns of entries headed 'freedom' in the main sequence of this last work, the librarian found, not the quotation his enquirer wanted, but a reference 'See also Liberty'. Under 'liberty' he found nine columns of quotations, but was able to locate in section IV 'Liberty: Its Defense' the sought-for saying: 'Eternal vigilance is the price of liberty', attributed to Wendell Phillips in an address before the Antislavery Society, 28th January 1852. A note added: 'It has been said that Mr Phillips was quoting Thomas Jefferson, but in a letter dated 14 April, 1879, Mr Phillips wrote: "'Eternal vigilance is the price of liberty' has been attributed to Jefferson, but no one has yet found it in his works or elsewhere ".' It has also been attributed to Patrick Henry.

Now he had the precise wording, the librarian decided to double check in ODQ and Bartlett. He was immediately surprised to find in the former (indexed under 'vigilance' but not under 'liberty') a slightly different wording and a completely different attribution: 'The condition upon which God hath given liberty to man is eternal vigilance', said by John Philpot Curran in a speech on the right of election of Lord Mayor of Dublin, 10th July 1790. With both the wording and attribution Bartlett was found to agree, but noting that the 'commonly quoted' version was the shorter one, as previously discovered in Stevenson.

It does happen on occasion that the enquirer can recall the author as well as the dimly recollected phrase: this can of course open up further avenues of search. The student will have noticed that books of quotations differ in their arrangement far more than do the general dictionaries, and that by offering a variety of approaches they tend to supplement rather than duplicate each other for this reason. The big three, Stevenson, Bartlett, and the *Oxford dictionary of quotations* demonstrate this particularly well, for while the first arranges its entries alphabetically by subject, the other two arrange them by author. In the ODQ, however, the authors are in alphabetical order; in Bartlett they are set out chronologically. Of course, each work has a very full index under individual words, and Stevenson and Bartlett have author indexes too.

Case 55: A reader in a college of education library came up to the desk with a copy of Samuel Butler *The way of all flesh*. She pointed to a page where the librarian read: 'Lord Macaulay has a passage in which he contrasts the pleasures which a man may derive from books with the inconveniences to which he may be put by his acquaintances'. 'Can you find me the original quotation?' the reader asked. Perhaps naturally, the librarian turned first to those dictionaries of quotations he knew were arranged by author. Robin Hyman *A dictionary of famous quotations* had 13 by Macaulay, there were four pages devoted to him in the *Oxford dictionary of quotations*, two pages in *Benham's* and two pages in the *Penguin dictionary of quotations*, but none of them seemed to suit, and in the indexes under 'books' there were far too many entries to follow up at this stage. In Bartlett the quotations are also of course grouped under authors, but the authors are arranged chronologically, so the index of authors had to be consulted first. The entry for Macaulay was asterisked, thus indicating that 'quotations from that author included as notes are so numerous that the editors considered it impracticable to give numbers of all the pages where they occur'. Mercifully, there were three pages of Macaulay quotations in the main chronological sequence, but again, none fitted the bill; once more the hundreds of entries in the Bartlett index under 'books' persuaded the librarian that these should be checked only as a last resort. Stevenson was then examined: here the main arrangement is by subject, but there is an index to authors. Beside Macaulay's name, however, was again found the dire asterisk, indicating that the number of his quotations is 'in excess of 150' and therefore no page references were given. This left only the subject approach. The 13 pages of quotations under 'books' are divided into ten subsections: of these the most appropriate seemed 'IV Books as friends and companions'. Here almost immediately was found a 13-line extract from Macaulay's *Essays* including the sentence: 'These friendships [with books] are exposed to no danger from the occurrences by which other attachments are weakened or dissolved'. With this the reader went away happily.

Clearly, the librarian unfamiliar with these varying patterns labours under a disadvantage. Other idiosyncrasies too are worthy of study, if he wishes to master his craft. As he will know, the *Oxford dictionary of quotations* is matched by the *Oxford dictionary of English proverbs*: he should also know that proverbs and phrases are deliberately excluded from the former, because they are dealt with fully in the latter. But if he studies the similar pair of volumes by Burton Stevenson, *Book of quotations* and *Book of proverbs, maxims and familiar phrases* he will find very considerable overlap and duplication. Similarly, the alert librarian should know that while *Benham's book of quotations* makes a feature of quotations from the Bible, *Hoyt's new cyclopedia of practical quotations* deliberately omits them; and that Stevenson excludes quotations from the Bible and from Shakespeare, leaving them to his *Home book of Bible quotations* and his *Book of Shakespeare quotations.*

Not many authors achieve such eminence as to warrant a whole dictionary of quotations devoted to their works, and where such tools exist the librarian will naturally turn to them with gratitude, *eg, Everyman's dictionary of Shakespeare quotations* (1953). There are many writers, however (usually of pure literature) who have had concordances of their works published: in recent years in particular the application of mechanical and electronic data processing methods has produced a spate of new titles, *eg,* D V Erdman *A concordance to the writings of William Blake* (1968); R C Williams *A concordance to the collected poems of Dylan Thomas* (1967). Because a concordance is normally exhaustive, indexing every occurrence of every word (except perhaps the very common) in an author's writings, whereas a dictionary of quotations is invariably selective, the searcher is usually well advised to try the concordance first. He does need, however, to watch for the partial concordance, which while comprehensive enough within its scope, does not extend to the whole of an author's work: for instance, S M Parrish *A concordance to the poems of Matthew Arnold* (1959) clearly does not cover his prose works.

Case 56: A phone call from the editorial office of a women's magazine asked for help in locating the passage in Dryden about Old Father Thames, but not a trace could be found in any of the dictionaries of quotations available (Bartlett, Stevenson, *Hoyt's,*

Penguin, ODQ, *Benham's*). Clearly this might be a case for a concordance, if one could be found. The library catalogue revealed nothing, but a consultation of Walford and Winchell discovered (in both) Guy Montgomery *Concordance to the poetical works of John Dryden* (1957). Fully aware that Dryden had also written prose, the librarian located a copy in a nearby university library. It turned out to be an early example of what has become increasingly common—a concordance produced by IBM machines. This particular example was rather more difficult to use than the conventionally printed kind, insofar as all the words were listed singly, without any context. However, applying what he knew of co-ordinate indexing, the librarian compared the four references to Dryden's use of ' Thames ' with the much larger number of uses of the word ' father '. There was only one which matched: ' AM 925 '. It took but a moment to interpret this as line 925 of *Annus mirabilis*, and when a copy of Dryden's poems was consulted this was found to be the first line of a four-line stanza: ' Old Father Thames rais'd up his reverend head . . .'

Frequently useful in tracing quotations by a specific author is a type of reference tool exemplified by W C de Vane *A Browning handbook* (second edition 1955); Maurice Lindsay *The Burns encyclopaedia* (1959); C H Whitman *A subject-index to the poems of Edmund Spenser* (1918).

Case 57: The librarian was called upon to assist an enquirer looking without success for the quotation by Sherlock Holmes in which he emphasises that the basis of his method of scientific detection consists in close attention to detail. As put, this enquiry did not give the librarian much to go on by way of keywords but did (by implication of course) offer the opportunity of an author approach. Turning therefore to the author-arranged quotation books the librarian drew blank at first with Bartlett (only a single column devoted to Sir Arthur Conan Doyle) but in the *Oxford dictionary of quotations* (nearly three columns) he soon ran to earth the appropriate quotation from *A case of identity*: ' It has been an axiom of mine that the little things are infinitely the most important '.

The reader, however, was quite definite: ' No, that isn't the one I am looking for '. Back with ODQ the librarian looked carefully through the rest of the quotations attributed to Conan Doyle, but to no avail. And then, rather than consult his other dictionaries of quotations arranged by author (*Benham's, Penguin, Everyman's, etc*), he made straight for Michael and Mollie Hardwick *The Sherlock Holmes companion* (1962). Fifty pages of this fascinating guide are devoted to 'A sampler of quotations': though there is no index, the librarian was soon able to run down in the section 'On detection and crime' what he was sure this time would be the desired quotation: 'You know my method. It is founded on the observance of trifles' (from *The Boscombe Valley mystery*). The reader confirmed that this indeed was what she had been looking for.

With major authors whose works are eventually published in the form of a collected edition there is a further source to check for the elusive quotation. In many cases the editor of the collection provides an index to the set, often in minute detail.

Case 58: A newly-appointed assistant librarian was asked to draft a reply to a letter just received containing the following request: 'Socrates believed that reliance on books was a bad thing for the memory. Can you document this for me?' His first thought was to look under 'books' in the indexes to the quotation dictionaries, but contact with sober reality in the form of entries to be scanned made him think again. His second and much more sensible approach was to look at the entries under 'Socrates' in those dictionaries arranged by author. Bartlett had eight, ODQ only two, and *Everyman's* had none. Two more were found in Hyman, but *Benham's* (as he learned when he consulted it) covers only British and American authors in its alphabetical sequence. None of these quotations, however, fitted the enquirer's description.

The only major quotation dictionaries in his collection not examined thus far were Evans and Stevenson, which are of course arranged by subject. They do have author indexes, and the reference librarian found some thirty page references to Socrates in Stevenson and eleven in Evans. They were not differentiated in any way, so by following them up one by one, he decided to try a short cut by seeing if he could trace a set of Socrates' collected works. He was brought up sharp by the library catalogue which seemed to suggest that there was none of Socrates' works in stock at all; although he was new to the library, this he simply could not believe. He turned for advice to that faithful standby *The readers' adviser: a layman's guide,* where all was made clear. He read: ' Socrates, like Jesus, left no writings of his own behind him. His teachings were entirely oral. What knowledge we have of his philosophy comes to us through the writings of his disciples, Plato and Xenophon '. Looking further to see if he could identify a good edition to consult, he saw that ' Jowett's translations are masterpieces: he made Plato an English classic '. This was obviously B Jowett *The dialogues of Plato* (fourth revised edition 1953) in four volumes; the library's set turned out to be the third edition of 1892 in five volumes, but it did contain what the librarian was looking for—a detailed 179-page index in the last volume. The entries under ' books ' were not relevant to the enquiry at all, but under ' memory ' there was a much more hopeful reference to Phaedrus, 274 E. The hunt sustained a temporary check when the volume containing this particular dialogue could not be found, but a substitute was soon located in the form of a separate edition, R Hackforth *Plato's Phaedrus* (1952). The reference was to a part of a whole section on writing, from which the librarian selected the following statement to include in his draft reply: ' [Men] will cease to exercise memory because they rely on that which is written, calling things to remembrance no longer within themselves, but by means of external marks; what you have discovered is a recipe not for memory, but for reminder '.

And as a last resort, provided the enquirer wishes the hunt to continue and is positive as to the author of the elusive phrase, the librarian can always turn to biographical sources, and in particular to the full-scale monograph biographies.

Case 59: In a hunt in a university library for chapter and verse for Dr Johnson's scornful remarks about those who insist on reading a book all the way through the librarian looked first at those dictionaries arranging quotations by author. *Benham's* was found to contain eight columns of Johnson quotations (with an extra column in the supplement), but none of them were what was wanted. Bartlett had 15 columns and ODQ had 19: both included a quotation from Boswell *Life,* 14 July 1763, which seemed a possibility: 'A man ought to read just as inclination leads him; for what he reads as a task will do him little good '. The enquirer, however, had no hesitation in rejecting it.

The next port of call, the *Penguin dictionary of quotations,* ran to 12 columns on Johnson, but again the only likely quotation was the one already given (but here dated 9 July 1763). Having by this time run out of author-arranged dictionaries, the librarian turned to Stevenson, which although arranged by subject does at least have an author index, but found Johnson's entry marked with an asterisk indicating that the number of quotations exceeds 150. The *FPA book of quotations* is similarly arranged, but the index did no more than lead to the quotation under ' reading ' already found in Bartlett and others, here without any date at all. The last source available was the *Faber book of aphorisms*: the author index gave 75 undifferentiated page references to Johnson, which the librarian did not feel inclined to follow up, so he turned to the main sequence, under the grouping ' writers and readers '. Scanning through the pages he found 10 scattered Johnson entries, none appropriate.

Having come to the end of the line by now, the librarian turned to his colleagues for help and was advised to consult the index to Boswell. This he found on the open shelves as the last volume of a six-volume set, *Boswell's Life of Johnson,* edited by George Birkbeck Hill and revised by L F Powell (1934-50). Immediately he found three references on ' reading books to the end '. The first referred to Johnson's own ' peculiar facility at seizing at once what was valuable in any book, without submitting to the labour of perusing it from beginning to end '; the second, to an account of Johnson's sharp retort to an enquiry as to whether he had read a book through: ' No, Sir; do *you* read books through?'. The third reference was to his plainly stated view (at the age of 75) on the advice given by someone to a young gentleman to read to the end of whatever books he should begin to read: ' This is surely a strange advice; you may as well resolve that whatever men you get acquainted with, you are to keep them for life. A book may be good for nothing; or there may be only one thing in it worth knowing; are we to read it all through?'

[With his enquirer well satisfied the librarian thought he would take the opportunity while he had Boswell before him of resolving

96

the conflicting dates in Bartlett and the ODQ on the one hand, and the *Penguin dictionary* on the other, for the quotation located earlier. As the text follows a chronological sequence it was a simple matter to locate the paragraphs describing the events of the day favoured by the *Penguin dictionary*: ' On Saturday, July 9, I found Johnson surrounded with a numerous levee, but have not preserved any part of his conversation '. This seemed more than conclusive, and the quotation was indeed found under the alternative date, Thursday, 14th July 1763.]

Forming a macabre sub-category of the quotation enquiries are those requests for the dying remarks of a particular individual. ' Famous last words ' casts a powerful spell: in old China it was the custom to engrave them on wood for permanent preservation. Modern librarians can find some of the more famous preserved in the phrase books—Stevenson, for example, lists many under ' death: last words ', and *Brewer's* has a list under ' dying sayings '—and there are at least two specific compilations.

Case 60: An enquiry about the last words of Dylan Thomas brought the surprising fact to light that he had no entries at all in the *Oxford dictionary of quotations*. Of the other compilations arranged by author, he was omitted from *Everyman's dictionary of quotations* also, but he had 16 entries in Bartlett (all from his *Collected poems*), 11 in Hyman *A dictionary of famous quotations,* and 25 in the *Penguin dictionary of quotations;* none of them, however, were ' last words '. He did not appear in the ' Dying sayings ' in *Brewer,* or in the section ' Death: last words ' in Stevenson's, or in the 5,000-entry ' Index of authors '.

Next consulted were Barnaby Conrad *Famous last words* (1961) and E S LeComte *Dictionary of last words* (1955). Though there was no entry in the latter, in the former was found what was wanted: ' I have had eighteen straight whiskies. I think that is the record '. As the source was given as John Malcolm Brinnin, the librarian presumed that the reference was to this writer's *Dylan Thomas in America* (1956), which he then examined. It was immediately apparent that these were by no means Dylan's last words (although to be fair to Conrad he does indicate this), for on the following morning he went for a walk and ' had two glasses of beer, chatting meanwhile with a truck-driver acquaintance '. Several later conversations were reported by Brinnin and the actual last words he recorded were ' Yes, I believe you '. In search of further confirmation (always a good idea with ' famous last words '), the librarian turned to the official biography by Constantine Fitzgibbon *The life of Dylan Thomas* (1965). The words quoted by Conrad appeared on the last page of the book and certainly were the last recorded by the biographer, but the accompanying text made it clear that the poet's death did not occur till five days later.

As this case shows, we are here in a region abounding in apocrypha: Stevenson warns that such sayings are ' always open to suspicion '. In the case of William Pitt the younger, Prime Minister of England, the enquirer can rely on the most commonly quoted ' Oh, my country! how I love my country!', or *Brewer's* and the *Dictionary of national biography* version, ' Oh, my country! how I leave my country! ', or he can follow the ODQ and Stevenson, both of which give his last words as ' I think I could eat one of Bellamy's veal pies '. One distracting habit, annoying to librarians, to which the dying are prone is to use quotations, especially from the Bible, instead of coining their own deathbed utterances. The great Earl of Strafford, for example, executed by Charles I in 1641, died with the words ' Put not your trust in princes ' on his lips, as *Brewer's* indicates. But as Bartlett will tell you, these words are from Psalm CXLVI, and (as the ODQ adds) appear also in the *Book of common prayer*.

It is not uncommon, as Bartlett points out, for a familiar quotation to differ from the original whence it derives. ' Fresh fields and pastures new ' was not what Milton wrote: his words were ' . . . fresh woods, and pastures new '. Shakespeare did not say 'All that glitters is not gold ', but 'All that glisters . . .' We are reminded by the ODQ that ' There is a fine old crusted tradition of misquoting not lightly to be broken and it might seem almost pedantic to deck these ancient friends in their true but unfamiliar colours '. This can place the librarian in a quandary as to what is the ' right ' answer in such a case. Misquotation is not always the explanation where the current form of a familiar phrase differs from its earliest known written appearance: the original may be in archaic English, or in a foreign language. Agreement may not be possible as to the original form: this is commonly so with anonymous, and particularly proverbial, expressions (see below). The best judge as to when the librarian has got close enough to the required original is usually the enquirer.

Case 61: The librarian found he had a number of versions to offer his enquirer when asked for the exact wording for an article in a weekly newspaper of what was described as the 'old' saying about beauty being entirely in the eye of the beholder. Stevenson *Book of quotations* gave it in the form 'Beauty is altogether in the eye of the beholder', attributing it to Lew Wallace *The Prince of India*, Bk iii, ch 6, p 178. The only clue as to date was obtained from the 'Index of authors' which described Wallace as an American general and novelist, 1827-1905. This attribution the *Oxford dictionary of quotations* confirmed (with the addition of the date 1893 and the alteration of the page reference to 78) but added an earlier and slightly different version omitting 'altogether', attributing it to Margaret Wolfe Hungerford 'quoted in *Molly Bawn* (1878)'.

The ODQ was followed exactly by Bartlett *Familiar quotations* (fourteenth edition 1968), although the phrase had been omitted entirely from the 1962 edition. He had however unearthed an even earlier reference with the same sense but substantially different wording: 'Beauty in things exists in the mind which contemplates them', traced to David Hume *Essays* (1741-42). With three versions for his reader to choose from, the librarian could have let it rest there, but more out of curiosity than duty he tried a few more quotation books. He could not find the sentence at all in *Everyman's*, *Hoyt's* or the *Penguin dictionary*, but when he found the Wallace wording attributed to Hungerford in Hyman *A dictionary of famous quotations* he decided to call it a day.

(*See also* case 54.)

Very commonly readers will bring quotations to the library, not to check up on the wording, but in search of *information* about the quotation itself. They may be curious about the context, the circumstances in which it was used; they may find the terminology obscure and wish to know its meaning; they may wish to know how the phrase has come down to us; but most usually they want to know who said it, and in particular who said it first, and when. It is in this interest in the origin of quotations that we encounter man's concern with the sayings of others at its most acute. In general, provided the reader has a specific quotation to search for the attack on the problem *via* the keyword indexes is quite straightforward.

Case 62: ' Who invented the phrase " the thin red line "?' sounded like an easy one, so the young assistant turned straight to the *Oxford dictionary of quotations,* only to find two separate sources given, without explanation. The first (undated) was Rudyard Kipling *Tommy*: ' But it's " Thin red line of 'eroes " when the drums begin to roll '. The second was from Sir William Howard Russell *The British expedition to the Crimea* (1877): ' [The Russians] dash on towards that thin red line tipped with steel '. No context or meaning was given, however, and as the assistant had been told always to double-check anyway, he tried Bartlett, where he found an earlier and more illuminating reference to its much earlier use by Russell (with slightly different wording) in his ' Correspondence to the London Times from the Crimea, describing the British infantry at Balaklava [October 25, 1854]'.

As expected, helpful background was furnished by *Brewer's dictionary of phrase and fable,* which agreed on Russell and added ' The old 93rd Highlanders were so described . . . because they did not take the trouble to form into a square. Their regimental magazine was later called *The thin red line.*' Stevenson was found to support Bartlett (with slightly different wording yet again), but interestingly referred to a letter in *Notes and queries* for 9th March 1895 from Russell himself claiming credit for the authorship of the piece. When the librarian followed this up he found Russell disposing of a rival claimant as follows ' If Mr Hems finds the phrase in Napier's " History ", I will eat the volume '.

[In 1970 *The thin red line* by John Selby was published, an account of Balaclava and the events surrounding it. In the Introduction the author admits only that Russell ' may have been the first to use the expression . . . There are, however, other possible claimants: for example, Sir Charles Staveley, commanding the 44th, wrote in his diary that he was in Balaclava when the firing broke out, and as he rode up to Kadikoi saw " the thin red line of the 93rd Highlanders fire their celebrated volleys ".']

Problems may arise with quotations containing vague or unhelpful keywords, and there will be instances where the obvious path is not always the most direct: it is vital to employ a flexible search strategy and be prepared to adopt it where circumstances suggest. Even where the sought-for quotation does contain obvious keywords, for instance, the search may not be all plain sailing. Such are the limitations, not to say idiosyncrasies of indexes to even the most respected reference books, that the user must constantly be prepared to vary his approach.

Case 63: The search for the author of the cosmic claim ' Give me a lever and a place to stand and I will move the earth ' began with the index to the *Oxford dictionary of quotations* under ' lever ' and under ' earth ', but to no avail. The substantial new *Dictionary of quotations* by Bergen Evans was tried next, under the same keywords, with similar results. Stevenson, however, revealed the author immediately (indexed under ' lever ' but not under ' earth ') as Archimedes of Syracuse. Further cross-checking through the volume identified him as the famous geometrician (287-212 BC), more renowned for his other famous quotation ' Eureka!' Stevenson added that the sentence was sometimes quoted as ' Give me where to stand and I will move the world ', but gave no supporting bibliographical references for either form. In the hope of a more precise indication of the original source (presumably Greek), the librarian turned to Bartlett, where an effort is usually made to include the original source of translated quotations. In contrast to Stevenson, the compiler here was found to have indexed the quotation under ' earth ' but not under ' lever '! The main entry did however furnish a specific source: Pappus of Alexandria *Collectio*. Still slightly puzzled at the omission of this striking quotation from a work like the *Oxford dictionary of quotations,* the librarian thought he would just check the entries under Archimedes in the main sequence. And there he found the quotation, in the original Greek, with an even more specific bibliographical reference: '*Pappus Alexandr., Collectio,* lib. viii, prop. 10, xi (ed. Hultsch Berlin, 1878) '. The English translation given was ' Give me but one firm spot on which to stand, and I will move the earth '. By now even more puzzled at his failure to trace this in the index at the start of his search, he checked again, only to find that the quotation was not indexed under *any* of the half-dozen possible keywords. It was only after quite a few moments' quiet study of this work, which he had used perhaps hundreds of times before, that he discovered at the very end the separate two-page Greek index, in which this quotation is indeed indexed, twice, under its Greek keywords. He also realised for the first time that the English translations, merely supplied to assist the reader, are deliberately left unindexed!

Case 64: The first problem faced by the librarian when asked ' Who was it said " How can I tell what I think till I see what I say "?' was the choice of a keyword to use in searching the indexes to the quotation books. A few moments' experiment with Stevenson *Book of quotations,* while not discovering the quotation, did suggest to him that the most likely search term to use was ' think '. Bartlett, Hyman and Evans were each consulted in vain, before (under ' think ') in the *Oxford dictionary of quotations* he came upon this reference to Graham Wallas (1858-1932) *The art of thought*: ' The little girl had the making of a poet in her who, being told to be sure of her meaning before she spoke, said: " How can I know what I think till I see what I say?" ' In Bartlett's very comprehensive index he could not find the phrase under ' think ' but ran it to earth under ' see ': The entry however gave a different source, W H Auden *The dyer's hand* (1962), which attributed the quotation as follows: ' The old lady, quoted by E M Forster—' How can I know..."'.

It was La Bruyère who said as long ago as 1688 that ' We come too late to say anything which has not been said already; ' and an ever-present hazard in the path of the librarian is the quotation requoted. As Bergen Evans points out ' authors are magpies, echoing each other's words and seizing avidly on anything that glitters ', and suspicions are often aroused as to whether the source to which one has traced a particular quotation is indeed the true fountainhead. It is a characteristic of memorable phrases that they are repeated, and the librarian often finds with chagrin that what he thinks is the ultimate origin of a quotation is no more than one of these repetitions. One surprising discovery by the editors preparing the 40,000-word second *Supplement* to the OED (due for publication in 1975) is that many of the seemingly new words and phrases that have become current in recent years have a far earlier origin: 'juvenile delinquent', for example, is found as early as 1818, and 'astronaut' as early as 1929. How this can happen is well illustrated by the case of Winston Churchill, one of the most prolific modern sources of memorable phrases. He tells us in *My early life* (1930) that as a young man it was his practice intently to study Bartlett *Familiar quotations,* 'an admirable work'. It was his opinion that 'The quotations when engraved upon the memory give you good thoughts', and the assiduous searcher can find many instances of lapidary Churchillian phrases that echo earlier quotations.

Case 65: A 'phone call one afternoon from the compiler of the 'Answers to correspondents' column in the local newspaper asked for help in tracking down the origin of the phrase 'iron curtain'. Thinking that a recently acquired etymological dictionary might serve the turn, the librarian was gratified to find in Ernest Klein *A comprehensive etymological dictionary of the English language* (1966): 'Coined by Winston Churchill in 1946 (in a speech at Fulton, Mo, USA)'. 'Just what I thought', replied the caller, 'but this letter I have claims it had been used long before that'. The phrase did not appear at all in the *Oxford dictionary of English etymology,* so dictionaries of quotations seemed the next best bet. In the *Oxford dictionary of quotations* the librarian found two separate entries, the first confirming Klein, giving Churchill's actual words as 'An iron curtain has descended across the continent' and the date as 5th March 1946; the second (with no cross-reference to the first quotation) quoting St Vincent Troubridge in the *Sunday empire news,* 21st October 1945: 'There is an iron curtain across Europe'.

Bartlett also attributed the quote to Churchill, but added in a footnote: 'According to the London Times, the expression " iron curtain " was coined by Ludwig Schwerin von Krosigk, Hitler's Minister of Finance, and was used by Goebbels in his propaganda material for some years before Churchill adopted it'. The *Penguin dictionary of quotations* indexed it under 'curtain' but not under 'iron', and gave sole attribution to St Vincent Troubridge; Stevenson indexed it likewise (with an incorrect page reference!), attributing it to Churchill. But it added the note: 'It was this use of the phrase by Churchill which popularised it, but it had been used in the same connection forty years earlier'. Quotations were given from H G Wells (1904), and one dated 1915 referred to Mexico having 'an iron curtain at its frontier'.

Clearly these were uses of the expression in a sense different from Churchill's, who was obviously referring to the division between the Communist and non-Communist worlds, so in an attempt to throw further light on the problem the librarian broadened his search to *Notes and queries* and to the general dictionaries. He soon discovered a correspondent in the former asking as early as 13th December 1947 'who invented the phrase?' The query was answered the next month by St Vincent Troubridge himself, putting in a claim for his own authorship. The phrase was not in the OED, or its *Supplement*, or in the main alphabet of the *Shorter Oxford dictionary*, but in the 1955 'Addenda' was found a reference to its use in a figurative sense in the 1817 *Journal* of the Earl of Munster, and, referring to Soviet Russia, as early as 1920. The actual quotation, attributed to Mrs Snowden, was 'We were behind the "iron curtain" at last'. Unlike the OED the *Shorter Oxford* does not give the full bibliographical source of its quotations, but after checking in the BM *General catalogue* the librarian felt able to give the source to his enquirer as Ethel Snowden *Through Bolshevik Russia* (1920).

[This deduction was later confirmed by the discovery of an entry in H W Fowler *Modern English usage* (second edition 1965), referring to 'an editorial note in the TLS (14 July 1961)'. By citing Mrs Snowden's book the editor closed a correspondence about the origin of the phrase that had been running for three months. The derivation had been given earlier in the series of letters as a translation of the German *der eisener Vorhang,* the fireproof iron theatrical curtain.

But the story did not end there. Later printings of the second edition of the *Oxford dictionary of quotations* were found to include in the 'Corrigenda' after the introduction a long note on 'iron curtain' quoting Ethel Snowden's use, but deriving the wider application of the phrase to countries within the Soviet sphere of influence from Goebbels' leading article dated 25th February 1945 in the weekly *Das Reich,* which was reported in the *Times* and the *Manchester guardian* on 23 . 2 . 1945 [sic]. The new Bergen Evans *Dictionary of quotations* (1968) included an interesting note about the phrase: ' The Russians, by the way, use it of us; they speak of *us* as being " behind the iron curtain ", and they may have invented the expression in this sense '.

More recently, the prefatory material to the fourteenth (1969) edition of Bartlett referred to the phrase as an instance where the familiar quotation differs from the original whence it derives. The entry in the body of the work not only showed how Churchill himself antedated his own use of the phrase at Fulton in 1946, by using it in a top secret telegram to President Truman dated 12th May 1945, but it also provided a reference earlier than Ethel Snowden's: ' With a rumble and a roar, an iron curtain is descending on Russian history ', Vasily Rozanov *Apocalypse of our time* (1918).

And yet despite all this and much more learned research which can be found reported in the pages of the journal *American speech* (*eg,* 30 1955 186-9; 26 1951 203), it was still possible for a former US ambassador and chief of White House protocol, Angier Biddle Duke, to write in the *Sunday times* of 3rd January 1971 of Churchill's Fulton speech, ' which became famous for the first use of the " Iron Curtain " phrase to describe Russian estrangement '.]

Tracing such quotations has been likened to opening a nest of Chinese boxes: the searcher is never sure that the latest to be revealed is indeed the last.

Case 66: A request received by the reference librarian one morning for the origin of ' Old soldiers never die, they only fade away ', was overheard by a colleague passing the enquiry desk: ' That's General MacArthur, when he was brought back from Japan by President Truman '. The librarian had of course been brought up to check everything, even the recollections of senior colleagues, so she turned to the dictionaries of quotations, where at first she found a pleasing unanimity. The *Oxford dictionary of quotations* attributed it to an anonymous ' War Song of the British Soldiers, 1914-18 '; the *Penguin dictionary of quotations* derived it from a ' Song of the

1914-18 War'; Bartlett referred to a 'War song, British Army [1914-1918]', *Hoyt's* to '*War Song,* popular in England. (1919)', *Benham's* to 'Song. c. 1914-1918', and Evans to 'Anon: British army song, 1914-1918'. Clearly, its use by MacArthur was yet another example of that librarian's curse, the quotation requoted. This was confirmed when Stevenson was consulted, where (in the Appendix) the quotation was found in a long extract from MacArthur's speech to Congress in 1951. This speech, however, added one more twist to the plot, for he described the quotation as 'the refrain of one of the most popular barracks ballads of that day', though the context made it quite clear that he was referring to a period 'before the turn of the century'. This point was taken up in the lengthy accompanying article: although the words first appeared in print in *Tommy's tunes,* published in London in 1917, it seemed likely that the General's memory was not playing him false and that the date was much earlier, possibly deriving in its barrack room form from a gospel hymn of about 1855, *Kind words can never die,* written by 'Sister' Abby Hutchinson. And as a final comment Stevenson quoted a letter from the Reference Librarian of the Music Division of the Library of Congress: 'I would be profoundly suspicious of any attribution to any person living or dead'.

An alternative fate that oft befalls a familiar saying is parody, as in the description of a White House dinner of 1877 where, it was reported, 'Water flowed like wine'.

Case 67: The enquirer seeking the origin of 'Nothing succeeds like excess' admitted frankly over the phone that he had used the phrase already in a speech, but that one of his friends had asked him where it came from. Promising to ring back as soon as possible, the librarian was sufficiently interested to check up first of all the origin of the phrase parodied, 'Nothing succeeds like success'. Surprisingly, this was not in the *Oxford dictionary of quotations,* but remembering the care taken to avoid overlap between this work and its companion *Oxford dictionary of English proverbs,* he decided that the phrase did have a proverbial sound, and so he made a check of the latter work. Here he immediately found the phrase, exactly as given, traced to its earliest appearance in English in

' 1867 Richardson *Beyond the Mississippi* 418 '. Turning to Bartlett, however, he came upon an earlier usage by Alexandre Dumas the Elder in *'Ange Pitou* [1854]. Vol. I, Page 72 '. This would, presumably, have been in French, and indeed in a footnote Bartlett did refer to an anonymous French proverb ' Rien ne réussit comme le succès'. Stevenson *Book of quotations* reinforced Bartlett, but also referred to an earlier oral usage, this time presumably in English, by Dr John C Warren of Boston in 1846 after operating for the first time on a patient under the influence of ether. The librarian reflected that these findings would make an excellent case study illustrating the difficulty frequently encountered of locating a definitive source for a particular quotation. In this particular instance an enquirer could choose from a) the first appearance in print in English (1867); b) the first appearance in print (1854); c) the first recorded oral usage (1846); or d) a proverbial origin, concealed in the mists of French history.

But this particular enquirer, of course, had asked for the origin of the parody phrase, so the librarian tried first of all Bergen Evans *Dictionary of quotations* which he knew made a feature of noting parodies and analogous quotations. Looking in the index under ' excess ', which seemed to him the most important keyword, he drew a blank, but under ' succeeds ' he was directed to the entry ascribing the words to Oscar Wilde *A woman of no importance:* ' Moderation is a fatal thing. Nothing succeeds like excess '. Curious as to why it was not indexed under ' excess ', he probed a little further, only to discover that it was indexed but under ' success '! Clearly this was an oversight of the indexer, who must have read the parody as its original, and indexed it thus.

[This finding is confirmed by Rudolf Flesch *The book of unusual quotations,* but *Cassell's book of humorous quotations* (1969), one of the most important recent dictionaries of quotations, seems to have slipped in tracing the phrase no further than the *Toaster's handbook,* compiled by Peggy Edmund and Henry Workman Williams, the first edition of which according to the Library of Congress *Catalog* was not published until 1914, fourteen years after Wilde's death. This lapse is the more inexplicable because this work is from the same American publisher and is closely modelled as to style, layout and typography on the great Stevenson, where the words are correctly attributed to Wilde.]

There are some parodies that are better known than the originals, but perhaps because it is so easy to twist a well-known saying, cheap parodies are legion and queries about them suffer a particularly high failure rate.

Case 68: 'Nothing is worth doing or well done which is not done fairly easily' was recognised as an obvious parody of the well-known 'If a thing is worth doing, it is worth doing well'. Stevenson and Bartlett agreed that the original quotation was Lord Chesterfield's, in his *Letters,* 9th October 1746: 'Whatever is worth doing at all, is worth doing well', but neither of them referred to the parody version. Neither could any trace be found in the *Oxford dictionary of quotations, Hoyt's, Everyman's, Benham's,* even Bergen Evans *Dictionary of quotations,* although this last did quote G K Chesterton's parody, 'If a thing is worth doing it is worth doing badly'. By this time the search had exhausted the library's stock of quotation books, and the reader's interest was declining markedly. The decision to let the matter rest there seemed to bring mutual relief.

It should be added, however, that there is another side to the coin of the quotation requoted, for enquirers are constantly surprised to discover how recent is the origin of many sayings that sound so much part of the language that they might have been in use for centuries.

Case 69: At the time of the 1971 negotiations on Britain's entry into the Common Market the librarian of a small public reference library was approached one lunchtime by one of the local shopkeepers holding the *Daily express* in his hand. He pointed to the page headed 'Should we speak French? . . . No', where the editor printed a selection from some of the 'thousands of letters from readers anxious to show their disapproval of French as the working language for the Common Market'. One of these letters, from a lady in Bromley, Kent, asked 'Where is our wonderful tradition "There'll always Be an England, And England Shall be Free"?' The shopkeeper's question was 'How old is that saying and who said it first?'

The librarian's first thought was that it sounded proverbial, and could be of venerable origin, but he could not trace it in *Stevenson's*

Book of proverbs or the *Oxford dictionary of English proverbs.*
Neither was it found in *Everyman's dictionary of quotations and
proverbs* or in Stevenson *Book of quotations.* Imagine his surprise
when he discovered that the *Oxford dictionary of quotations* traced
it back no further than ' Song of Second World War, 1939 ', attributing it to Hughie Charles. Cross-checking quickly with Bartlett to
be sure, he found this confirmed, with the addition of the name of
Ross Parker. The *Penguin dictionary of quotations* also gave the
two names.

Like verification enquiries, described above, questions about the
derivation of particular quotations often produce conflicting evidence, and the librarian has difficulty in providing the single
' right ' answer that the enquirer expects. Again his best plan is to
turn to the enquirer for a decision on the question, for example, of
how closely the form of the quotation as the enquirer has it and the
form as given in the reference books must coincide.

Case 70: The obvious source to try when asked for the origin of the
proverb ' Every cloud has its silver lining ' was the *Oxford dictionary
of English proverbs,* but none of the instances given there matched
word for word : The earliest example was 1634 Milton *Comus* ' did
a sable cloud Turn forth the silver lining ', but the first occurrence
in the form closest to the phrase as given was 1885 Gilbert *Mikado*
' There's a silver lining to every cloud '. *Brewer's dictionary of phrase
and fable* included the saying, but gave an explanation only : ' There
is some redeeming brightness in the darkest prospect '.

Among the quotation books, the *Penguin dictionary* did not have
the phrase at all, Evans and *Hoyt's* referred only to Milton, and
Benham, though he gave the quotation in precisely the form that
the enquirer had given, did not attribute it to any source, quoting
only the Milton version. Bartlett, however, quoted a well-known
alternative version : ' There's a silver lining/Through the dark
cloud shining' from Lena Guilbert Ford *Keep the home fires burn-
ing* [1915]. The *Oxford dictionary of quotations* also quoted Ford.
Finally, in Stevenson, which would have been consulted first if it
had been to hand, were found no fewer than 13 distinct quotations
(indexed under ' cloud ' but not under ' silver '), including Milton,
Gilbert, and Ford. The only one in exactly the form specified was

from Don Marquis *certain maxims of archy*. This was undated, but the index of authors revealed the author as an 'American journalist, humorist and poet (1878-1937)'.

By now the librarian had come to suspect that he was being over-meticulous in his hunt for the precise form of words the enquirer had used. He therefore reported his findings, leaving the decision to him.

(*See also* case 95).

It is obvious, so vast is the field, that no book of quotations can even approach comprehensiveness: thus, as Louis Shores tells us, 'No library can have too many of them'. The inevitably selective nature of such tools means that they duplicate each other much less than might be expected. In each case the editor or compiler has had to make a subjective decision about the inclusion of a particular item, and while there is obviously little disagreement and therefore some overlap where the really renowned phrases are concerned, there is plenty of scope left for the individual slant. The *Oxford dictionary of quotations* is 'primarily intended to be a dictionary of *familiar* quotations . . . popularity and not merit being the password to inclusion': 'familiar' is defined as such as 'might be found at some time in one or other of the leading articles of the daily and weekly papers'. Similarly, Robin Hyman *A dictionary of famous quotations* concentrates on 'what is likely to be familiar to the general reader', and the most famous tool of all, originally compiled in 1855 by John Bartlett, is actually entitled *Familiar quotations*. By way of contrast, Rudolf Flesch *The book of unusual quotations* claims that 'any resemblance between this book and a standard collection of " familiar " or " famous " quotations is purely coincidental . . . it begins, so to speak, where Bartlett leaves off '. And Bartlett's major American rival, Burton Stevenson *Book of quotations* speaks even more plainly: 'the phrase " familiar quotations " is all but meaningless '.

What this means in practice for the librarian on a quotation hunt is that he must not slacken his pace merely because he has drawn so many blanks: so long as there is another compilation to check, he must retain the hope that the next editor might be the one to regard the elusive quotation worthy of record.

Case 71: In a university library a member of the staff of the English department appealed for help in tracing the origin of the phrase 'Only connect'. He had, he said, already tried the quotation books. Possible search terms, of course, were only two in this case, so the librarian felt sure he could rely on the search having been thorough. The works that had been consulted were Stevenson *Book of quotations, Oxford dictionary of quotations,* Bergen Evans *Dictionary of quotations, Everyman's dictionary of quotations and proverbs,* Benham's *book of quotations, Hoyt's new encyclopedia of practical quotations,* and Robin Hyman *A dictionary of famous quotations,* which the enquirer had found shelved together. The librarian was able to draw his attention also to *Brewer's dictionary of phrase and fable,* the *Oxford dictionary of English proverbs,* Stevenson's *book of proverbs, maxims and familiar phrases,* and the four volumes of the *Words and phrases index,* but to no avail. A blank was also drawn with the *Oxford English dictionary* and its 1933 *Supplement.*

And then reviewing the sources she had checked, the librarian noticed the absence of Bartlett *Familiar quotations.* Upon investigation she learned that it was away at the binders, but as she knew it was such a useful source she took the trouble to telephone the local library to ask if they would check it for her. Persistence had its reward when she learned that according to Bartlett the quotation is from E M Forster *Howard's end* (1910). This work she knew as a moderately long novel, so she enquired further as to the exact page reference, only to be told that Bartlett specified only the chapter (22), although the entry did add half a dozen lines of context.

Case 72: 'I would like you to trace a quotation for me, but I am not too sure of the wording' had a familiar ring to the information officer taking the telephone call in an industrial library. As she expected, it was for an after-dinner speech one of the company's executives was preparing: a few moments' conversation elicited the fact that it was not really the precise derivation he wanted tracing but simply who said it, and the correct wording. He thought it was something like 'I am not so think as you drunk I am'.

Although the library was mainly scientific and technical, the small ready-reference collection held a handful of quotation books for just such queries as this: the *Oxford dictionary of quotations,* Bartlett *Familiar quotations,* and *Cassell's book of humorous quotations.* The information officer was not unduly perturbed to draw a blank with all three; she merely rang the local public library for help. It was only when they reported that they had consulted without success Stevenson, *Benham's,* Rudolf Flesch *The book of unusual quotations, Hoyt's,* and *Brewer's dictionary of phrase and fable,* that she felt a sense of impending doom.

Gathering her wits together, she calmly reviewed the situation with the help of Walford. Of the dozen or so quotation books listed that had not been checked, only two or three seemed making an effort to hunt down: Evans *Dictionary of quotations* was priced at $15, *Everyman's dictionary of quotations and proverbs* at £1.12½ —about one-fifth of the cost of Evans—and the paperback edition of the *Penguin book of quotations* at £0.60. On her next trip into town she visited her usual book shop, looked up the *Penguin,* and promptly bought it. Returning to the library she was able to read out to her enquirer the quotation he wanted (he had in fact got it word perfect) and its source, Sir John Squire (1884-1958) *Ballade of soporific absorption.*

[The quotation is also to be found in Evans and in *Everyman's.*]

It is also useful to remember that earlier editions of the standard works may contain entries discarded from the later for a variety of reasons; the second (1953) edition of the *Oxford dictionary of quotations,* for instance, reports the dropping of 250 quotations because they seemed no longer familiar. Used with care (for it may well be that the entries have been rejected because they are inaccurate), such earlier editions can occasionally help out with an elusive phrase.

Case 73: A college of education lecturer had been working for some time on the dictionaries when she came to the librarian's office for help. 'I am tracing the origin of a number of common sayings in English, and I have run into a problem you may be able to help me with.' She had found the phrase she wanted, 'As fit as a fiddle ' in the *Oxford English dictionary,* but the earliest quotation illustrating its use was dated 1882. The reader was sure it was older than this, but the other dictionaries in the library shed no light on her problem.

The librarian first tried *Brewer's dictionary of phrase and fable:* as he might have known, the meaning was given (' in fine condition ') but no derivation. And so the books of quotations were tried: it was not in Bartlett, Evans, *Hoyt's,* the *Penguin dictionary of quotations,* but in *Benham's* it was traced (not indexed under 'fiddle' but under 'fit'), with a reference to John Ray *Compleat collection of English proverbs* (1670, 1742, 1767, *etc*). The *Oxford dictionary of quotations* did not list the phrase, but the sight of the first (1941) edition shelved side by side with the later reminded the librarian of the hundreds of quotations it contained that were omitted from the second edition. It was therefore with some satisfaction that he found the phrase included in the first edition, attributed to William Haughton (*fl* 1598) *English-men for my money.* Assuming that the reason for its later omission was its proverbial cast, he turned to the latest edition (1970) of the *Oxford dictionary of proverbs,* to receive confirmation of his findings, with the additional information that a discussion of the proverb could be found in volume 192 of *Notes and queries.*

As mentioned above (page 95) the search will often lead the librarian beyond the phrase books into the biographical sources, once a suspicion as to author has been raised. From clues given in the quotation it is also possible sometimes to hypothesise the time and circumstances of its use and so narrow the area of search.

Case 74: 'Railways will only encourage the lower classes to move about needlessly' was the elusive quotation that had exhausted both the library's collection of quotation books (Stevenson, Bartlett, ODQ, *Benham's,* Hyman, *Cassell's,* Evans) and the young reference librarian's mental resources. She had also tried general phrase books like *Brewer's dictionary of phrase and fable,* that vast store of quotations the *Oxford English dictionary,* and the last fifty years of *Notes and queries.* It was therefore somewhat despairingly that she turned to her older colleague, asking 'Have you ever come across this one before?' To her surprise, the question was greeted with a smile: 'I am almost certain it is the Duke of Wellington, and if it isn't it should be, because it sounds like him' But he was not able to suggest a source that had not already been tried and could only offer to help in checking through any likely biographies that they could find. The reference library had none in stock (it was a medium-sized borough library), but the lending library catalogue revealed six. The latest and most substantial (571 pages) was the first volume of the Countess of Longford's two-volumed *Wellington* (1969-), but the catalogue entry (a BNB card) gave the title as 'The years of the sword' which seemed to suggest that it dealt with his years of active service before 1815, and as it was not on the shelves it could not be consulted anyway. However in Philip Guedalla *The duke* (1931) the index immediately revealed a promising reference to Wellington's opinions on railways. These turned out to be as reactionary as one could wish (*eg*, 'If I could attain the object, no lady should ever go by a Train, at all events without protection'), but did not include the sought-for quotation. The other four were also available and were scanned in turn : none of them had any entry under 'railways' in the index, and so the chapter headings and text were examined. Of course the Duke was born in 1769 and was therefore already about 60 when the first railways were being built, so the two librarians concentrated their attention on the later chapters, dealing with the last twenty or thirty years before his death in 1852. Richard Aldington *Wellington* (1946) covered this period in the last three of his 26 chapters, but a careful check revealed nothing at all on railways. Leonard Cooper *The age of Wellington* (1964) gave only seven pages to the Duke's last 20 years, and a close examination was also fruitless, as was a similar perusal of Sir John Fortescue *Wellington* (third edition 1960). It was only when the young librarian caught sight of the 'Bibliographical note' at the end of S G P Ward *Wellington* (1963) that she was persuaded to abandon the search incomplete. The note read: 'A great deal of myth has attached itself to the Duke, and much time can be wasted in attempts to trace apocryphal stories, remarks mistakenly ascribed to him or others quoted out of context'.

This last instance well illustrates a feature of quotation queries that is only too familiar to the case-hardened reference librarian— their high rate of failure. This distressing trait they share with biographical questions, and for the same reason, which is that both areas of investigation are 'open-ended': in theory, any remark made by anybody could be the subject of a reader's enquiry, just as a biographical query could be about anyone who has ever lived. And just as the biographical dictionaries list only the renowned, the quotation books preserve only the most memorable sayings. Very frequently indeed does the librarian exhaust all his reference tools without finding the quotation he wants.

Case 75: ' With twenty-six soldiers of lead I will conquer the world ' was the stirring sentence which began a long and fruitless search. The enquirer had found it printed without attribution as the frontispiece to J R Biggs *An approach to type* (1949), and he wanted to know its source. One by one the quotation books were tried, in vain: Stevenson, the *Oxford dictionary of quotations* (and the two companion books of proverbs), *Hoyt's, Benham's, Everyman's,* the *Penguin dictionary of quotations,* Evans, Hyman, the *FPA book of quotations,* and even *Brewer's dictionary of phrase and fable.* Bartlett had an undated quotation from F W Goudy (1865-1947) *The type speaks* which came near: ' I am the leaden army that conquers the world—I am TYPE ', but the librarian agreed with the enquirer that this sounded like a derivative of the original.

The OED and its 1933 *Supplement* was tried under all the significant words, *Notes and queries* was searched (*via* the indexes), and the four-volumes of *Words and phrases index* so far published were also scanned. The Biggs book was examined page by page, and a number of others on typography were more perfunctorily examined. Purely by chance the quotation was found at the heading of a chapter in Percy Freer *Bibliography and modern book production* (1954), but the attribution was ' author unknown'. Somewhat despairingly the bibliographies were checked, and through the *Cumulative book index* a typography textbook by H E Jackson *26 lead soldiers* was traced, published in 1937 by Stanford University Press, but no copy could be traced locally. The Library of Congress *Catalog* entry gave no clue as to the derivation of the title. *Book review digest* located three reviews, only one of which (*Publishers weekly* for 1st May 1937) was accessible: this was exceedingly critical, taking the author to task for a number of errors, in particular his description of England's first printers, ' Wynkyn de Worde and his successor William Caxton '. The reviewer (Hellmut Lehmann-Haupt) did however congratulate the author on his ' brilliant title ', perhaps not realising that it was not original. But there the hunt had to be abandoned.

[Had the librarian located a copy of Jackson's book it would have served no purpose. A careful check of its 228 pages reveals no reference at all to the quotation, other than the title of the book itself.]

It is encouraging to note, however, that there are compensating features to enquiries about quotations. All the best textbooks on reference work go to some lengths to impress upon the student the necessity for the librarian to ascertain precisely what it is that the reader requires before he begins his search; the reference process is not simply a matter of answering questions, and the reference interview has a crucial role to play in determining the enquirer's real problem. In the case of queries about quotations or other phrases (as also in the case of biographical questions), it is usually a simple matter to ascertain the precise subject of the enquiry. However vague the reader's information, the *form* of an enquiry about a phrase or about a person is clear and unmistakable, and the reference interview is correspondingly brief.

The quotation books also vary in the amount of information they give with each entry. All too often the source is merely indicated, without a full bibliographical reference. Context and background information are also sparse or even absent in many cases, and the librarian may be obliged to extend his search beyond the quotation books. Hardly ever is the meaning of a particular quotation given, even with quite obscure phrases, and yet queries about meanings are quite common, especially from children. As was noted above, works like *Brewer's dictionary of phrase and fable* can be invaluable here, even though they may not give precise derivations or specific bibliographical references.

Case 76: A simple-sounding request in a university library from one of the lecturers for the exact wording of Occam's Razor had the librarian floundering at first. Observing this, the enquirer was kind enough to explain what the librarian should have asked him in the first place: that Occam's Razor was a statement or law propounded by William of Occam, a famous medieval philosopher.

The librarian first thought he would try those quotation books arranged by author, but he could not find his man under either ' William ' or ' Occam ' in the *Oxford dictionary of quotations,*

Bartlett *Familiar quotations*, the *Penguin dictionary of quotations*, or Hyman *A dictionary of famous quotations*. Turning next to those subject-arranged dictionaries with author indexes he drew a blank both with Stevenson *Book of quotations* and Evans *Dictionary of quotations*. And then once again as so often *Brewer's dictionary of phrase and fable* came to the rescue with the entry (under 'Occam's Razor'): ' " Entia non sunt multiplicanda praeter necessitatem " (entities ought not to be multiplied except from necessity), which means that all unnecessary facts or constituents in the subject being analysed are to be eliminated. Occam dissected every question as with a razor.'

Not all readers calling upon the librarian's help have a particular phrase in mind. On the contrary, many come seeking *inspiration* in the shape of a quotation appropriate to a particular occasion, to use in a speech or debate, for instance, to inscribe upon a gift or in an autograph album, to adorn a gravestone or ceremonial tablet, to affix at the head of an article or chapter, to use as a book title. Such enquirers obviously feel comforted to know that other, wiser voices have thus expressed sentiments with which they agree. The more worldly enquirer, often a writer himself, seeks such quotations ' to give a pleasing touch of erudition or to save the trouble of thinking for himself ', as the ODQ frankly admits. The only possible approach here is by subject, and fortunately there are several excellent compilations so arranged. An approximation to a subject approach can also be made by way of the keyword indexes.

Case 77: The reference librarian of a busy town library received a note from his chief to the effect that one of the members of the library committee who was also chairman of the housing committee wanted some help with his speech at the opening ceremony of a new housing development. In particular he was looking for some suitable quotations about the place of the home in modern society. The librarian, an experienced man, knew exactly where to look— the main sequence of Stevenson *Book of quotations,* where the arrangement is by subject. Here, under ' home ' he found over six pages, with a ' see also ' reference to ' house ' with two further pages. Many of the examples were obviously unsuitable—there were a dozen or so on 'Home: its drawbacks'—but he was able to make a fair selection for typing and forwarding to the alderman.

There are also specialised tools, fashioned for just this purpose, *eg,* Maud Van Buren *Quotations for special occasions* (1938); H V Prochnow *Speaker's handbook of epigrams and witticisms* (1955); Allen Andrews *Quotations for speakers and writers* (1969). Useful too are collections of aphorisms such as W H Auden and Louis Kronenberger *The Faber book of aphorisms* (1962): not primarily reference books, they are more akin to anthologies of verse, for dipping into, or even for continuous reading. Very highly selective, admittedly partial, they can be difficult to consult, but do on occasion produce the perfect gem of a phrase to adorn a particular setting.

Case 78: A history lecturer in a college of education visited his library to ask for help with a book review he was writing. What he required specifically was a 'punchy' (to use his own phrase) quotation from a well-known writer about history books to start off his own piece, and he had looked through the page-and-a-half on history in Allen Andrews *Quotations for speakers and writers* without finding anything to suit. Stevenson was found to have four pages under 'history', although only a minority of the quotations were about *books* on history. To the librarian some of these at least seemed striking and vigorous enough: 'History, with all her volumes vast, Hath but *one* page' (Byron); 'It is pleasanter to read history than to live it' (Walpole); 'Anybody can make history. Only a great man can write it' (Wilde). But the enquirer was not happy with any of these.

The fact that the last example was quoted from the *Aphorisms* of Oscar Wilde reminded the librarian of the *Faber book of aphorisms*, where he found no fewer than 14 pages devoted to history. The lecturer spent what seemed like an enjoyable half-hour over the volume before getting up to leave. In response to the librarian's enquiring look he showed him the quotation from Anatole France he had finally chosen: 'All the historical books that contain no lies are extremely tedious'.

Although we all know what a proverb is, no one has ever produced a satisfactory definition. In the Introduction of the *Oxford dictionary of English proverbs* we read that 'men who have worked for years on the subject have hardly bettered the dictionary definition . . . " a short pithy saying in common use " '. The scholarly editors of one of the most respected American collections advise 'It might be better, indeed, to attempt no exact definition of proverb but to rely on the common and received understanding of what is likely to be found in a book called a Dictionary of Proverbs or the like '. In fact the student will have noticed, if only from the cases so far discussed in this chapter, that the compilers of some of the reference books make no attempt to distinguish between quotations and proverbs, as their titles sometimes indicate, *eg,* John Bartlett *Familiar quotations: a collection of passages, phrases and proverbs; Benham's book of quotations, proverbs and household words; Everyman's dictionary of quotations and proverbs.*

There are differences, it is true, between quotations and proverbs. A quotation is basically literary in origin, a passage cited in a book, play, speech, *etc.* It is normally available in written form, either from the very beginning of its life or from shortly afterwards. It follows that it can in most cases be attributed to a particular author, and a specific date, and that it exists in a single definitive form (although it may be misquoted later). A true proverb, on the other hand, is part of oral tradition, basically a saying, passed on by word of mouth. Literary warrant is often incomplete or absent. Owing its origin in many cases to the common people it follows that only occasionally can it be attributed to an individual, or to a particular date. As Stevenson *Book of proverbs* puts it, 'Rarely indeed is one permitted to sit in at the birth of a proverb, or to name its author'. All this means, furthermore, as the *Oxford dictionary of English proverbs* points out, 'many proverbs have not a precise, invariable, and generally known and accepted form'.

All this, of course, the librarian must contemplate. But when faced, particularly at the outset of an enquiry, with questions about phrases like 'Something old, something new; something borrowed, something blue'; 'Bell, book and candle'; 'Dead men tell no tales'; or 'Three people can keep a secret, if two are away'; he has no means of knowing in advance which will turn out to be quotations and which proverbs, for readers tend to bring the library the same kind of problems of verification, information, and inspiration with

119

both. Fortunately, as we have seen, many of the reference tools he has to consult draw no distinction, and so he is able to proceed with an open mind. It is a sensible policy when on such a hunt to look on all phrase books as fair game; only when the librarian gets a sharp scent of the proverbial should he aim first at the specialist compilations of proverbs. Even here, however, he will notice that the compilers are obliged by the very nature of their materials to compromise to some extent: although it agreed that proverbs are in origin non-literary, Stevenson's *Book of proverbs* has really no alternative to its stated course of action: 'The English quotations have been taken from literary sources where possible, with their exact location indicated'. Similarly, the *Oxford dictionary of English proverbs* states as its purpose 'to cite for each entry the earliest literary reference in manuscript or book, with a few examples from later centuries'. In solving those enquiries asking about the origin of a proverb the librarian must remember that it will normally have had a vigorous life in common speech, perhaps for many years, before it becomes enshrined in print. This is the explanation for the hundreds of proverbs ascribed for instance to Cervantes, of which he was merely the transmitter.

Case 79: To the young librarian asked about the history of 'There isn't room to swing a cat' the phrase sounded very modern, even slangy, so he was mildly surprised to find it derived in Burton Stevenson *Book of quotations* from Charles Dickens *David Copperfield,* volume ii, chapter 6. Confirmation was immediately forthcoming from Bartlett (though here the chapter was numbered 35—obviously quoted from another edition), together with the date, 1849-50. The *Oxford dictionary of quotations* was a little more informative, quoting the phrase as 'there wasn't room to swing a cat there', and adding a few lines of the context for good measure.

Clearly, the evidence pointed to Dickens as the coiner of the phrase, but the enquirer was not satisfied: what precisely was the significance of the phrase? And why a cat particularly? *Brewer's dictionary of phrase and fable,* which according to Walford has 'few rivals in its coverage of phrases and adages', proved most enlightening: 'Various explanations have been suggested . . . Swinging cats by their tails as a mark of sportsmen was at one time a favourite amusement'. However, perhaps the most plausible explanation would derive the phrase from the cat-o'-nine tails, in view of the restricted space on board the old wooden ships where the 'cat' was a common method of punishment.

And then, on consulting the OED as he usually did in such cases, the librarian was amazed to discover (in the entry under 'cat') a 1771 quotation from Smollett *Humphrey Clinker*, over threequarters of a century before Dickens: 'At London, I am pent up in a frowsy lodgings where there is not room enough to swing a cat'. Dickens, it seemed, was merely making use of an expression that was probably common currency. Was then Smollett the originator of the phrase? Continuing the search in the quotation books, the librarian drew a blank with *Benham's* and with *Hoyt's*, but found that Evans quoted Smollett. *Words and phrases index* led him to *Notes and queries* for 1925, which also referred to Smollett, pointing out that he was at sea as a surgeon 1741-3, but going on to ask ' Is there no earlier example of the phrase?' No reply was forthcoming, but on reflection the librarian now felt he could detect a proverbial ring, and sure enough, in the *Oxford dictionary of English proverbs* was found a quotation dated 1665, implying that it was already a common expression by that time: ' They had not space enough (according to the vulgar saying) to swing a Cat in '.

Case 80: The librarian asked to help trace the originator of the phrase ' the thin end of the wedge ' knew the enquirer as a regular reader, an English teacher by profession. He therefore asked him had he tried anywhere himself, and received the reply: ' I have looked in all the quotation books but I can't find it '. Further enquiries revealed that he had looked under ' thin ' but not under ' wedge ', which (as the least familiar, and in this case the most important, keyword) the librarian himself would have preferred as his main search term. However, on rechecking the librarian too drew a blank with Stevenson, Bartlett, ODQ, *Hoyt's*, Evans and *Penguin dictionary of quotations*. There was an entry in *Brewer's dictionary of phrase and fable*, but as so often it comprised only an explanation: 'An action, innovation, etc., of apparently small consequence which may lead to major undesirable developments '. In *Benham's book of quotations*, however, and in Robin Hyman *A dictionary of famous quotations*, the phrase was found: in both instances it was without any attribution at all, but the entries did furnish a hint that opened up new possibilities, for *Benham's* included it among the proverbs and Hyman specifically described it as a nineteenth century proverb.

Checking immediately in the *Oxford dictionary of English proverbs,* the librarian found the phrase traced to a chapter heading in Trollope *Dr Thorne* (1858), in the form ' The small end of the wedge '. He had to admit surprise in learning that it was so recent, although well aware that Trollope may have been the first to set down a familiar phrase in literary form. Stevenson *Book of proverbs* was found to confirm the Trollope reference, as was the OED, although the earliest quotation given by the latter using the precise form ' thin end . . .' was from the *Graphic* of 20th December 1884.

There is possibly one feature of proverb enquiries distinguishing them from queries about quotations: more frequently the librarian is asked for the meaning of the saying. This can be quite difficult to find, for (as with the quotation books) the books of proverbs concentrate on the form and the source of the proverb, often to the exclusion of more than the barest context, and sometimes without reference to the meaning. Yet some proverbs are profoundly obscure, *eg,* ' The fathers have eaten sour grapes, and the children's teeth are set on edge '; 'An old wise man's shadow is better than a young buzzard's sword '.

Case 81: In a busy children's library one evening a young reader approached the desk for help with her homework. She wanted to know the meaning of the saying to teach your grandmother to suck eggs. The librarian knew only vaguely what it meant, but was confident she could find an explanation among the reference books in the adult library. Its proverbial ring sent her first to the *Oxford dictionary of English proverbs,* where she found the phrase traced as far back as a 1707 translation from the Spanish—but with no explanation. Indeed she observed that such explanations of the meaning, although not absent, are very few and far between. With Stevenson *Book of proverbs* it was the same story: the earliest written usage being 1707, but without any meaning. It was not until she left proverbs and quotation books to consult *Brewer's dictionary* *of phrase and fable* that she found what she wanted : ' Said derisively to some one who tries to teach his elders or the more experienced '.

And like quotation queries, when it is background information that the enquirer wants the librarian is often obliged to extend his search beyond the phrase books.

Case 82: When asked for information about ' Jack Robinson ' of the famous proverb, the reference librarian was not disposed at first to take the enquiry seriously. It was necessary for the reader to explain that there was a real Jack Robinson and she wanted to know something about him. Upon enquiry she did disclose that she had tried ' some of the proverb books ', without success, although she had found the actual proverb listed in two of them. The librarian was not surprised at this, for he knew that such background information as she required was not usual in the dictionaries of proverbs, but he did take the trouble to check again in the *Oxford dictionary of English proverbs,* where the earliest indication of its use was in Maria Edgeworth's novel *The absentee* of 1812—but there was no information about Jack. Knowing the *Oxford English dictionary* to contain an unexpected hoard of proverbs, he was pleased to discover (under ' Jack ') a much earlier reference to the proverb's use in Fanny Burney *Evelina* (1778). This was also the earliest reference given by Stevenson *Book of proverbs,* which went on to add, ' though Miss Burney uses this as an ordinary and well-understood saying, no earlier instance of its use has been discovered '.

Always a good source for background information, *Brewer's dictionary of phrase and fable* suggested itself next, and was found to provide several pointers. According to *Grose,* for instance, the original Jack Robinson was in the habit of paying flying visits to his neighbours; no sooner was he announced than he was off again. According to Halliwell *Archaic dictionary* (1846) the phrase derived from ' an old play '. But Brewer added that this old play had never been identified, and he was sceptical about these accounts. He mentioned the Fanny Burney reference, and the early nineteenth century popular ditty by Thomas Hudson about Jack Robinson the sailor who returned to find his lady married to another.

Books of quotations were consulted next. No doubt because proverbs are left to the *Oxford dictionary of English proverbs* the phrase was not found in the *Oxford dictionary of quotations*. Bartlett had the Fanny Burney reference; *Hoyt's* referred to Halliwell, Grose, and Hudson 'the English singer' who 'made popular the refrain'; Stevenson said 'many tales have been invented to explain the origin of this phrase, but none convincing'; *Benham's* stated firmly 'the origin of this proverbial phrase is unknown'.

Undeterred by this dogmatic utterance, the librarian decided to widen the search by trying the biographical angle. In the *Dictionary of national biography* he found ten John Robinsons listed; in the entry for 'Robinson, John (1727-1802)', a Westmorland politician, he read, 'Sheridan, when attacking bribery and its authors, retorted in reference to shouts of "name, name", by looking fixedly at Robinson on the treasury bench, and exclaiming, "Yes, I could name him as soon as I could say Jack Robinson"'. At last he seemed to be getting somewhere, and the thought struck him that a check of *Notes and queries* might unearth more evidence, this being just the kind of problem to delight the readers of that invaluable journal. He was amused to discover that the origin of this proverb had been queried in its pages many times, the first as far back as 1852. All the suggested explanations he had so far encountered in his search he found repeated, with several more ingenious alternatives. The story about Sheridan appeared in the volume for 1909, this time traced to Lady Dorothy Nevill *Reminiscences,* where she goes on to say: 'thus originating the saying still current at the present day'. This seemed like the end of the line, until the librarian discovered on checking that these *Reminiscences* were not published until nearly ten years after DNB: it seemed possible that Lady Dorothy may have been drawing on the DNB entry, or on a source common to both. She was, however, bluntly contradicted by the note a little later in *Notes and queries,* which attacked her explanation as 'one of the innumerable fictions invented after the fact. The phrase is quoted as a stock one by Miss Burney in 1778, in "Evelina". Sheridan was first returned to Parliament in 1780, so that his speech could not have "originated" the saying.' There the trail ended, leaving not only a disappointed reader but also a crestfallen librarian, for he had failed to find what he was asked for, he had revealed an important omission in one of his most cherished reference books, and he had exposed a most misleading story in another.

[It should be added that the surprising omission of the Fanny Burney reference from the first edition of the *Oxford dictionary of English proverbs* (even though it had been quoted years before in the OED) was remedied in the second.]

Among the phrases that enquirers bring to the librarian for assistance, besides quotations and proverbs, it is possible (though not easy) to distinguish epigrams, aphorisms, maxims, adages, mottoes, slogans, catch-phrases, and so on. The student will find, however, that the dictionary defines them all in pretty much the same terms, and he should heed Logan Pearsall Smith's advice that ' these distinctions of the rhetoricians are not of much importance and have seldom been observed in the current usage of the words '. And in any case, faced in practice with an enquiry about phrases like ' Go to it!' or ' The secret of being a bore is to tell everything ', or ' There is no such thing as a pretty good omelet ', or 'Any port in a storm ', or 'The French language is a pianoforte without a pedal ', the librarian should be heartened to remember that they are often found treated together with quotations and proverbs in many reference books, *eg, Benham's book of quotations, proverbs and household words,* Bartlett *Familiar quotations: a collection of passages, phrases and proverbs,* and Stevenson's *Book of proverbs, maxims, and familiar phrases,* where the compiler ' has not concerned himself with fine-drawn distinctions . . . He has permitted himself the widest latitude of inclusion '.

Clearly, the number of possible permutations of words into phrases is virtually infinite and thus no phrase book can even begin to approach the comprehensiveness claimed for the individual words of a language by the major dictionaries. The compiler of such a book is obliged to be highly selective, to choose only those phrases which are particularly memorable, or pointed, or wise, or felicitous, or traditional, or merely familiar. It is for this reason, like the quotation books, that phrase books overlap to a lesser degree than might be imagined.

Among the most difficult phrases to trace are those that have entered the public consciousness *via* the mass media, such as ' Say it with flowers ', ' I don't mind if I do ', ' We try harder ', ' Come with me to the Kasbah ', ' I'm only here for the beer '.

Many of these, of course, on the stage, on radio, TV, and films are spoken not written, and are therefore more akin to proverbs than quotations (although technically they are neither). Even those few that do appear in cold print are usually in the newspapers or mass circulation magazines, and are untraceable through the usual indexes. They include catch-phrases from variety shows, advertising jingles, snatches from popular songs, and the slogans of politicians. In due course, if they survive, they do appear in the phrase books, *eg*, ' It's that man again ' (from the BBC comedy series scripted by Ted Kavanagh), ' Dr William's pink pills for pale people ' (advertisement), ' Ta-ra-ra-boom-de-ay! ' (title of 1891 song by Henry J Sayers), ' Wait and see ' (used repeatedly in speeches in 1910 by H H Asquith), all of which appear, perhaps surprisingly, in the *Concise Oxford dictionary of quotations.*

The librarian's difficulty is with those phrases of recent coinage that have not as yet been accorded such status. One or two new compilations, such as Bergen Evans *Dictionary of quotations* (1968), emphasise modern quotations, and at least one specific attack has been made on the problem by J B Simpson in *Contemporary quotations* (1964), who has confined himself to the period since 1950, gleaning his quotations from newspapers, magazines, speeches, sermons, theatre, TV, *etc.* An even more specialised collection is Valerie Noble *The effective echo: a dictionary of advertising slogans* (1970), which lists 2,000 examples from the print media of the previous five years, many of which (as the preface points out) ' live on as separate entities even though they once originated as campaign themes ', such as ' schoolgirl complexion ', ' even your best friend won't tell you ' and ' a diamond is forever '. Even so, in this area of investigation, the librarian must be prepared for many fruitless searches.

Case 83: A phone call from a sub-editor on the local newspaper asked for the originator of the description ' gnomes of Zurich ' as applied to Swiss financiers. There was nothing in the dictionaries (OED, *Shorter Oxford, Webster's third, Random House*) so the librarian turned to the quotation books. Bartlett, ODQ, Stevenson, Hyman, Evans, *Hoyt's, Benham's* were all checked, but to no avail.

The four volumes that had thus far appeared of *Words and phrases index* and the last half-dozen general indexes to *Notes and queries* were similarly unproductive. Trying as a last chance the bibliographies the librarian immediately found in the title index volume of *British books in print* a work by Fehrenbach called *The gnomes of Zurich: inside story of the Swiss banks,* a copy of which was soon run to earth in the library's collection. A 300-page work, published in 1966, it was not immediately helpful, for neither the index nor the preface and introduction referred to the phrase at all. Quailing at the prospect of a hunt through the whole text, the librarian began to scan the first chapter. On page 16 he lighted upon the first mention of the phrase in a description of the period of financial crisis in November 1964: 'There was a strong and bitter feeling among British government Ministers that the pound was the victim of deliberate sabotage by Swiss bankers . . . George Brown, Economic Minister and Number Two man in the cabinet, came out of a meeting and snapped: "The gnomes of Zurich are at work again". The remark was widely repeated in the lobbies of the House . . .'

[In due course the phrase made its expected appearance in the more usual search tools: the 1970 centenary edition of *Brewer's dictionary of phrase and fable* contains an entry which reads 'an uncomplimentary name given to those financiers of Zurich controlling international monetary funds. The phrase became popular after its use in November 1964 by Mr George Brown'. Reference is made to Fehrenbach's book (although no date is given), from which a further quotation is given illustrating the use of the words.]

(*See also* cases 69, 95.)

This previous case also illustrates one source of memorable phrases that is of particular interest to librarians: titles of books. It is not unusual to find a book which has, in the words of the *Times* about J K Galbraith *The affluent society* second edition 1969, 'headed simultaneously into the list of best sellers and the dictionary of quotations'. Instances that spring to mind are *A room of one's own* (by Virginia Woolf), *Gentlemen prefer blondes* (by Anita Loos), *The shape of things to come* (by H G Wells), and *The call of the wild* (by Jack London). In desperate cases it is always worth remembering that the title volumes of bibliographical tools like *British books in print* and its American counterpart, *Books in print* have on occasion ended a long search.

Case 84: The librarian of a county headquarters reference library was puzzled to receive from one of the branches a subject request form asking for the origin of the phrase ' catcher in the rye '. He had indeed read J D Salinger's remarkable novel of this title some years ago, and his desk copy of the *Reader's adviser* told him that it had been published in 1951. It had not crossed his mind that there could be any other source for the phrase, but he dutifully checked in the dictionaries (OED, *Webster's third, Brewer's*) and the quotation books (Stevenson, ODQ, Penguin, Hyman, *Hoyt's, Benham's,* Bartlett). The sole mention was found in this last work, quoting from Salinger's book: ' little kids in this big field of rye . . . I have to come out from somewhere to catch them . . . I'd just be the catcher in the rye '.

Case 85: When asked who was known as the ' handsomest young man in England ' the young assistant librarian's thoughts turned first to the biographical sources. A moment's reflection, however, was enough to convince her that the form of the question gave her no possible lead into these sources, and she realised that she must search for the origin of the quotation. But this was to prove no easy matter: within ten minutes she had exhausted the library's quotation books (Stevenson, Bartlett, ODQ, Evans, Hyman), *Brewer's dictionary of phrase and fable, Words and phrases index,* and the last fifty years of *Notes and queries.* When she turned to her colleague for help, all she could suggest was ' Why not see if it's the title of a book?' This line she had not tried with quotations before and it would not have occurred to her unprompted, so she turned to the bibliographies with some scepticism. She was not encouraged when she drew a blank with both *British books in print* and *Books in print,* but she persisted with the more recent volumes of the *Cumulative book index* and the *British national bibliography.* And then in the 1965-1967 *Cumulated index* of the latter she located a book of this title. Looking up the main entry she discovered that this was a biography of Rupert Brooke by Michael Hastings, published in September 1967. She was able within a matter of days to borrow a copy from a neighbouring library. She found the work to be a lavishly illustrated popular biography, and learned that it was W B Yeats who thus described Rupert Brooke.

[It is interesting to note that this book *never* appeared in *British books in print* (which was issued annually from 1967), presumably because it was not published when the 1967 volume appeared and it had not gone out of print by the time the subsequent annual issue was compiled.]

As always with quotations, however, the librarian needs to be on the watch for the borrowed phrase, particularly prevalent among book titles.

Case 86: When John Braine (himself a former public librarian) published his first novel *Room at the top* in 1957 there were many enquiries about the source of his title. It did not appear in *Brewer's,* Stevenson, Bartlett, *Hoyt's, Everyman's, Benham's,* or in the *Oxford dictionary of quotations.* A search back through the general indexes to *Notes and queries* was suggested. The practice adopted by this invaluable work of listing quotations only under the first word almost caused the searcher to miss the relevant index entry, which was not under ' Room . . .' but (spotted merely by chance on the same page) under ' There is always room . . .' This referred to a query posed in the number for 20th April 1946 by the compilers of the *Oxford dictionary of quotations,* no less, asking for the source. Their plea was answered less than two months later: the sentence originated as the reply given by Daniel Webster (1782-1852), the great American statesman, when advised not to become a lawyer as the profession was overcrowded, ' There is always room at the top '. Reference was made to Edward Latham *Famous sayings and their authors* (second edition 1906).

[In due course the quotation appeared in the second edition of the ODQ (1953): perhaps by some oversight only the first edition (1941) had been checked in the course of the search.]

Case 87: All that ' cakes and ale ' recalled to the librarian in a college of education was the title of a novel by Somerset Maugham. He had been asked for the origin of the phrase, and was interested to learn from the quotation books (Stevenson, Bartlett, ODQ, *Benham's*) that it was originally Shakespeare's, who in Act II, Scene 3, line 123 of *Twelfth night* had put into Sir Toby's mouth the words ' Dost thou think that because thou art virtuous, there shall be no more cakes and ale? '

Thus far so good, but to satisfy his own curiosity he continued the search in an attempt to discover the precise meaning. Right away the OED told him that the phrase was used figuratively to mean a ' good thing ', quoting as the earliest instance of its use the Shakespeare passage already found. In *Brewer's Dictionary of phrase and fable* he found not only confirmation of the meaning, given as ' a good time ', but also the one and only reference to Somerset Maugham's novel.

[There is some evidence that the phrase is older than Shakepeare. Attributed to Aesop (and therefore, presumably, translated from the Greek) is ' Better beans and bacon in peace than cakes and ale in fear '. Stevenson *Book of proverbs* goes back as far as c4000 BC to 'Ani *Papyrus: Book of the dead*. Ch.i, 1.34 ' for the sentence (presumably translated from Egyptian hieroglyphics) ' Give cakes and ale to perfect souls '.]

(*See also* cases 62, 75, 96, 97.)

The fact mentioned at the beginning of this chapter that dictionaries concentrate on individual words must not be allowed to obscure the extent to which the great unabridged dictionaries cover phrases. These may be proverbial or particularly striking phrases, but they also include those groupings of words which have appeared together so regularly that they have themselves become basic units of the language. This is well illustrated by the practice of the *Oxford English dictionary,* which treats as *main words* ' all those compound words (and phrases) which from their meaning, history, or importance, claim to be treated in separate articles ', *eg,* ' leading article ' ' laughing gas ', ' low water '. With those general combinations of words where each element retains its full meaning, *eg,* ' to melt in the mouth ', ' mock auction ', ' on the spur of the moment ', or with those of more specialised significance, but which are still explicable in connection with their cognates, *eg,* ' straw vote ', ' soup kitchen ', ' state paper ', the OED is more selective, giving only specimens at the end of the main article. Hence it is much more difficult to guess whether a particular phrase is likely to be included in the OED and its imitators than a particular word. The librarian is bound to sympathise with the editors in their problem: 'There is . . . considerable difficulty in determining to what extent combinations are matters for the lexicographer, and to what extent they are merely grammatical'. Nevertheless, those that are selected for inclusion are illustrated by quotations and it is always worth while trying the OED when on a search of this kind.

Case 88: 'This phrase, "the answer's a lemon", where does it come from?' was the question, and the books of quotations were tried first, starting with the big three: Stevenson *Book of quotations,* Bartlett *Familiar quotations,* and the *Oxford dictionary of quotations.* Not a trace was found, and a search of the *Penguin dictionary of quotations,* Evans *Dictionary of quotations, Cassell's book of humorous quotations,* Hyman *A dictionary of famous quotations,* and *Hoyt's new cyclopedia of practical quotations* proved equally fruitless. This was virtually a clean-sweep of the library's total stock of quotation books, for one only remained to try: *Benham's book of quotations, proverbs and household words.* Nothing was found in the index to the main sequence, but the librarian remembered enough about the layout of this long-established work to recall that the 'Supplement' (unlike Stevenson where there is a combined index) had its own special index. There the phrase was revealed: 'Lemon' is slang for something undesirable. The saying is therefore a scoffing reply'. As to its origin, however, all the entry had to say was 'American (c.1910)'.

Nevertheless, this was obviously a pointer to the next sources to check: *A dictionary of American English* and Mathews *Dictionary of Americanisms.* The actual phrase, surprisingly perhaps, was in neither, though the latter had an entry for the 1863 use of 'lemon' as a slang term for 'a worthless person or thing'. Changing tack slightly, the librarian turned next to such dictionaries of American slang as he had available. He soon discovered that L V Berrey and Melvin van den Bark *The American thesaurus of slang* was not designed to answer questions of this kind, giving neither dates nor attributed quotations. Harold Wentworth and S B Flexner *Dictionary of American slang,* on the other hand, was more helpful, including among its five meanings for 'lemon' two which could be appropriate: 'A sharp verbal thrust, criticism, or retort *c 1900*' and 'Something unsatisfactory, inferior, or worthless. *Colloq. since c 1925*'.

All that *Brewer's dictionary of phrase and fable* had to say was 'A senseless and ridiculous repartee: used as a form of reply to some particularly silly and unanswerable conundrum'. When *Notes and queries* was tried the librarian was intrigued to read in the issue for 9th March 1942 that someone had posed exactly the same query, but without getting any answer. Then as a final and not very hopeful throw he looked up the *Oxford English dictionary*. Among the two columns devoted to 'lemon' one definition was '*slang* (orig. *US*). Something bad or undesirable'. The earliest date quoted for its use in this sense was 1912, but among the quotations was one by 'Michael Arlen' dated 1922: 'The answer was a lemon'.

(*See also* cases 79, 82, 87.)

It is one of the most intriguing phenomena of language that where words in phrases are concerned the whole can be much more than (and sometimes very different from) the sum of the parts. A clay-pigeon, for instance, is not a pigeon, neither is it made of clay; an Adam's apple is not an apple and has little to do with Adam; a blind worm is not a worm, and is not blind; the cat-bird seat (see *Webster's third*) has nothing to do with cats, birds, or even catbirds. Where it is the meaning of such phrases that the reader requires, the dictionaries are invaluable, for they invariably include a definition.

Case 89: The librarian, asked for the meaning of 'bought in', had never met the phrase before, and admitted as much to the reader. Obviously anxious to help, the reader produced a newspaper with the report of an art auction. A number of items, all miniatures, were described as being 'bought in'. The librarian's first move was towards the *Oxford English dictionary,* where (not under 'bought' but under 'buy') he found that the term 'to buy in' dates from 1642 and means 'To buy back for the owner, *esp.* at an auction when no sufficient price has been offered'.

But of course the unique and irreplaceable role the OED plays in enquiries of this kind is as the repository of almost two million

132

quotations, which is many more than the contents of all the major dictionaries of quotations *put together.*

Case 90: It is well-known that ante-dating the OED quotations is a favourite pastime of many literary gentlemen, and the young librarian realised he might be face-to-face with one such would be antedater when an enquirer produced a newspaper clipping from the *Sunday times.* This described progress towards the second supplement of the OED, due in 1975, and the item causing the problem was the statement that one of the new entries would be for the phrase ' dirty work at the crossroads ' which was ' attributed to P G Wodehouse, 1914 '. (To be strictly accurate the newspaper report said ' crosswords ', but the enquirer assured the librarian that this was just a misprint.) ' I am sure it is much older than that, but the dictionaries of quotations are not much help ', the librarian was told.

He soon ascertained that the enquirer had found for himself the entries in Stevenson and Bartlett. The former ascribed the phrase to Walter Melville *No wedding bells for him,* but without date. The index of authors described him as 'American song-writer ', but again omitted dates, although they were given for other authors. Bartlett *Familiar quotations* was even less positive than this, including the quotation in the 'Anonymous ' section at the end, where it was merely 'Attributed to Walter Melville's melodrama, *The girl who took the wrong turning; or No wedding bells for him* '. A footnote added ' In *Notes and queries* (London) '—again with no indication whatsoever of date.

The enquirer had been fortunate in his choice of quotation books, for the librarian drew a complete blank when he searched all the others: *Oxford dictionary of quotations; Hoyt's new cyclopedia of practical quotations; Penguin dictionary of quotations;* Robin Hyman *A dictionary of famous quotations;* Bergen Evans *Dictionary of quotations.* Even the recent and likely-sounding *Cassell's book of humorous quotations* proved no help.

Turning next to follow up the *Notes and queries* clue given by Bartlett, the librarian had no choice, in the entire absence of any hint as to date, but to check back systematically through the indexes. Fairly quickly, in the 14th *General (ie,* cumulated) *index,* covering July 1929 to June 1935, an entry was located. This revealed itself in the issue for 22nd July 1933 as a query from a correspondent at Princeton University asking for the origin of the phrase! The only reply this evoked, a little later, was a suggestion connecting it (obviously very confusedly) with the custom of burying suicides at crossroads with stakes through their hearts! This was obviously not the reference Bartlett was drawing on, but surely if the phrase had been noted in an earlier issue of the journal the editor would have mentioned it? This line of enquiry was therefore temporarily abandoned, and a different tack tried.

On the off-chance that the phrase might be proverbial in some way, the *Oxford dictionary of English proverbs* was checked, without success. Not surprisingly, the phrase was found in Stevenson *Book of proverbs,* for as the compiler tells us, ' In order to make the work complete, many so-called " familiar quotations " have been added '. Attribution was as expected, the same as in Stevenson *Book of quotations,* but there was the additional note : ' (c. 1900) See Notes and Queries, ser.xii, vol.iv, p.25.' This looked as if it might be the elusive Bartlett reference, and when checked in the library's set it turned out to be three replies in the issue for January 1918 to a query posed the previous month asking for the origin of the phrase. The most specific derived it from ' one of Walter Melville's clever melodramas at the Lyceum—either " The girl who took the wrong turning " or " No wedding bells for him " '.

In an attempt to discover a more precise date, the librarian next tried to track down the American song-writer, Walter Melville. *Who was who in America* seemed the obvious source, now conveniently furnished with a collective index to the 80,000 names in all the five volumes covering 1607 to 1968, but Melville's name did not appear. Neither was he traced in the *Dictionary of American biography.* He had no entry either in the Library of Congress *Catalog of books/National union catalog* which was checked as far as 1967. Rather puzzled at this the librarian's thoughts turned in the direction of a more specific biographical source *Who's who in the theatre,* which Walford had told him had started in 1912. This first edition the library did not have, but in the second edition (1914) and fourth edition (1922) Walter Melville was described as ' author, actor, and theatrical manager ', born in London in 1874, himself the son of a long-established theatrical manager, and manager of the Lyceum theatre since 1909. Among the dozen or so of his melodramas listed was *The girl who took the wrong turning,* and in the

134

appendix 'Notable productions and important revivals of the London stage' the date was pinpointed at 1st October 1906 at the Standard theatre and 26th December 1910 at the Aldwych. The entries suggested to the librarian that Melville was clearly a figure of some importance in the history of the London theatre, so he essayed a glance at the *Oxford companion to the theatre* (third edition 1967), where he found an interesting entry by W Macqueen Pope. Apparently something of an amiable eccentric, together with his brother Frederick, Walter Melville amassed a great fortune from their joint theatrical enterprises, dying in 1937.

Of the same kind of value, in their specialised ways of course, are the other great dictionaries compiled on the lines of OED on historical principles, and including as a matter of course a whole range of illustrative quotations. That vigorous, inventive and unmistakable variety of the English tongue spoken in North America has contributed so many striking phrases to the common stock that it should be routine in any search to include *A dictionary of American English* and M M Mathews *A dictionary of Americanisms*. The librarian should, however, take care to distinguish the illustrative quotations used in compilations such as this, which are genuine quotations collected from the literature, dated and specified with chapter and verse, from those illustrative examples specifically written by the compiler of a dictionary to demonstrate the use of a word or phrase (as, for example, in the *Random House dictionary of the English language*).

Case 91: When asked 'Where did the black bottom get its name?' the librarian immediately assumed that she was being asked about the dance of that name popular in the 'twenties. As it happened, she was right, but she did take the precaution of checking with the enquirer just to be sure. *Webster's third new international dictionary* gave two meanings for 'black bottom'—'a tract of low lying land with black soil', and 'an American dance popular from 1926 to 1928 with sinuous movements of the hips and rocking steps'—but did not explain how the dance came to be so-called. Mathews *Dictionary of Americanisms* was more helpful: defining the term as ' a form of Negro clog dance involving prominent movements of the

135

hips', it illustrated this with a *New Yorker* quotation of 9th October 1926 which in effect linked the two *Webster's* definitions. The dance was 'constructed to simulate the movements of a cow mired in black bottom river mud '.

Margaret Hutchins advises: ' Quotations are a type of question in which it is especially desirable to call in the aid of other people, for much of the success in tracing them depends on the memory of former reading . . . That this need for help from outside is often felt and expressed is evident from the large proportion of questions in *Notes and queries* and its imitators that are about quotations. Consequently indexes to these series should always be consulted before the quest is either abandoned or referred elsewhere.'

Case 92: The young librarian in search of the origin of the jocular catch-phrase ' Tennis, anyone? ' turned to *Notes and queries* only after a well-nigh fruitless search through the quotation books. Nothing had been traced in Stevenson, the *Oxford dictionary of quotations,* Hyman, *Hoyt's,* Evans, or even in *Cassell's book of humorous quotations.* The only ray of light had been shed by Bartlett, quite early on in the search, where the phrase was attributed, incredibly, to Humphrey Bogart! No date was given, the only explanation reading ' His sole line in his first play '. Biographies of Bogart (preferably an autobiography) would have been the logical sources to try next, but first the librarian turned to *Notes and queries.* It did not take him many minutes to discover in the issue for September 1962 someone else posing the very query that he was pursuing. The writer knew no more than that the phrase was from a modern play. This provoked a number of replies over the succeeding months, the most informative coming in the April 1963 issue from a correspondent at Harvard: ' The device of clearing the stage by calling out, "Anyone for tennis? " or " Tennis anyone? " was associated with the early Broadway career of Humphrey Bogart, where in the mid-twenties he was brought on, as a sort of recurring joke, in a number of plays in white tennis clothes with a racquet in hand, a smile, and the traditional line '. No actual play was referred to, nor was there any clue as to its pre-Bogart use, but in the June 1963 issue attention was drawn to a line in Ber-

nard Shaw's play *Misalliance*: 'Anybody on for a game of tennis?'
Finally in October 1963 another correspondent referred to the use
of the phrase in a *New Yorker* cartoon ' about ten years ago '.

These investigations had clearly revealed enough information
about the phrase to content the enquirer, who went away more than
satisfied, but they left the young librarian pondering. To him the
case seemed an excellent illustration of the difficulty (already encountered above) of stating definitively the origin of a phrase.
Even assuming that Shaw was the first to use it on the stage, he
cannot have been the inventor: the cry must have sounded across
tennis-courts and through drawing-rooms on numerous late Victorian and Edwardian summer days. And in any case, it was unlikely
that this *literal* origin was what the enquirer (either in the library or
in *Notes and queries*) was really after. The really interesting feature
of the phrase was that it became a standing joke, as its use in the
New Yorker cartoon would indicate: it was more than likely that
enquirer after its origin really wanted to know the origin of its
humorous connotation. And on the best evidence so far adduced
this would seem to have emerged during the 1920's from the playing
of the young Humphrey Bogart.

(*See also* cases 73, 86, 90.)

Founded in 1849, and now a monthly, *Notes and queries* is certainly the oldest, as well as the best known example of its kind.
Since 1923 its title-page has proclaimed that it is ' for readers and
writers, collectors and librarians ', and its pages are well worthy of
study. It is a source well-tapped by the editors of many dictionaries
of quotations, proverbs, and phrases; indeed it serves as a forum
and exchange for unsuccessful quotation-hunters, and if Barry Pain
is right and ' imitation is the sincerest form of flattery ' then *Notes
and queries* clearly has a throng of admirers. There have been two
separate *American notes and queries*—the first, which ran from
1941 to 1950 is now defunct—and similar publications can be
found in other countries also, *eg*, France. Invaluable for enquirers
in the field of local history are the numerous local imitators such as
*Bedfordshire notes and queries, Devon and Cornwall notes and
queries*, now mostly extinct.

137

Case 93: The originator of the claim 'What Manchester thinks today, England will think tomorrow' was being unsuccessfully searched for by a university lecturer in politics. He understood that the statement related to the former practice in parliamentary elections of the boroughs polling some days before the counties, with the consequence that any swings or trends noticeable in a large industrial city such as Manchester might well presage similar nation-wide movements. But in his hunt for the first use of the phrase he was having no success at all, and so he turned for help to his local city library.

It seemed to the librarian that it could equally well be a proverb or a quotation, so he determined to check both sources, starting with the *Oxford dictionary of English proverbs* and Stevenson *Book of proverbs*. Unsuccessful there, he moved next to the quotation books: Bartlett, and Stevenson, and the ODQ had nothing to show, but in *Benham's* he found among the political phrases and illusions the statement 'What Lancashire thinks today, England will think tomorrow'. No attribution was suggested, the entry merely stating that it was a 'Nineteenth-century saying, found in various forms, " Manchester " (or Birmingham) being occasionally substituted for " Lancashire " '.

None of the other quotation books or phrase books (Hyman, Evans, *Brewer's*) mentioned the saying, and neither did *Words and phrases index,* so the indexes to *Notes and queries* were scanned. One reference was soon found, but when followed up in the issue for 20th November 1926, it was revealed as an enquiry as to who first used the phrase! As no reply was indexed the librarian assumed that this was one of the many queries that go unanswered. He did note, however, that the enquiry had come from G L Apperson: the name struck an immediate chord, and a glance at the index to Walford showed why. This was the compiler of *English proverbs and proverbial phrases: a historical dictionary* (1929), a pioneering work of scholarship and one of the bases of the *Oxford dictionary of English proverbs*. It seemed likely that he had written to *Notes and queries* in the course of preparing his dictionary, but he must have been unable to track down the phrase for the librarian discovered on checking that he had not included it.

It occurred to him at this point that the local approach might pay dividends in this case, for the enquiry clearly had a local connection. He was aware of the existence of local imitators of *Notes and queries,* and a few moments search of the library's shelves revealed a number of volumes of the short-lived [Manchester] *City news notes and queries.* The indexes to these volumes proved to be extraordinary compilations, inconsistent, incomplete, and quite inadequate, so the librarian felt that fortune was indeed smiling on him when he traced an entry in the volume for 1878, as follows: ' The Marquis of Salisbury, when Secretary for India, at a dinner given to him at the Queen's Hotel, Manchester, I think by the Chamber of Commerce, used the expression, " What Lancashire thinks today, England will think tomorrow ". Since then the authorship of the phrase has been attributed to him. In the *Daily news* of Wednesday, in a letter by Mr Walter Wren, the eminent " coach ", Lord Salisbury is said to have borrowed the sentence from Mr Cobden. Can anyone say when, where, and in what connection Mr Cobden used the words? ' This query appeared in the issue for 31st August 1878; it appeared again in the 28th December issue, in a list of ' The unanswered queries of the past year '.

A new vista was thus opened to the librarian and his enquirer, and the *Concise DNB* (part II) confirmed that Salisbury was Secretary for India in 1866-7 and again from 1874-8 under Disraeli. But this was the political field in which the enquirer was an authority, and by mutual agreement it was decided that he would from that point resume his own investigations, first by checking on Salisbury's movements to see when he was in Manchester, and then narrowing the focus to contemporary newspaper reports of his speech.

Case 94: Even *Notes and queries* does not contain the source of *every* elusive quotation. When asked for the origin of ' Home, James, and don't spare the horses ', the young assistant conscientiously worked through the quotation dictionaries: Stevenson, Bartlett, the *Oxford, Benham's, Hoyt's,* Evans, the *Penguin,* and even *Cassell's book of humorous quotations.* No mention of the phrase was to be found, neither was it in *Brewer's dictionary of phrase and fable,* the *Oxford dictionary of English proverbs,* or the OED.

Recalling what she had been told, she then turned to *Notes and queries.* Within moments she had unearthed two references, only to discover that both of them were queries asking for the source: the first (in the issue for 28th September 1935) asserted ' The modern song uses a quotation which is much older and was known during the war ', and the second (21st November 1942) claimed ' I connect it with a drawing in *Punch*, and the tang of it is Thackeray or his period '. But neither of these correspondents received any reply to their requests. At this stage the assistant took her problem to a senior colleague. ' Yes, I have had this before ', he immediately replied, ' Look at this ', and he showed her the note in the preface to the *Oxford dictionary of quotations,* where the quotation was given as an example of those cases where ' every effort to trace their source has failed '.

As this last case might suggest, perhaps the most immediately profitable way of taking Margaret Hutchins' advice to call in the aid of other people is for a librarian to consult his colleagues. The collective memory of an alert reference team is an informative source to tap for all kinds of enquiries, but in no case will such rich dividends be reaped as with queries about elusive quotations, especially where memory is backed up by a staff information index.

Case 95: A phone call received in a large city reference library from a TV producer asked for the origin of ' the boys in the backroom '. Mistakenly, as it turned out, the librarian made first for the quotation books, searching fruitlessly through Stevenson, Bartlett, ODQ, *Benham's, Hoyt's,* Hyman, Evans and even *Cassell's book of humorous quotations.* It was not until he tried the very recent centenary edition (1970) of *Brewer's Dictionary of phrase and fable,* that he found the phrase defined as ' the unpublicized scientists and technicians in World War II who contributed so much to the development of scientific warfare and war production, and since applied generally to such anonymous laboratory workers '. The derivation was given as a speech by Lord Beaverbrook (24th March 1941): ' To whom must praise be given . . . to the boys in the backroom '.

Justifiably pleased that his persistence had been so rewarded, he was on the point of calling back his enquirer when a colleague stopped him: ' Marlene Dietrich used to have a song about " the boys in the back room ", and I am sure it was before the war '. The library catalogue showed two fairly recent biographies of Dietrich: Leslie Frewin *Dietrich: the story of a star* (1967) was found to lack an index, and although there was a list of her films there was no corresponding list of her songs: John Kobal *Marlene Dietrich* (1968) was also without an index, but in the 'Filmography and discography' the librarian soon ran to earth the film *Destry rides again* (1939), in which she sang 'The boys in the back room' (Decca, Capitol, and three Columbia record numbers quoted). Having pinpointed the film and the date, the librarian turned back to Frewin, where he read that the film had been released a few weeks after the outbreak of World War II, and that her number, 'See what the boys in the back room will have' soon became a popular hit.

The librarian was obviously faced with what is a common dilemma in determining the 'origin' of phrases. Clearly, Marlene Dietrich had used the words of the phrase before Lord Beaverbrook: equally clear they had for her a different meaning, for *Destry rides again* (as its title suggests) is a Western. It was theoretically possible, therefore, for both of them to be the originators of the phrase: Dietrich of the phrase itself, and Beaverbrook of the phrase with the specialised meaning. It is interesting to note that this specialised meaning, referring to behind-the-scenes research workers, is now the primary (and possibly the *only* current) meaning, at least in British usage, as the dictionaries show. The 1956 'Addenda and corrigenda' to the *Shorter Oxford dictionary,* for instance, has an entry defining 'back-room boys (girls)' as 'a group of men (women) engaged in secret research', quoting Beaverbrook again, this time dated April 1941: 'The boys in the back rooms, who do not sit in the limelight'. The supplement to Eric Partridge *A dictionary of slang and unconventional English* gave a similar definition, describing the phrase as journalistic jargon dating from around 1941, and becoming a general colloquialism in 1943, mostly in a Services' context until the end of the war. It is worthy of note, however, that Harold Wentworth and S B Flexner *Dictionary of American slang* (1960) gives only the earlier meaning: 'Those politically wise; politicians, their staffs and friends'.

Case 96: A caller on the phone in a busy city library wanted information about the word (or phrase) 'uptight', which he claimed he was encountering more and more frequently. He wanted to know the meaning and where it came from, so the librarian turned first to the dictionaries. None of the major dictionaries (OED, *Shorter Oxford, Webster's third, Random House*) included the term, and neither did the more specialised sources to which he turned next: Mathews *Dictionary of Americanisms,* Partridge *Dictionary of slang and unconventional English, Brewer's dictionary of phrase and fable,* Berrey and van den Bark *The American thesaurus of slang,* Wentworth and Flexner *Dictionary of American slang.*

It was *Words and phrases index* which provided the first clue to a possible explanation with its entry for 'wound up tight'. Looking up the reference given in the journal *American speech,* 29 1954 104, the librarian read that it was a hot rod term from the Pasadena area, meaning 'running at maximum rpm in a particular gear'. He was not too happy with this as a likely explanation, but as he had come across no other he consulted his colleagues. 'That's strange', said one, 'but I came across an example only the other day'. It took him but a few minutes to locate it in the novel by James M Cain *The postman always rings twice* (1934), where Frank Chambers (the narrator, who tells the story in the first person) says 'So I'm in the death house, now . . . I'm getting up tight now'.

And in the absence of any information more precise than this, the librarian could do no more than report his incomplete findings to his enquirer.

[*Uptight* was the title given to a film about black militancy made by Jules Dassin in the US in 1968, and the title index volumes of recent annual issues of *Books in print* reveal two books with this title —John Gimenez and Charles Meredith *Uptight* (1967) and Dick Winfield *Uptight* (1967)—as well as a third including the term: Carter Brown *Uptight blonde.*]

A recent addition to the librarian's armoury in this area is the computer-produced *Words and phrases index* (1969-), specifically compiled by librarians to assist librarians and others to trace information on such topics as ante-datings, new words, new compounds, new meanings and other published research supplementing the OED. The aim of the volumes so far published is to cover publications from 1925, and the journals indexed include *Notes and queries.*

Case 97: 'When did the phrase " across-the-board " first come into use, and exactly what is its meaning? Is it slang? ' was the query posed in a university library. The enquirer had with him in a file

142

two carefully mounted clippings from the *Sunday times*, one dated 29th January 1967, the other 16th February 1969: the first referred to 'an across-the-board service to children in schools', the second to 'across-the-board cuts in gas tariffs'. The phrase could be found in none of the dictionaries consulted (OED, *Shorter Oxford, Webster's third*, Mathews *Dictionary of Americanisms*, under either 'across' or 'board'. *Brewer's dictionary of phrase and fable* was likewise checked without success. With some misgivings the quotation books were also tried: first the big three, Stevenson, Bartlett, and the ODQ; then Bergen Evans, the *Penguin dictionary*, Robin Hyman—but to no avail. Then the librarian thought to try the newly-acquired *Words and phrases index*, which he had noted but not used before. And there he found two references to 'across-the-board': one of them he was unable to follow up because his library did not have the journal cited (*Publications of the American dialect society* for November 1951), although he did draw it to his enquirer's attention. The other reference was to the *Britannica book of the year* for 1948, page 804, which turned out to be the regular entry 'Words and meanings, new' which librarians and other word-hunters find so valuable. The entry for 'across-the-board' was brief, but gave the enquirer precise answers to his questions: It read as follows: '*adj.* Touching or effecting all parts of (a system); general, as, "an across the board wage increase" (1945)'.

This at least was something for his enquirer, but the librarian recalled he had not checked any of the dictionaries of slang: Eric Partridge *A dictionary of slang and unconventional English* proved unfruitful, but there was a 19-line entry in Harold Wentworth and S B Flexner *Dictionary of American slang*. In addition to the meaning and usage described by *Britannica* (said to have been in 'Mainly labor union and political use; since c1940') it traced the phrase back to c1935 as 'A type of horse-racing wager in which equal amounts of money are bet on the same horse to win, place, and show', referring to a 1956 book by T Betts *Across the board: behind the scenes of racing life*. The actual derivation of the term was the electronic totalizator board, showing all the details of each race such as the odds on each horse, the total bets to win, place, and show, *etc*.

[The *Random House dictionary of the English language*, the most recent major dictionary, published in 1967, has two separate and unconnected entries for the phrase, giving three related meanings, and one illustrative quotation, but no dates, and no explanation as to its origin.]

As a glance at Walford or Winchell will confirm, most of the world's major languages have, like English, their own dictionaries of quotations, proverbs and other phrases, *eg*, Paul Dupré *Encyclopédie des citations* (1959); Eberhard Puntsch *Zitatenhandbuch* (second edition 1966); Giuseppe Giusti and Gino Capponi *Dizionario dei proverbi italiani* (1956). Similar works can be found too for a number of other languages, particularly those possessed of a vigorous literary tradition, *eg*, T Vogel-Jorgensen *Bevingede ord* [Danish] (fourth edition 1955). Obviously, in appropriate cases and where the librarian has access to such tools, they will form the first line of attack on questions about foreign quotations and the like. Most libraries perhaps will not have available a wide range of such titles, and so it is well to remember that the general foreign-language dictionaries can play a role here, similar (but on a smaller scale) to the part OED plays for English quotations, proverbs and phrases.

In coping with readers' enquiries in this area the librarian needs to be aware of two possible complications. The first concerns the question of translation: we know that it was Adolf Hitler who said 'My patience is exhausted '; that Rousseau wrote ' Man was born free, and everywhere he is in chains '; that Aesop warned ' Don't count your chickens before they are hatched '; that General Mola invented the phrase ' the fifth column '; but all these are merely translations of what was really said in the original German or French or Greek or Spanish. It is important for the librarian to remember this, even when his enquirer does not, and in cases where the exact wording or the precise origin of a quotation is asked for he must be quite sure what he is about, but if it is obviously an English version that is required (as in case 53) he can call upon not only Stevenson, Bartlett, *Hoyt's* and the rest, which include quotations like these from many tongues translated into English, or the ODQ and the *Penguin dictionary* which give foreign quotations in their original tongues with English versions appended, but also those specialised tools concentrating specifically on English versions of foreign quotations, *eg*, Norbert Guterman *A book of French quotations with English translations* (1963); T B Harbottle *Dictionary of quotations (classical)* (third edition 1906).

144

It is worth pointing out that an equivalent is not necessarily the same as a literal translation, indeed in some cases it bears little or no relation to the original text. What a good equivalent does match of course is the *sense* of the version in the other language. The French version of 'To call a spade a spade' is 'Appeler un chat un chat' (to call a cat a cat); the Spanish say 'Decir el pan pan y el vino vino' (to call bread bread and wine wine). Many proverbial phrases, 'To carry coals to Newcastle' for instance, would be meaningless if translated literally, yet there are quite exact equivalents in French: 'Montrer le soleil avec un flambeau' (to show the sun with a torch); German: 'Eulen nach Athen tragen' (to carry owls to Athens); Spanish: 'Vender miel al colmenero' (to sell honey to the beekeeper); Italian: 'Portare vasi a Samo' (to carry vases to Samos); and even Latin; 'Noctuas Athenas afferre' (to carry owls to Athens).

This distinction between equivalents and translations is important to watch for in enquiries about any foreign phrases, especially idioms: for instance, the French version of 'To take French leave' is 'Partir à l'anglaise'.

A particular variety of this translation complication occurs with proverbs. As has been noted above (page 119), many proverbs do not have a precise form: there cannot therefore be a precise translation. On the other hand, it is a feature of many proverbs that they are international, with equivalents in many languages, deriving perhaps from some common stock. The librarian has available to help him here special multilingual compilations of proverbs on a comparative basis, *eg,* Augusto Arthaber *Dizionario comparato di proverbi* (new edition 1952) which gives the Latin, French, Spanish, German, English, and ancient Greek equivalents for almost 1500 Italian proverbs. Useful also with day-to-day enquiries are those similar compilations which group foreign proverbs by subject but give them all in their translated English form, *eg,* Henry Davidoff *A world treasury of proverbs from twenty-five languages* (second edition 1961).

The second complication to watch for concerns those foreign quotations and other phrases that have been absorbed intact into the English language, *eg,* 'Plus ça change, plus c'est la même chose', 'In vino veritas', 'Sturm und Drang'. Since the reason so many have retained their original form is that there is no adequate English equivalent, it follows that a concise translation may be difficult to

145

produce, and the enquirer may have to make do with an extended and perhaps even roundabout explanation. Once again some of the general phrase books do contain foreign examples in the original languages; there is in addition a selection of special-purpose dictionaries, *eg,* Kevin Guinagh *Dictionary of foreign phrases and abbreviations* (1965), H P Jones *Dictionary of foreign phrases and classical quotations* (1908).

Case 98: When asked what a *carpe diem* poem was, the assistant in a university library had to ask his enquirer for more information. He was shown the phrase, in a book on English literature, with the explanation that the enquirer guessed it must be a special kind of poem and that the phrase was probably Latin or Greek. He knew enough to recognise Latin when he saw it, so he turned to the special section of Latin quotations in *Benham's book of quotations, proverbs and household words,* where he found it translated as 'seize the present day', and attributed to Horace: 'Dum loquimur, fugerit invida Aetas: carpe diem'. *Brewer's dictionary of phrase and fable* confirmed both the translation and the attribution, but gave the second half of the quotation: 'Carpe diem quam minimum credula postere', and added by way of further explanation 'Enjoy yourself while you have the opportunity'. For good measure, Stevenson and the ODQ were checked: both gave the full quotation (*ie,* both halves), but spelt the last word 'postero'.

This information proved sufficient for both the librarian and his enquirer to agree on what constitutes a *carpe diem* poem; the example that sprang to both their minds was 'Gather ye rosebuds while ye may ...' by Robert Herrick.

[The phrase can also be found as an illustrative example in Sir William Smith *A smaller Latin-English dictionary* (third edition 1933) and in C T Lewis and Charles Short *A Latin dictionary* (1879), and Evans *Dictionary of quotations* considers it one of the most famous of quotations.]

Where enquirers seek more than an explanation of the meaning, such as for instance the derivation of a phrase or the date of its introduction into English, the librarian may have to range further than the phrase books. Here it is useful to remember that the great unabridged general dictionaries do contain foreign words and phrases, which they often treat every bit as fully as English terms. Once again the *Oxford English dictionary* is the model here: it is illuminating to study the care with which foreign words and phrases are distinguished into denizens (fully naturalized as to use, but not as to form, inflexion, or pronunciation), aliens (names of foreign objects, titles, *etc*, which we require often to use, and for which we have no native equivalents), and casuals (of the same class, not in habitual use, which for special and temporary purposes occur in books of foreign travel, letters of foreign correspondents, and the like). To use foreign dictionaries for these phrases can be fraught with danger: their meaning in English may differ substantially from the meaning they have in their original language.

Case 99: When asked some years ago ' Where does *éminence grise* come from?' the librarian turned first to what he thought were the most appropriate sources (as listed in the edition of Walford then current): as H P Jones *Dictionary of foreign phrases and classical quotations* (1908) and Maxim Newmark *Dictionary of foreign words and phrases* (1950). He also tried a likely-looking work listed by Winchell, W F H King *Classical and foreign quotations* (third edition 1904) and the more recent Kevin Guinagh *Dictionary of foreign phrases and abbreviations* (1965). In none of these did the term appear, neither was it found in the scholarly OED-like C A M Fennel *The Stanford dictionary of anglicised words and phrases* (1892). Remembering that most dictionaries of quotations include foreign examples, he next scanned Stevenson, the ODQ, Bartlett, *Hoyt's*, *Benham's* (with its special section of French phrases), the *Penguin dictionary*, Evans, and Hyman, not forgetting *Brewer's dictionary of phrase and fable,* to no avail.

By now in a state of mild alarm, he thought to try one or two general dictionaries, where he was immediately encouraged to read it defined in the *Concise Oxford* as ' confidential agent, esp. one who exercises power unofficially', with an indication that the term (French for 'grey cardinal') was originally applied to Cardinal Richelieu's private Secretary. But, as the enquirer immediately asked, ' Why grey? and why cardinal?' The librarian turned therefore to consult the much fuller etymologies in the OED, but was once more surprised to find no entry; neither could he trace it in the 1933

Supplement or in the *Shorter Oxford* (including its 1955 'Addenda '). *Funk and Wagnalls new standard dictionary* he knew had a special appendix ' Glossary of foreign words, phrases, etc.', but once again he drew blank. Finally, to his relief he found within the space of a few lines in *Webster's third* all that the enquirer wanted; namely, that ' grey eminence ' was the nickname of Père Joseph (François Le Clerc du Tremblay, d. 1638), a French monk and diplomat who was confidant of Cardinal Richelieu, the French statesman (d 1642) who was styled *Eminence rouge* (' red eminence '). The term of course related to the colours of their respective habits and to the unofficial power exercised by Père Joseph.

[It was not until the publication in September 1966 of A J Bliss *A dictionary of foreign words and phrases in current English* that the librarian came across a possible explanation for the puzzling absence of the term from the most obvious sources. Bliss makes a point of including etymology and date of introduction into English, together with notes on points of interest and ' a certain amount of encyclopaedic information ', referring where appropriate to the OED and *Stanford*. Though his entry on *éminence grise* is not as full as *Webster's third*, he does add one item which might account for the fruitlessness of the early search : despite its venerable French origin, the term was not introduced into English until the twentieth century.

Nevertheless, the phrase must have been known in England in its original meaning well before this. *Words and phrases index* refers to *Notes and queries* for 1964 where the *Westminster review* of 1838 is quoted on Richelieu's ' celebrated secret agent, known by the soubriquet of *L'Eminence grise*—Father Joseph, the capuchin friar '.]

Most research workers in the humanities would agree with their librarian-helpers that phrases, and quotations in particular, are among the most baffling items to search for. But they would probably also agree, because of their common delight in *le mot juste*, that success in such a hunt has a sweetness all its own.

3
books about people

MAN'S FASCINATION with language is matched only by his interest in people. Preachers, publishers, journalists, film and television producers, and many others with their professional fingers on the public pulse will tell you that biography is one of the most popular forms of information, inspiration, and recreation. Louis Shores informs us that 'Almost all analyses of reference questions by frequency show that questions on biography are at or near the top of the frequency list'.

In fact it can be downright misleading to think of biography as a subject in the same way as chemistry or numismatics are subjects. E C Bentley's clerihew that 'Geography is about maps, but biography is about chaps' presents too naive a view (as I am sure its author knew). Biography pervades all subjects; indeed according to some it goes further, for Emerson's view was that 'There is properly no history; only biography'. Perhaps because biography is totally pervasive of the whole field of human knowledge, biographical questions in libraries encompass all the different categories of enquiries that have been distinguished by writers on reference work (see, for instance, *Case studies in reference work,* pages 10-26). Among the commonest are the *factual enquiries* (more descriptively 'fact-finding' enquiries), where the reader is seeking a specific piece of information.

Case 100: 'Was the "Admirable Crichton" a real person?' was an enquiry no doubt from a reader familiar with J M Barrie's play

149

of the same name (or possibly a film version of the play). The librarian had no idea of the answer, but was fortunate enough to pick upon *Webster's biographical dictionary* to consult first. Only one Crichton was listed among its 40,000 names, James, 1560?-1582, 'Scottish prodigy of learning and athletic accomplishments known as " the Admirable Crichton ", an epithet from the Scottish poet John Johnston's *Heroes Scoti* (1603) '.

Case 101: The assistant in a county branch library who was asked for Patrick Campbell's title guessed that her enquirer was interested in the columnist and TV personality (and not, for instance, in either of the two of that name who figure in the *Dictionary of national biography*, Mrs Patrick Campbell, the famous actress and first Eliza Doolittle; and *Sir* Patrick Campbell, distinguished naval officer). Going together to the reference alcove, they examined what she thought was sure to provide the answer, one of the few reference books to become a household word, *Debrett*. Entitled in full *Debrett's peerage, baronetage, knightage, and companionage,* this work certainly would have solved the problem except for the fact that the entries in the peerage section are under the titles and not under family names. There is, it is true, an index to peers' names with references to their titles, but, as the assistant discovered, it is to surnames only and Campbell happens to be the surname of several noble lords. Rather than follow up each reference individually in the main sequence, she dropped *Debrett* and took up *Who's who* instead, guessing that Patrick Campbell would rate a place as a writer, if not as a peer. She was right, for his entry under 'Campbell, Patrick' referred her immediately to '3rd Baron Glenavy '.

Specific facts are notoriously difficult to verify and facts about people can be particularly elusive. Though a person's life may be packed with incident, only the most infinitesimal fraction can ever be recorded, and even this is usually done long after the event. It so often pays to check one biographical source against another; not only to eliminate factual errors but also to detect significant omissions. Even those reference tools that rely upon the biographees themselves for their information are not immune; indeed they may be particularly prone to sins of omission: in *Who's who in America,*

150

for instance, Theodore Roosevelt made no reference to his unsuccessful attempt on the presidency in 1912, and entries in *Who's who* sometimes fail to mention previous marriages. Dates of birth too are notoriously liable to fluctuation, particularly (it is said) in entries self-compiled by women. Where usually reliable reference works contradict each other, the librarian may need to go beyond them, back to the original sources if possible, endeavouring in the words of Margaret Hutchins 'to find information whose origin is as close as possible to the subject, in place and in time'.

Case 102: A student who explained he was doing research on the early novels of Evelyn Waugh came to one of the librarians in a large university library. He wanted to know whether it was true that Waugh failed his degree at Oxford. He had already discovered contradictory evidence in newspaper reports at the time of the novelist's death: the *Daily mail* of 11th April 1966, for instance, said that 'he left without taking a degree', but the *Guardian* of the same date referred to 'a modest degree'.

Obviously no longer in the current *Who's who*, Waugh would have to wait some years to appear in the *Who was who* volume covering the 1960's, and for his presumed place in the *Dictionary of national biography* even longer. His last (and, of course, self-compiled) entry in *Who's who* (for 1966, the year of his death) was non-committal on the topic of his degree, merely referring to the fact that he was educated at Hertford College, Oxford. All that the long entry in *Twentieth century authors* (1942) had to say about his university career was that he was Senior History Scholar at Hertford; in the biography at the end of the article and also in the *First supplement* (1955) were a number of references to books and papers on Waugh, but the librarian doubted if they would be worth following up in this instance. In *Chambers' biographical dictionary* the only reference in the 26-line entry to his scholastic achievements said that 'he turned naturally to writing when he left Oxford', and the *Times* obituary (traced *via* the *Index to the Times*) was also silent on his degree, but both mentioned an autobiography *A little learning,* published in 1964.

It seemed time to go back to primary sources, in this case the annual *Oxford University calendar* with its alphabetical list of members of the university and their degrees. Evelyn Waugh's name

151

could not be found in the current issue at all, but it was only after closer study that the librarian grasped the point that graduates are only included automatically in this list for eight years after matriculation. Remembering that (according to *Who's who*) Waugh was born in 1903, the librarian surmised that he would have matriculated about 1921 or 1922, graduating three years later. Examining the earlier volumes of the *Calendar* in the stacks, he found in the 1924 Class Lists that the examiners 'In Historia Moderna' had placed him in Class III. Obviously, then, he had passed his examination, but why were the magic letters 'BA' missing beside his name in the list at the end of the volume, whereas all his fellows (even those in Class III) had BA after theirs? One answer suggested itself when the librarian checked the third place in the volume where he expected to find Waugh's name—in the list of scholars at Hertford College. One feature marked his name out from all the other scholars—the letter 'H' following lhe date of his matriculation (1922), where the rest of the names had the letter 'M'. This indicated that he had matriculated in the Hilary Term (*ie*, beginning in January) rather than in the more usual Michaelmas Term (*ie*, beginning in October). By the time he took the examination in Summer 1924 therefore he would have been one term short of the full three years' residence necessary to graduate—despite having satisfied the examiners.

Confirmation from the author himself came on page 208 of the first volume of his autobiography—of which the librarian was now able to relish the deliberately ironic title (*A little learning*): 'I was uneasily aware as I left the Examination Schools that the questions had been rather inconvenient . . . My father decided that a Third Class BA was not worth the time and expense of going up for a further term.'

A common variety of biographical enquiry within this category is the straightforward identification problem, where the reader has little more than the name (and sometimes not even that) and he seeks the librarian's aid in placing this name in time and space—in other words, he simply wants to know who he is, poet or peasant, prince or pauper.

Case 103: By sheer coincidence two consecutive enquiries in the same morning asked about famous prelates although only in the case of the second was his calling explicit in the question, and in neither case was the librarian aware of their fame. What was explicit in the first enquiry, however, was its retrospective cast, as indicated by the use of the past tense: ' Who was Mandell Creighton? '. The enquirer pronounced the surname to rhyme with Dayton (of which more anon), but providentially the librarian had asked him to spell it, which he was able to do. Without further enquiry, the librarian made straight for Hyamson *A dictionary of universal biography,* which he knew excluded living persons but yet listed more names than any other biographical dictionary. Sure enough, Creighton was there, briefly characterised in the single-line entry as Bishop of London and historian, 1843-1901. The coded references indicated that articles on him could be found in the first supplement to the *Dictionary of national biography* and the 1911 edition of the *Encyclopaedia Britannica,* and an obituary in the appropriate *Annual register.* Familiar with the strengths of DBN the librarian guessed that a Victorian bishop was just the type to rate a full entry (in fact he got ten columns), but the enquirer seemed satisfied with what he had seen in Hyamson—he now had Mandell Creighton ' placed '. The librarian was a little reluctant to give up quite so soon, so he reached for *Chambers' biographical dictionary* shelved next to Hyamson. Here the entry (at twelve lines) was a little more informative, referring at the end (as is the usual practice in this useful work) to the ' Life (1904) by his wife '. The reader studied this politely, but showed interest only in the information that Creighton was pronounced to rhyme with Brighton.

The next enquirer asked ' Who is Cardinal Brown? '. On this occasion the librarian did not ask the enquirer to spell the name (though it might have saved him a little time if he had!), and he assumed from the use of the present tense that he was in search of a contemporary. The Anglo-Saxon surname was not very much help—the man could be British, American, Canadian or Australian (to name but a few). The name could even be spelt Braun—which opened up another range of possibilities. A non-national who's who was obviously the answer. Immediately to hand was the new *Who's who in the world.* After fruitlessly scanning the 34 Browns, the librarian came upon half-a-dozen Brownes, in the midst of which he found the one he wanted, Michael David. The 9-line entry began by characterising him as 'clergyman', which seemed a trace under-stated, as it went on to describe him as Master-General of the Dominican Order and a Cardinal since 1962. The entry said he was educated at Rome and Fribourg University, and included his Rome address, but puzzlingly, it neither gave his place of birth nor his nationality, in which the enquirer seemed particularly inter-ested. Taking a chance, therefore, the librarian tried *Who's who*. Here he learned that Michael Browne had been born in County Tipperary and educated (before he went to Rome) in Cashel. And so the Cardinal was not British, or American, or Canadian, or Australian, or even Anglo-Saxon at all—he was an Irishman!

Occasionally encountered are identification queries with a special twist: where there are two (or even more) candidates with the same name, each at first sight matching the enquirer's specifications.

Case 104: 'Can you find me the address of William Craig? He's a politician', was a very simple problem for the reference librarian of a small Scottish public library. Literally within seconds she had available for her enquirer the twenty-line *Who's who* entry for the Rt Hon William Craig, Northern Ireland MP and former Minister, including his Belfast home address.

'No, no!' was the reader's immediate response, 'the one I want is a Scot'. The librarian pointed to the next entry, twice as long as the first, under the indubitably Scottish name William Stuart McRae Craig, Emeritus Professor of Paediatrics and Child Health at the University of Leeds, currently with an East Lothian address. But this was still not the one—and there were no more William Craigs in *Who's who*.

'Do you know anything more about him?' was the obvious question to put to the reader. 'I think he is a baillie', he replied. As a Scot the librarian knew what the *Concise Oxford dictionary* would otherwise have told her, namely, that a baillie is a Scottish municipal magistrate, the equivalent of an English alderman. Pressing the reader to cudgel his memory further, she eventually extracted the information that the William Craig they were looking for might come from Aberdeen. Passing over the *Local government manual and directory* (which is restricted to England and Wales), straightaway in the *Municipal year book* in the Scottish burghs section she consulted the Aberdeen entry. The address of Baillie W P Craig was given as 4, Fraser Street, Aberdeen AB2 3XS.

(*See also* cases 127, 133, 136.)

Less common is the reverse, where two separate characters in the course of the investigation merge into one.

Case 105: An enquirer who called the reference library on the phone one evening admitted frankly that he wanted to settle a bet. He had become involved over a drink in a friendly argument about Sandy Brown, the clarinettist and band-leader. His companion maintained that he was the same man as the Sandy Brown who was well-known as an expert on acoustics for the BBC. Asking the reader to hold the line, the librarian reached for the latest *Who's who,* but Sandy Brown was not to be found, even under 'Brown, Alexander'. He thought he would have to arrange to call back, when his eye fell on the recently acquired *Who's who in the world.* Quickly checking, he was more than a little surprised to find a thirteen-line entry, indicating that Sandy Brown, Fellow of the Royal Institute of British Architects, was not only responsible for the 'acoustic design of most radio and TV studios in UK', but was also the recipient of the *Melody maker* top clarinettist award for 1962-70. The librarian could not help but recall the words reported by the Evangelist, 'A prophet is not without honour, save in his own country'.

A very large number of biographical queries in libraries are *subject* enquiries, that is to say 'material finding' enquiries, asking for 'something on' (or perhaps less hopefully 'anything on') the person sought for.

Case 106: The young librarian in a college of education library made quite a fool of herself at first when approached by a student 'looking for something on Milner's kindergarten', for her immediate response was to ask the student if he knew where it was. Her unspoken assumption that it was some kind of infants' school provoked some merriment, but eventually the enquirer sobered up sufficiently to explain that Milner was a famous British colonial administrator and his 'kindergarten' was his team of assistants. The librarian asked for time to look, and retired to recover her composure and discover something about Milner. *Webster's biographical dictionary* soon identified him as Alfred, 1st Viscount Milner (1854-1925), a German-born British administrator in South Africa, but there was no mention of a 'kindergarten' in the fourteen-line entry. *Chambers' biographical dictionary* had almost twice as much, including five lines of bibliography, but again the 'kindergarten' was conspicuous by its absence.

By now, however, she knew the year of his death, which enabled her to go straight to the 1922-30 *Dictionary of national biography* volume, where she found an extensive (thirty columns) but most readable account of his life. In the midst of it she came upon this sentence, describing his negotiations in Britain in 1901 whilst on leave from South Africa: 'He also chose a band of keen young men, fresh from Oxford or Toynbee Hall, soon to be famous as "Milner's kindergarten", to help him in starting his schemes of reorganisation and social reform in the new colonies'. She noticed in the bibliography at the end of the article several references to likely-looking books on his work in South Africa.

Clearer now as to what was required, she consulted the library catalogue under Milner—to no avail. BNB was more helpful, drawing her attention to a 1970 work, originally published in the US two years earlier by a university press: Walter Nimocks *Milner's young men: the 'kindergarten' in Edwardian imperial affairs*. First ascertaining that the reader was prepared to wait, the librarian immediately ordered a copy. When it arrived three weeks later she was interested to find it a thorough and substantial work, with a frontispiece in the form of a group photograph of twelve members of the 'kindergarten'. The ten-page bibliography included notes for the researcher on the members' private papers, and the text contained this comment: '. . . one would assume that the students of Edwardian history had produced a considerable body of monographic literature on the subject. This, however, is not the case. Though an unpublished PhD dissertation and three articles have appeared . . . "this curious band has yet to find its rhapsodist".'

Whether the student saw himself in this role or not, the librarian was not certain: there was no doubt, however, from his reaction to her production of the book that in his view at least she had redeemed her initial *faux pas*.

If about contemporary figures, a goodly minority of these enquiries in all types of library will be found to come from chairmen or hosts responsible for ' a few words of introduction ' about prospective speakers or guests. What is usually needed here is a *curriculum vitae*, but on occasion it is helpful to locate sources of a more informal and even gossipy nature, to add flesh to the bare bones of, say, a typical *Who's who* profile. This is where those biographical tools which indicate further sources are so useful.

Special care has to be taken when a person is the subject of a request for ' something on ', for it will be found that enquirers are not always interested primarily in information of a biographical nature. Very often what they really want is something on *the work* of the man they are after, whether he is a bridge-builder, or a composer, or a designer of comic postcards.

Case 107: ' Have you got anything on Donald McGill?' was at first taken by the unsuspecting librarian at its face value. He did manage to extract from the reader the information that McGill was an artist, but he seemed either unable or unwilling to reveal more. Neither *Who's who* nor *Who's who in art* had an entry for him, and he did not figure in the most comprehensive list of artists the library possessed, Emmanuel Bénézit *Dictionnaire critique et documentaire des peintres, sculpteurs, dessinateurs et graveurs de tous les temps et tous les pays*. Returning to general sources the librarian tried in quick succession (but unsuccessfully) *Webster's biographical dictionary, Chambers' biographical dictionary* and *Who's who in the world*.

The reader had been observing this performance with diminishing interest; in an attempt to sustain his morale the librarian (who was quite willing to continue the search) asked ' What sort of thing were you looking for?' The reply was startling: ' I don't really want anything on the man himself. It's his drawings I am interested in.' Quite obviously, even if an entry had been found in *Who's who*, it would have been useless in this instance. What was wanted was an extended account, in a periodical article, for example. Perhaps *Art index* would be the best source to try? But first he thought he might as well complete his search in the biographical sources by working through *Biography index,* subtitled ' a quarterly index to biographical material in books and magazines '. It was here at last that he encountered the first mention of his quarry: described as an ' English post-card designer ', he had an article devoted to him in *Time* for 26th October 1962. This journal was unavailable in the library and so could not be consulted immediately, but from the dates following McGill's name in the heading (1875?-1962) the librarian guessed that the article was quite probably an obituary tribute. Continuing the search, however, he found a further reference, to a 127-page book: Arthur Calder-Marshall *Wish you were here: the art of Donald McGill* (1966). He was suitably chagrined to find that his library already had a copy on its shelves, with a card in its catalogue under ' McGill, Donald '. Although the book described its subject as ' the greatest practitioner of the comic postcard, and especially of the seaside postcard ', the librarian was comforted to learn that he was not alone in his ignorance. In an essay on the art of Donald McGill in *Horizon* for February 1941 George Orwell had commenced by admitting ' Who Donald McGill is, I do not know. He is apparently a trade name.' Most consoling of all were the full-colour reproductions of some dozens of McGill's choicest postcards.

A small proportion of biographical queries turn into *research enquiries* when the librarian finds he has exhausted the reference tools at his disposal and is obliged to turn to primary sources and even to manuscript and private sources. So carefully have names been recorded down the years (in parish registers, for instance, and rate-books), and so often, comparatively speaking, do we find letters and other personal documents preserved that biographical research often beckons encouragingly. But in most libraries, perhaps, the pressure of time forces the reference librarian to draw back once he nears the limit of organised knowledge, leaving his enquirer to plot his own route through the uncharted seas of pure research.

Case 108: In a large research library one of the readers, a clergyman, came to ask for help in tracing information on William Webb Ellis. As he explained, his main claim to fame is as the almost legendary boy in the football game at Rugby School who picked up the ball and ran with it, thus inventing Rugby football (and, in due course, American football). As they made their way towards the biographical reference shelves, the reader added ' I have already tried most of those '. And so he had, for Ellis was not to be found in DNB (or its supplements, which the librarian was careful to check), *Chambers' biographical dictionary, Webster's biographical dictionary,* or *Lippincott's universal pronouncing dictionary of biography and mythology.* He had drawn blank with the indexes too: Hyamson *A dictionary of universal biography,* Riches *An analytical bibliography of universal collected biography,* Arnim *Internationale Personalbibliographie* and *Biography index* from its commencement in 1946.

Clearly it was going to be necessary to explore primary sources. Assessing what they had to go on, the librarian could not make it amount to more than firstly, the name; secondly, the connection with Rugby School; and thirdly, the vague impression that the famous incident took place sometime in the 19th century, probably in the first half. Lining all these up seemed to point in the direction of the *Rugby School register, 1675-1849.* The name of William Webb Ellis was immediately found in the index, referring to the entrances for Midsummer 1816, where he was described as aged nine in November and a son of Mrs Ellis of Rugby. A footnote by the editor further described him as an exhibitioner at Brasenose College, Oxford, and rector of Laver Magdalen, Essex. His date of death was given as 24th January 1872. Little enough in truth, but sufficient for the alert librarian to be able to guarantee finding further entries in Foster *Alumni Oxoniensis, 1715-1886* and in *Crockford's clerical directory,* with the distinct possibility of an obituary in the *Times* and of an appearance in Boase *Modern English biography.* Taking these one by one, he found that Foster described him as the second son of James Ellis of Manchester, gentleman, gave the dates of his matriculation and graduation (BA and MA), confirmed the date of his death and added his ministry of St George's, Albemarle Street, London to the rectorship in Essex listed by the *Rugby School register.* He drew a blank with the *Times,* no entry appearing in the *Index* either in the ' Deaths ' or under Ellis, but was gratified to find an entry in Boase. This remarkably useful work concentrates on those who died in the half-century after 1850 and is invaluable for many figures of local or temporary

159

importance omitted from DNB. To what had been already discovered it added the approximate date of his birth, November 1807 (which the librarian had already calculated from the entry in the *Rugby School register*); the rectorship of St Clement Danes, Strand, from 1843 to 1855; a list of his publications, all of a religious nature, *eg, Dangerous errors of Romanism* (1853); and a reference to a portrait in the *Illustrated London news* for 1854. This turned out to be an engraving 'from a daguerreotype by Beard', one of a number of similar portraits of other clergymen used to illustrate a symposium of Fast-day sermons. Finally, *Crockford's* was consulted—the 1865 issue being chosen—but the brief entry was found to furnish no fresh information.

Several further possible avenues invited exploration. Local newspapers in Essex would probably have an obituary. Manchester directories might throw light on where his father used to live in Manchester. Similar sources in Rugby could perhaps locate his mother's address. His publications (including those in the British Museum but not listed by Boase) could be studied. And as for unpublished sources, there would be parish registers (for his baptism as Manchester?), his marriage certificate (if any), his will (almost certainly), as well as a whole host of possibilities and probabilities at Manchester, Rugby, Oxford, London, and Essex. But at this point, having revealed these further avenues, the librarian decided that his part in the investigation was at an end.

With those biographical enquiries that are really genealogical, *ie,* concerned with the tracing of ancestors, librarians in all kinds of libraries have learned to be even more cautious. So numerous are such enquiries and so specialised the work, that with all but the most straight-forward many librarians as a matter of policy will do no more than direct the readers' attention to such works as the Society of Genealogists *Genealogists' handbook* (fourth edition 1967), or P W Filby *American and British genealogy and heraldry: a selected list of books* (1970), with the recommendation that they consult a professional genealogist.

Case 109: A very simple-sounding enquiry in a small-town reference library was one asking for the present descendant of Sir Walter Scott. The librarian first made sure that what the enquirer really wanted was the senior descendant, the head of the family, the current heir to the title (for the librarian recalled that the *Sir* in this instance signified 'baronet', a hereditary title, rather than merely 'knight' which is a title dying with its holder). Turning to the latest *Burke's genealogical and heraldic history of the peerage, baronetage and knightage* (to give it its full name), she hesitated at first in case it was a Scottish title, but on reflection decided to plunge into its thousands of pages, fairly confident that the baronetcy was a United Kingdom creation. To her amazement she discovered no less than five Scott titles, all baronetcies: Scott of Beauclerc, of Great Barr, of Rotherfield, of Witley, of Yews. Of these the first seemed the most likely contender, for the current holder was named Sir Walter Scott, fourth baronet. Then she noticed that the title had only been created in 1907 (the first baronet also being Sir Walter). Before investigating the others she thought it would be useful to check in DNB when the great Sir Walter was made a baronet. In the course of scanning his long entry she came across one sentence which made her quest superfluous: 'Scott has no descendants except the Hon Mary Monica Maxwell Scott, daughter of [James Robert] Hope-Scott, and her children'. The likelihood was that for lack of a male heir the title had become extinct.

Returning therefore to *Burke's peerage,* she checked the list of extinct titles at the end. She quickly located the Constable-Maxwell-Scott baronetcy only to discover a 'see' reference to 'Norfolk, D.' This was indeed a surprise, for the Dukes of Norfolk, as their seven-page entry proclaims, 'stand next to the Blood Royal, at the head of the Peerage of England'. After no little searching among the quite complicated small-print lineage the librarian eventually located Mary Monica Maxwell-Scott, and from that all was plain sailing. Though all her eight children (four sons, four daughters) had died, the two daughters of her eldest son were both living. Of these, the elder was Patricia Mary Maxwell-Scott, born 11th March 1921— the great-great-great-granddaughter of Sir Walter Scott himself. Confirmation that this was indeed the 'descendant' the enquirer was seeking was provided by the address given for her: 'Abbotsford, Melrose, Roxburghshire'—the great house that Sir Walter had built in the Scottish baronial style on the banks of the Tweed. The librarian recalled the words used by DNB, 'It was at Abbotsford that Scott was in his glory'.

Like questions about quotations (see page 116 above), biographical enquiries are almost invariably simple *in form*. They may be far from simple to answer satisfactorily, but even the most inexperienced librarian can usually *understand* a request for biographical information, whereas a problem in the field of international law or chemical engineering may need a great deal of elucidation before the search can be started.

Fortunately for the librarian, this interest that people have in people has ensured for many years now the provision of a comprehensive battery of biographical reference sources, and close on five thousand can be found listed and annotated in R B Slocum *Biographical dictionaries and related works: an international bibliography* (1967). So long as the person enquired about is of some notability, whether he be living or dead, the chances of locating an entry for him in one of the standard works are good.

Case 110: An enquiry in a large public library was prompted by a few sentences from the introduction the recently published work by Harry Ludlam *A biography of Dracula: the life story of Bram Stoker* (1962): ' My quest for Bram Stoker began seven years ago. More than biographical research it developed into work of detection, with patient investigation of the vaguest clues. For the fact was, after the ravages of the two world wars the more usual sources of research had long vanished: memories had dimmed; records had been destroyed or lost. And, though Count Dracula had found a niche in most of the world's reference books, his flamboyant creator did not merit a single mention. Not even in Dublin, his birthplace ... Nothing was ever written about Bram Stoker.'

The reader could not believe that such a well-known writer had been ignored by the biographical reference tools, and he sought the librarian's help. The librarian began with Hyamson (1951)—and immediately found an entry for Stoker, Irish journalist, actor, and miscellaneous writer. Reference was made to J S Crone *A concise dictionary of Irish biography* (1937); when consulted a twelve-line entry was found and it was noted that the place of publication was *Dublin*. Briefer entries were found for him in both *Chambers' biographical dictionary* and *Webster's biographical dictionary* (1943). Having learned that the date of his death was 1912, the librarian

162

looked up *Who was who, 1897-1916,* and found no fewer than 38 lines on him!

Biography index drew his attention to an entry for Stoker in F N Magill *Cyclopedia of world authors* (1958), which reminded him to check in *Twentieth century authors* where he found a two-column entry, including a very clear photograph and an eleven-line bibliography of works by and about him. Finally when he checked the 1912 *Index to the Times* he located an obituary notice.

Technically too, long years of experience have seen to it that these tools reach an enviable level of sophistication in contents, arrangement, methods of updating, *etc.* And in the more modern works standards of accuracy are commendably high. This is not the place to discuss in detail the well-nigh infinite permutations possible in biographical dictionaries—contemporary/retrospective, national/international, specific/general, popular/scholarly, descriptive/evaluative—but the student will learn to recognise a standard pattern, observable in most major countries. The twin pillars of such a national system are usually a general quick-reference who's who of the living in one volume and a more extended multi-volumed scholarly dictionary of eminent figures of the past.

The pattern established in the late nineteenth century by the archetypal (British) *Who's who*—the only example that does not need to distinguish itself by a qualifying phrase—has been followed by most developed countries. We now have not only *Who's who in America* but also *Wer ist wer, Qui est qui, Wie ist dat, Chi è, Quién es quién, Hvem er hvem, Quem é alguém,* and many others. Designed to answer a wide range of questions about each country's eminent men and women of the day, the self-compiled entries usually display in standardised format a non-critical summary of the vital facts about their subjects. The best examples (*eg, Who's who* and *Who's who in America*) take the greatest care in selecting names for inclusion: fame based solely on sporting achievement is not sufficient, and the merely notorious (as opposed to the famous) are excluded. Conviction of any crime usually eliminates automatically. *Who's who* keeps its basis of selection a closely guarded secret; *Who's who in America* is slightly more revealing, insisting that inclusion is on the basis of ' reference value '. This is annoying to some, and one British publisher in recent years has brought out

163

a rival entitled *Who really is who.* Close attention is paid to regular updating (*Who's who* annually, *Who's who in America* every two years).

Case 111: ' Can you find me Hugh McDiarmid's address?' was the very simple telephone query received in a college library one morning. Before the assistant had time to enquire further, the caller anticipated her with ' He's a Scottish poet '. Knowing that addresses are always given by *Who's who* (and that the entries are updated annually by the subjects themselves) she took the volume to the 'phone. 'Hugh McDiarmid' turned out to be a pen-name, for the entry referred her to Christopher Murray Grieve. At the end of the 43 lines on him (two-thirds of them listing his writings) his address was given as The Cottage, Brownsbank, by Biggar, Lanarkshire.

Case 112: A 'phone request for the name of the Bishop of Birmingham was one which could obviously be answered by the current *Who's who.* It was not until the librarian opened the volume that he saw that the problem was not so simple as at first sight, for there appeared to be more than one candidate. Under ' Birmingham ' he found no fewer than five names listed: Most Rev George Patrick Dwyer, Archbishop (RC); Rt Rev Lawrence Ambrose Brown, Bishop (C of E); Rt Rev George Sinker, Assistant Bishop (C of E); Rt Rev Joseph Cleary, Auxiliary Bishop (RC); Rt Rev A J Emery, Auxiliary Bishop (RC). Back at the telephone he explained this to his caller, who asked him to read out the names. When he got to Bishop Sinker, he heard her cry ' That's the one! Thank you very much!'.

With supersonic travel and communication satellites now commonplace, the restriction of names in a who's who to citizens of one nation alone makes less and less sense. Indeed for years now *Who's who in America,* for instance, has included a number of foreigners, some of whom have never set foot there, but who have ' reference interest to America '. Similarly, in *Who's who* can be found entries for Wernher von Braun (German-born NASA administrator), Maurice

Chevalier (French stage and film actor), V M Molotov (Soviet diplomat), and many others who are clearly not British.

Useful though this departure is, the need is still felt even in the largest libraries for an international who's who, not only for names from those countries without a national who's who, but also for those enquiries when the country of the person sought for is not known. Long established here is the annual *International who's who*, covering 120 countries and endeavouring to include everyone whose name is known outside his own country. More limited in coverage and furnishing minimal data is the *International year-book and statesmen's who's who*. Offering a very strong challenge to both of these is the sturdy newcomer from the *Who's who in America* stables. Entitled *Who's who in the world*, its first 1971-1972 edition claims 25,000 entries from 150 countries, which puts it into first place immediately, at a selling price, however, about equivalent to the other two put together.

Case 113: When asked ' Can you find me something on Eisenstaedt, the great photographer?' the librarian first enquired whether it was information on his photographs or on the man himself that was wanted. Once it was clear that biographical details were needed, the librarian turned first to his extensive shelf of who's whos. He was too canny automatically to assume that a German name meant he should first consult either *Wer ist wer* or the English-language *Who's who in Germany* (in neither of which Eisenstaedt appears, as a matter of fact!), and so he turned to the *International who's who*. Unsuccessful there he tried *Who's who in the world*, to be rewarded by a 17-line self-compiled entry on this German-born ' photo journalist ', resident since 1935 in the United States. Making a note of his three books there listed, the librarian turned to *Biography index* in search of something to round out the spare outline thus drawn. Without difficulty he found a string of suitable articles from *Time* and *Life* and similar journals.

Each of these current dictionaries of international biography is compiled on the basis of questionnaires completed by the biographees themselves. This is perhaps the appropriate place to remind the student that here is also the arena for the vanity publication. In addition to the eminently respectable works just discussed, examples will be found of who's who-type publications designed chiefly to be sold to those listed in them. People are picked for inclusion not on merit alone, but in the hope that they will eventually purchase a copy of the work, preferably in the much more expensive de luxe edition with the name of the owner embossed in gilt.

The pattern for the other leg of a national system of biographical reference was also set in late nineteenth century Britain with the huge assembly of narrative accounts of dead notables entitled (like *Who's who*), with supreme Victorian indifference to similar ventures in other countries, the *Dictionary of national biography*. Scholarly, evaluative, fuller and more rounded, the articles were signed by their distinguished contributors and equipped with lists of sources consulted. It aimed to include all those who 'have achieved any reasonable measure of distinction in any walk of life'. Taken as a model by many later works, *eg, Dictionary of American biography, Dictionary of Welsh biography, Dictionnaire de biographie française, Dictionary of New Zealand biography,* despite its faults (which are many), it can still stand as an archetype worthy of close study, as well as an indispensable reference tool.

Case 114: A young woman known to the library staff as a local teacher came into a small public library one evening and spent several minutes looking at the shelves of Greek and Latin literature. Eventually she approached the desk: ' I wonder if you can help me. I am trying to trace the criticisms that A E Housman made of the German Latinists for their blunders in Manilius, but I can't find anything on the shelves.' The librarian decided to approach this very specific enquiry from the biographical angle, *via* A E Housman (whom, it must be confessed, he had always thought of as a poet only, author of *A Shropshire lad*).

He struck lucky with the first book he consulted, *Chambers' biographical dictionary,* where he found a brief but surprisingly readable account of this remarkable scholar and poet who failed his degree finals at Oxford yet went on to become Professor of Latin successively at University College London and the University of Cambridge. The article described how he spent nearly thirty years (1903-30) on the text of Manilius, but spoke of his ' waspish irascibility towards other scholars, especially those who uncritically accepted the earliest known text', and concluded with a nine-line bibliography, including his *Collected works* (1939) and a 'Life' by Grant Richards (1941).

Both of these sounded worth exploring but neither was in the library, so he turned to DNB in the hope of an entry. Having discovered from *Chambers'* the date of Housman's death (1936), he was able to go straight to the 1931-40 volume, where he soon located the extensive entry. On the matter of his edition of Manilius he read: 'The preface to Book I was a challenging assertion of Housman's views on scholarship. Its ruthless wit and unanswerable severities enchanted his juniors, although they were less pleasant reading to some of his seniors and contemporaries . . . In the fifth volume he dealt trenchantly with Manilian literature of the past three decades.'

Here then was a precise location for the criticisms the enquirer was seeking. All that remained was to furnish a specific bibliographical citation to set the interlending machine in motion. Furnished with the help of the 1940 *Reference catalogue of current literature* (predecessor of *British books in print*) it read *M Manilii Astronomicum,* ed A E Housman (Cambridge University Press, second edition 1937) in five volumes.

[The first edition of this remarkable work appeared at intervals from 1903 to 1930, each volume in an edition of four hundred copies produced at Housman's own expense and sold at much less than cost price. In his preface to the fifth volume he noted that ' only the first [volume] is yet sold out, and that took 23 years; and the reason why it took no longer is that it found purchasers among the unlearned, who had heard that it contained a scurrilous preface and hoped to extract from it a low enjoyment'. After his death Cambridge University Press took over publication of the whole series. As examples of his assessment of the German editors the following are typical extracts: ' They say he was born of human parentage; but if so he must have been suckled by Caucasian tigers . . . Not only had Jacob no sense for grammar, no sense for coherency, no sense for sense, but being himself possessed by a passion for the clumsy and the hispid he imputed his disgusting taste to all the authors whom he edited . . . The promptness with which these scholars defend the corrupt and the ease with which they explain the inexplicable are at first sight a strange contrast to the embarrass-

167

ment they suffer where the text is sound and the difficulty they find in understanding Latin . . . By this time it has become apparent what the modern conservative critic really is: a creature moving about in worlds not realised. His trade is one which requires, that it may be practised in perfection, two qualifications only: ignorance of language and abstinence from thought.']

Forming a special category of reference source are the biographical indexes and bio-bibliographies. Strictly speaking they are not biographical sources at all, for, as is the case with many indexes and bibliographies, their actual information content is sparse, or even non-existent; their function is to direct the user to material on their subjects. But they make excellent starting points, particularly where the enquirer is unable to furnish much by way of clues as to period or place for the man he wants. Perhaps the most widely useful of these is A M Hyamson *A dictionary of universal biography,* which has the great value of inclusiveness, listing far more names than any other comparable work. As its compiler points out, it 'is not a volume of biography'—indeed his policy of 'one person one line' makes this clear for all to see—but it serves as a one-place index to the contents of DNB, DAB, and a couple of dozen other major biographical sources covering 'all ages and all peoples'. Excluding living persons, it is obviously not so totally universal in scope as *Chambers'* or *Webster's,* but could be the first port of call in many enquiries about figures of the past.

Case 115: A request in a small university library for something on 'Bagford the biblioclast' set the librarian thinking. She had no idea what a biblioclast was (which is nothing to be ashamed of as the word does not appear in the *Concise Oxford dictionary*) and had to ask her enquirer. 'Oh, it's a man who breaks up books', was the quite accurate but not very helpful reply. In something of a quandary where to look first she tried the most comprehensive list of names she knew, Hyamson *A dictionary of universal biography.* The only likely candidate seemed John Bagford, English antiquarian and book collector, 1650-1716. The coded entry indicated that he was treated in both DNB and *Nouvelle biographie universelle.* Better known by its later title *Nouvelle biographie générale,* this 46-volume work edited by Hoefer was found to have a brief eleven-line entry with no mention of biblioclasm. DNB on the other hand characterised him immediately as 'shoemaker and biblioclast', going on to explain that he attracted the soubriquet by compiling an 'enormous collection of title-pages and other fragments in sixty-four volumes folio, which has procured him the . . . emphatic maledictions of all who object to the mutilation of books'. The entry practically filled the column, ending with two references to further sources of information.

(*See also* case 103.)

Between the current who's who and the retrospective dictionary of national biography is sometimes found an important intermediate category of source listing names withdrawn from the former on death but who have not yet had chance to get into the latter. *Who's who* again furnishes the model here with its half-dozen volumes of *Who was who*.

Case 116: An enquiry from an aggrieved academic followed on the publication in 1971 of the 'first full scale study of the university teaching professions to appear [in Britain]', A H Halsey and M A Trow *The British academics*. What had annoyed him was a comparatively minor aside on page 206, where in a discussion on the status of academics in society, mention is made of prestige based on 'popularity or notoriety as an expositor in the mass media. Professor C E M Joad would perhaps be the archetypal case here.' The enquirer was sure that Joad was never a professor and wanted the librarian to help him confirm it.

The librarian was just old enough to remember Joad's great days as a popular pundit in the press and on the radio, particularly in the long-running 'Brains trust' programme. He was certainly known as 'Professor', indeed his was probably the name most likely to spring to the mind of the man in the street when he pictured a university professor. The most convenient source to check was probably *Who was who*.

Here, in the 1951-60 volume, he found that Joad had been Reader in Philosophy and Head of the Department of Philosophy at Birkbeck College in the University of London. There was no mention of a professorship, although as a DLitt he was certainly entitled to call himself Dr Joad. From the date of his death (9th April 1953) as given in *Who was who* it was a simple matter to trace his obituary *via* the *Index to the Times*, but once again the librarian could not find in the half-column appreciation any mention of his holding a professorial chair.

Checking in the *Commonwealth universities yearbook* for the year of his death, the librarian found the same story. He was listed as a Reader in the Department of Philosophy, with an asterisk to signify that he was Head of the Department. By way of contrast, in the Department of Physics immediately below, the Head of the Department, J. D. Bernal, was unequivocally designated as Professor.

Finally, in the current *Birkbeck College calendar* the librarian found a list of former professors, including those deceased, from which Joad's name was conspicuously absent.

[Joad has a place in the DNB volume for 1951-60, published in 1971. Based on 'Private information: personal knowledge' the long account avoids referring to him as a professor. The entry in *Chambers' biographical dictionary* actually states: 'He upset academic circles by using the title of professor in journalism'. Now Halsey (Professorial Fellow of Nuffield College, Oxford) and Trow (Professor of Sociology at the University of California, Berkley) have succumbed to the spell of the mass media and enshrined 'Professor' Joad in what is likely to become the standard work on the British academic.]

Of course most of those whom death eliminates from the current listings *never* attain the pantheon of their country's retrospective dictionary, for the criteria of selection are so different. *Who was who, 1951-60,* for instance, lists perhaps 10,000 names withdrawn from *Who's who* during the decade, but the compilers of the *Dictionary of national biography, 1951-60* have decided that no more than 760 citizens are fit to be immortalized in its pages. There are also the unfortunate few removed from *Who's who* for reasons other than death: these never even get into *Who was who*.

Case 117: 'Can you find me something on Canon Jenkins of Oxford?' was a simple enough query, although the librarian was somewhat aghast when he encountered the veritable army of Jenkinses in *Crockford's clerical directory,* most of them Welsh. Only one of them, however, met the twin specifications of the enquirer—a canon and at Oxford—and this was Canon David Edward Jenkins, fellow, chaplain and praelector in theology at Queen's College Oxford from 1954, whose address was given as 366, Woodstock Road, Oxford. The reader's response was discouraging: ' Oh, no, no! This isn't the man I want at all! He was a famous Oxford " character "; died a few years ago.'

Suitably chastened to realise that he had neglected one of the cardinal rules of reference work in failing to extract all pertinent information from the reader at the outset, the librarian thought he would make a fresh start with *Who was who.* Without much difficulty he soon identified this man as Canon Claude Jenkins, 1877-1959, Canon of Christ Church and Regius Professor of History. The long article was strictly confined to the bare facts, as expected, the only hint of anything unusual being the recreations listed: ' walking, climbing, and collating MSS '. In the hope of a more rounded and human portrayal (which was obviously what the enquirer wanted), the librarian tried the recent DNB volume covering the decade of his death, 1951-60. He was surprised to find that he had not been included: he felt sure that had Canon Jenkins been Regius Professor fifty years earlier a place in DNB would have been assured.

He was even more shaken to learn that the *Times* had apparently reported his will but not his death, until it struck him that if he *had* died on 16th June 1959 (as stated in *Who was who*) his will could not possibly have been probated by 22nd June (as reported by the *Times*). The librarian surmised therefore that the *Who was who* date was a simple misprint, June for January—and so it proved. An earlier *Index* soon directed him to the full-column obituary in the *Times* for 19th January. Headed ' Church historian and Oxford eccentric ', it proved to be ideal for the reader's purpose, a concise but readable summary of the life and work of ' a scholar of almost legendary learning . . . a character whose idiosyncrasies lent variety and amusement to [Oxford] society '.

It is hardly ever the case that the enquirer has nothing but a name to offer the librarian, but if there truly are no further clues at all as to period, or nationality, or sphere of activity then the librarian turns first to the handful of universal biographical dictionaries that are restricted neither by time nor place nor subject and which include the quick and the dead alike. Should he feel that the person sought for is comparatively modern he would be well advised first to consult *Webster's biographical dictionary* and *Chambers' biographical dictionary*.

Case 118: ' We have been asked to find out about Geiger of the Geiger counter; can you help us? ' was the plea from a small group of children in a busy city library. The librarian took them over to the biography shelves and took down *Who's who in the world,* because he had learned to his cost that German names were by no means confined to Germans. His prudence was justified by the three Geigers that he found—George Raymond, an American philosophy professor, Louis Bertrand, a French philosophy professor, and Rupprecht, a German painter—although none of them fitted the enquirer's specification.

Only then did it strike him that he had unconsciously made an assumption about Geiger, unwarranted by anything the children had told him, namely that he was still living. Perhaps he was, as the Geiger counter, used for measuring radioactivity, was obviously a modern device; but then again, perhaps he was not. He decided to try *Webster's.* Here, in the entry for Ludwig Wilhelm Geiger, German oriental scholar, he noted a very brief mention of ' His son Hans (1882-1945), physicist; interested esp. in radium research '. This find was confirmed by the slightly longer account in *Chambers'* describing him as a ' German physicist . . . investigated beta-ray radioactivity and with Müller, devised a counter to measure it '.

He had his man ' placed ' now, but this was only the start; half-a-dozen lines would not satisfy a posse of curious youngsters. He checked quickly with Hyamson, without success, and then tried *Neue Deutsche Biographie,* the G volume of which had been published in 1963, where under the full name of Johannes [Hans] Wilhelm Geiger he found a column entry with half a column of bibliography, by and about him. This was better, but he had known that the children would not be able to read the German, and had only checked to see if it gave him any further leads—which it didn't!

Perhaps there was an article in English on him in a periodical? Here he was on surer ground, for in the course of a check through

Biography index he encountered a reference to what turned out to be just the thing: a short article by A T Krebs, with portrait and autograph, in *Science* for 27th July 1956.

Such handy single-volumed all-embracing compilations are extraordinarily useful for many other kinds of biographical enquiry also, and have a particular value in home or office. Lacking the stereotype format of the who's who type of work or the more leisurely pace of the great national biographical sources, their entries are obliged to aim at (in the words of Lytton Strachey) 'a brevity which excludes everything which is redundant and nothing that is significant'. An even more difficult choice faces their compilers in deciding who to include, if considerations of time and place and subject are to be ignored. *Webster's* claims that its 40,000 names 'have been selected as objectively as possible', but *Chambers'* admits quite frankly that in choosing its 15,000 biographies 'Our method has been to ask ourselves the question " Is he (or she) likely to be looked up? " and to answer it as honestly as possible'.

Case 119: 'What's the Code of Hammurabi? ' was the very quick-reference query put over the 'phone in a college of technology library. The librarian had a vague idea about it being a code of laws, and was positive about Hammurabi being the man responsible. She therefore decided to look him up first. She was less certain about the spelling, but found that *Webster's* had anticipated her by giving three different versions of the name of this 'Greatest king of the first dynasty of Babylon (c1955-1913 BC) . . . his codification of the laws and edicts was discovered in 1901, one of the most important " documents " [it was carved in stone] in history of human race '. To this *Chambers'* added the location of the inscribed tablet in the Louvre, although disappointingly (and unusually for *Chambers'*) did not refer to any further source.

Ringing back with these few basic facts, and offering to look further, the librarian discovered that they more than satisfied her enquirer.

The two classic sources in this field of universal bibliography are the great French 19th century compilations J C F Hoefer *Nouvelle biographie générale* (1853-66) in 46 volumes and J F Michaud *Biographie universelle* (second edition 1843-65) in 45 volumes. Rivals for many years, their differences culminated in a law suit for piracy, but they remain today unequalled as scholarly sources. Their value, even more than a century after their publication, is evidenced by the recent facsimile reprint edition of Hoefer and the microfiche edition of Michaud. For the librarian fortunate enough to have access to them they furnish long signed articles with bibliographies on over 50,000 of the great of all ages and countries.

Case 120: The problem that the librarian encountered at first in his search for details of the life and work of Diophantus of Alexandria was not that he was obscure and therefore not to be found—indeed as the reputed inventor of algebra he was quite famous and appeared in all the books—but that so little appeared about him in the standard biographical sources. *Webster's* had no more than three lines on him, placing him in the third century AD (or later), and giving his chief work as *Arithmetica* in thirteen books, six of which are extant. *Chambers'* was a little more forthcoming, referring the reader to 'Heath's *Diophantos of Alexandria* (1885; enlarged 1910)'. Various other works, including some subject sources like the *Oxford classical dictionary*, were all found to have entries, but none extended to more than a few lines. Finally, the librarian turned to Hoefer *Nouvelle biographie générale* where he was gratified to find two columns of close print, including eleven lines of bibliographical references.

[Had the librarian turned first to Hyamson he would have been directed to Hoefer immediately.]

Many experienced reference librarians can relate instances, to their cost, where they were led astray by assuming at the outset of one of these very open enquiries that the subject was a real person. This is not always a valid or even a plausible assumption, and the librarian should always bear in mind that the art of biography had its origins in the early accounts of legendary gods, kings, and heroes. Our modern counterparts are the fictional characters that people the pages of novels or plays, about whom queries will occasionally be posed as if they were indeed flesh and blood. Convenient to

174

consult in cases of doubt are titles such as the three-volumed *New century cyclopedia of names* and Joseph Thomas *Universal pronouncing dictionary of biography and mythology,* often known as *Lippincott's.* Like *Webster's* and *Chambers'* they are universal in scope, but they also include many fictional names.

Case 121: When faced with a request for the name of the original Marathon runner, the librarian realised that his biographical dictionaries were not going to be of any help, arranged as most of them were alphabetically by name and not by subject. He turned therefore to a more specialised source, a subject dictionary (or to be strictly accurate, a subject encyclopedia, despite its title); he found eleven lines in the *Oxford classical dictionary* on the famous battle of Marathon in 490 BC—the first Greek victory over Persia—but no mention of a runner. A little surprisingly he found a general encyclopedia more enlightening; in *Britannica* in addition to an article on Marathon (the battle) he found an article headed ' Marathon race (modern) '. He read that this ' commemorates the legendary feat of a Greek soldier, who in 490 BC is supposed to have run from Marathon to Athens, a distance of 22 mi. 1470 yd., to bring news of his countrymen's victory over the Persians '.

So the feat was merely legendary! But did the legend tell us the runner's name? An obvious source to consult was *Brewer's dictionary of phrase and fable*: here the librarian learned that the result of the battle ' was announced by courier, sometimes called Pheidippides, who fell dead on his arrival '. Feeling that he would like to see this confirmed, he looked up Pheidippides in the *New century cyclopedia of names,* which intermingles 100,000 proper names of all kinds—people and places, literary and historical, biblical and mythological, real and imaginary. The entry read: 'Athenian athlete. When the Persians landed at Marathon, Pheidippides was sent as courier from Athens to Sparta, asking the city's help against the invader. According to Herodotus, he covered the distance of about 150 miles in two days. Pheidippides is sometimes confused with the runner, whose name is not preserved, who brought to Athens the news of the Greek victory at Marathon.'

In a case like this the librarian could do no more than present his findings to his enquirer, and let him make up his own mind who the original Marathon runner was.

But as this case shows, the line between fact and fiction, truth and legend, real and imaginary, is not always so easy to draw, which explains the long entries in the sober pages of the *Dictionary of national biography* for names such as Robin Hood ('legendary outlaw, has been represented as a historical personage') and Arthur ('the real or fabulous king of Britain').

Queries about people who have leapt into prominence only recently pose their own particular problems. As virtual unknowns six months previously, obviously they will not be found in the standard reference sources, even if compiled annually like *Who's who*. Many of them never appear in these sober volumes, if their fame is of the transitory kind bestowed by the mass media on 'personalities' from the twin worlds of sport and show-business. And vast numbers of people 'in the news', particularly if they are discovered on the wrong side of the law, very quickly find themselves out of the headlines, and permanently. And yet, as librarians know, readers will ask about them. In most cases, perhaps, the best sources are non-biographical, in particular the newspapers (especially if indexed) and the news digests such as *Keesing's contemporary archives* and *Facts on file*.

Case 122: At the time of the attempted assassination of Rudi Dutschke, the German student leader, in early 1968, world interest focussed on Axel Springer, whose West Berlin headquarters of his newspaper and magazine empire came under attack from rioters. Then and for months afterwards enquiries were received by libraries for information about him.

A commercial librarian attempting to satisfy such an enquiry soon learned that the basic sources were no more than minimally informative. *Who's who in Germany* (which is in English) gave a mere fourteen-line drily factual summary—less than it gave, for instance, to Rudolf Springer, a professor at the University of Munich, and about the same as it gave to Ferdinand Springer, book dealer. *Wer ist wer* (in German, of course) was similarly restrained—as of course is expected in works of this kind—about this man, regarded by many as one of the most influential figures in West Germany.

What the enquirer wanted to fill out the picture was comment, background, a portrait perhaps. The best source for this is the current press, and so the librarian made for the indexes to the *Times* and the *New York times*. The former led him to an article by David Hotham (dateline, Bonn) ' The Springer press empire, a target of hate ', with a portrait of Axel Springer, in the *Times* for 15th April. The *New York Times index* referred him to a similarly illustrated article in the *New York Times magazine* for 17th March 1968.

It is in this context that an experienced American reference librarian has described the *New York Times index* as one of the best single keys to biography in the library, and it is interesting to note that one of the most recent attempts to furnish information on ' prominent personalities . . . unknowns who become overnight celebrities . . . controversial figures other biographical services may not cover at all ' is based on this great newspaper. The *New York Times biographical edition* each week provides some twenty loose-leaf profiles selected from the previous week's issues of the paper, together with monthly, quarterly, and annual cumulative indexes. Of the more traditional biographical reference sources outstandingly useful is the H W Wilson monthly *Current biography*: though covering no more than a couple of dozen names in each issue it does concentrate on those thrust recently into the limelight, treating each very fully. Its cumulated *Yearbook* and decennial indexes adds to its retrospective value. Less well-known, particularly outside the US, is the *Monthly supplement* to *Who's who in America,* which is international in scope, deliberately concentrating on people ' in the news '.

Case 123: A problem similar to the one encountered in the previous case faced the librarian asked for ' something on Hugo Hefner ', like Axel Springer a ' magazine publisher ', according to *Who's who in America*. Buried among the thirteen lines of basic personal and career data in that entry, the young librarian noticed the name of *Playboy,* the magazine that has made Hugo Hefner into the sort of publisher asked about in libraries.

To her he seemed an ideal candidate for attention by *Current biography*. A check of the indexes confirmed her hunch, revealing that he had featured in the September 1968 issue between the Archbishop of New York and the widow of Ernest Hemingway. Extending (with portrait and list of references) over four columns, this account described *Playboy* as the 'most successful magazine publishing venture in the mid-twentieth century in the United States'.

It is important for the librarian to be able to distinguish those biographical queries where the enquirer does not merely desire some 'information' about a person, but wishes to read about his life. These are but particular instances of that general category of reference service known as readers' advisory work, as described in *Case study in reference work* (pages 22-26). Although the form of the request as posed may be identical with that of a material-finding query, what the reader usually wants is a good solid volume to take home and settle down with by the fire (or by the air-conditioner). Here we are bibliographically in the realms of *individual* biography, not collected biography, but provided that the enquirer knows who he wants to read about, and always assuming that a book-length biography exists, meeting his needs is a simple task, for most library catalogues enter such works under biographee as well as biographer, as the published British Museum *General catalogue of printed books* demonstrates so well.

Case 124: An unusual instance of a specific request for an individual biography was an approach made in a small university library by a reader with a copy of the *Penguin book of Victorian verse* in his hand. On page 343 in a brief note on John Davidson (1857-1909), a Scottish poet 'of extended talent never fully realized' and who committed suicide by drowning, it was stated: 'He left instructions in his will that no biography of him was to be written'. The reader wanted to know whether such a biography had in fact ever been attempted.

Obviously the entries in the second supplement to DNB and in *Encyclopaedia Britannica,* and his obituary in the *Annual register* (all indexed by Hyamson) were not biographies in this sense, so the librarian turned first to the BM *General catalogue.* In the main set amid the thirty different John Davidsons there distinguished, 'Davidson (John) *the Poet*' stood out by reason of the number of his entries, although only two works *about* him were listed: Hayim Fineman *John Davidson: a study of the relation of his ideas to his poetry,* a fifty-one-page thesis published at Philadelphia in 1916,

178

and Gertrud von Petzold *John Davidson und sein geistiges Werden unter dem Einfluss Nietzsches* (Leipzig, 1928), neither of which could be described as biographies. In the *Ten-year supplement, 1956-1965,* however, were two titles that appeared more promising: R D Macleod *John Davidson: a study in personality* (1952) and J B Townsend *John Davidson: poet of Armageddon* (1961). Indeed both reader and librarian felt it was worth while trying to borrow copies of these two works for further study.

When in due course they arrived, the first turned out to be a 35-page pamphlet published in Glasgow on the occasion of the centenary of the poet's birth. Macleod confirmed the existence of the unusual provision in the will and added, 'A number of biographers have thought of Davidson as a subject for biographical study but so far his life has not been written ... American and other researchers have been and are at work, and inhibitions based on Davidson's own wish are likely to be less strong as the years pass.'

Townsend was obviously one of the workers referred to, for his book, one of the Yale University Studies in English, was based on his PhD dissertation. There was no index entry under 'will', but on scanning through the pages the librarian found where Davidson's words were quoted: 'No one is to write my life now or at any time'. The author went on to recount how the poet also left instructions that manuscripts of all his unpublished writings, including letters, should be destroyed. These instructions were carried out. The librarian wondered whether Townsend would attempt to justify his disregard of the poet's wishes. His musings were stilled when he came upon the following: 'On October 22, 1909, Davidson's executors announced in the *Times* . . . a ruling by the Principal Probate Registry that, since the will had not been witnessed, the deceased had died intestate . . . As for the other provisions of the document, no one has ever been bound by them legally or morally.'

For the librarian the field of individual biography (including autobiography) has one special problem—the diffuseness of its boundaries. What is one to make of such works written in the guise of fiction, whether novels or plays, *eg*, Robert Graves *I, Claudius*; Nikos Kazantzakis *Saint Francis*; Rolf Hochhuth *The soldiers* (Winston Churchill); Robert Bolt *A man for all seasons* (Thomas More)? Or those fictional works that are barely-concealed autobiographies, such as Thomas de Quincey *Confessions of an English opium eater*? How about works that are primarily 'subject' books but are treated by the author in such a way as to be as revealing as any autobiography, *eg,* Winston Churchill *The second world war*? And does biography comprise correspondence, journals, confessions, memoirs, reminiscences, and the like?

More difficult is the subject approach to individual biography in those cases where the enquirer has no specific name in mind. The *Subject-index of the London Library* uses the sub-heading 'biographies' under the subject with which the biography is concerned and William Matthews is one who has made a particular contribution to this area with his bibliographies of *British autobiographies* (1955), *British diaries* (1950), *American diaries* (1945), and *Canadian diaries and autobiographies.* (1950).

It was precisely because 'No present reference tool provides this information on the scale needed' that in 1969 the H W Wilson Co published M E Nicholsen *People in books: a selective guide to biographical literature arranged by vocations and other fields of reader interest.* Designed for everyday use rather than retrospective bibliographical completeness this work was actually produced in response to the demand from librarians, themselves spurred on by enquiries from their readers for 'biographies of chemists from Russia, or eighteenth century French poets, or life stories of victims of polio, or biographies of twentieth century Brazilians' (Preface).

Case 125: A research student in a university library told the librarian he was looking for lives of Chartists. After a few moments' enquiry the librarian had determined from his reader that what he wanted was not simply biographical information on people who had taken part in this great nineteenth century British working-class movement, but separate 'lives' of individual Chartists, especially those written by themselves, *ie,* autobiographies. Clearly, if the enquirer could furnish the names of a few prominent Chartists, it might well be that the library card catalogue, or better still, the British Museum *General catalogue of printed books* would do the rest. It emerged in the discussion, however, that he had already thought of this; indeed, he had tried it with two or three sample names (John Fielden, James Bronterre O'Brien, George Julian Harney) without success. What he really hoped the librarian could provide him with ideally was a ready-made list of such biographies (and autobiographies).

A bibliography of the Chartist movement was the thing to look for first, and Besterman *World bibliography of bibliographies* the place to try. This is of course limited to separately-published bibliographies, but even so the librarian was astonished to find only one work on Chartism in the whole five volumes, a very specialised catalogue from the Newport Public Library on *John Frost and the Chartist movement in Monmouthshire.* Making straight for the biographical sources, therefore, he tried first the subject index he remembered at the back of *Chambers' biographical dictionary.* In the ' History ' section he found under ' Chartism ' a sole reference to the six-line entry on Thomas Slingsby Duncombe, the radical MP who actually presented the Chartist petition to Parliament. The entry concluded (as so often in *Chambers'*) with a brief bibliographical note: ' See Life (1868) '. This was a start, at any rate—if Duncombe could be considered a real Chartist!

Changing tack, he next consulted the *Subject-index of London Library,* choosing this not only because of the subject access it provides to individual biographies but because he knew that Chartism, as a nineteenth century political movement, was squarely in the centre of the London Library's very broad subject interests, and would be very well represented in its collections. Taking note that the four volumes of the *Subject-index* only go up to 1953, he checked in each under ' Chartism: biographies '. And in each he found names listed, eleven in all, including one which figured twice. Following these up as instructed in the author catalogue, he soon had the titles and dates of the sought-for biographies, including a good selection of autobiographies, *eg, The life of Joseph Barker written by himself* (1880), W J Linton *Memories* (1895), Thomas Frost *Forty years' recollections* (1880).

At this point he remembered William Matthews *British autobiographies* (1955) in whose excellent index he soon found references to six Chartist autobiographies, four of which he had already traced in the London Library *Subject-index,* but two of which were new.

[This was clearly not a complete tally, but doubtless proved adequate for the reader's immediate purposes. It is interesting to note that had a more conventional bibliographical approach been made, by way of, among others, *Writings on British history* (which of course does not include works published before 1901), one book that would have been revealed is G D H Cole *Chartist portraits* (1941), comprising twelve chapters each devoted to a leading Chartist. Of course, this collection of biographical sketches would not have met the enquirer's specification of individual biographies and autobiographies, but the detailed bibliographical notes would have been found interesting because for half of his selection Cole is obliged to say repeatedly 'It is curious that there is no Life of [Richard] Oastler'; 'There is no published Life of [Ernest] Jones'; 'It is extraordinary that there is no Life of [Feargus] O'Connor'.

It should be added that in the thirty years or more since Cole wrote these words some of the desiderata have been supplied, *eg,* Donald Read and Eric Glasgow *Feargus O'Connor, Irishman and Chartist* (1961). There is no entry for Chartists in M E Nicholsen *People in books.*]

Midway between the comparatively brief accounts in the biographical dictionaries and the more leisured studies in the book-length biographies are the chapter-length treatments in works of collective biography such as C P Snow *Variety of men, Plutarch's lives, etc.* Usually compiled with some common theme in mind, some of the more recent collections are included in *People in books,* but the major retrospective index analysing over 56,000 accounts from 3,000 volumes is P M Riches *An analytical bibliography of universal collected biography* (1934).

In numerical terms the overwhelming majority of biographical reference works concentrate on people in specific occupations or other specialised groups, *eg, American men of science,* H M Colvin *Biographical dictionary of English architects, 1660-1840* (1954), the *Law list.* It would be inappropriate here to discuss them in detail, for they are subject sources, but it should be pointed out that they have certain advantages over the general biographical tools in some instances. As specialist sources they can be expected to include more names from their specific field than works attempting to cover the whole of knowledge; indeed, some claim to be comprehensive —which no general biographical dictionary ever could be—as, for instance, *Crockford's clerical directory* for the Anglican clergy, or the *Biographical directory of the American Congress. 1774-1961.* Usually, too, they are able to give more detail in each of their entries, and can reasonably be expected to be more accurate and more reliable, compiled as many of them are from sources closer to the original than are some of the general works.

As to type, they follow fairly closely the pattern of the general biographical dictionaries, falling into two main groups. Current figures are well provided for in the who's who type of work, whether or not those words actually appear in the title, *eg, Directory of American scholars, Medical directory, World who's who in commerce and industry*. Self-compiled, frequently updated, in standardised format, the entries in the best of these works (as in the three listed) show a commendable standard of reliability.

For figures of the past the searcher sometimes finds available more substantial retrospective compilations, with bibliographical references, attempting in some cases to do for musicians or chemists or saints what DBN does for Englishmen, *eg, Bryan's dictionary of painters and engravers* (1903-5) in five volumes; Sir Lewis Namier and J N Brooke *The House of Commons, 1754-90* (1964) in three volumes.

Case 126: In search of details of the life of Bartholomäus Bruyn the librarian drew blank with Hyamson and *Chambers'*, but found a two-line mention in *Webster's*: ' 1493?-?1555. German religious and portrait painter '. The entry in the *New century cyclopedia of names* extended to ten lines, but this was still not sufficient for the reader, who revealed that she was an art student making a special study of Bruyn. Turning therefore to a specialist source they were disappointed to find no more than a dozen lines in *Bryan's dictionary of painters and engravers*, although there was appended a handy list of paintings and their locations. Trying an even more specialised source, particularly appropriate for a German painter, they next consulted the 37-volume Thieme-Becker *Allgemeines Lexikon der bildenden Kunstler*, described by Winchell as ' the most complete and authoritative dictionary of painters '. The librarian had taken the precaution of ascertaining that the student did have some German, so he was gratified to find no fewer than seven closely-packed columns of text, together with an extensive bibliography.

Not all listings accept this dichotomy between the living and the dead. Like *Chambers' and Webster's* in the field of universal biography, a work like *World who's who in science* (1968) despite its title includes names both past and present, ranging from 1700 BC to 1968 AD.

Biographical indexes too are found in some special fields, giving the bare minimum of biographical data necessary for identification, and concentrating on directing the enquirer to further sources of information, *eg, Mallett's index of artists* (1935-40), N O Ireland *Index to scientists of the world from ancient to modern times* (1962).

One important category of biographical source in specialised areas is not matched in the general field—the directory. Whatever may appear on their title pages (for many directories are described as something else, and a number of so-called 'directories' are not directories at all), a directory is basically a list of names and addresses. Perhaps the most frequently encountered examples are membership directories, of learned societies, of professional institutions, and the like, *eg,* Institution of Chartered Accountants in England and Wales *List of members,* but in this group also fall titles such as the *Army list.* It could be said that it is stretching a point to categorise these as biographical sources, for the information given with each entry is usually meagre, often no more than name, qualifications, post held, and address. They are primarily location tools: indeed some are arranged in subject order, *eg, Imperial calendar and civil service list,* or by place, *eg, Teachers of history in the universities of the United Kingdom.* Where they score, however, is in their inclusiveness, for within their limits they are non-selective, listing all members in good standing. This can be important in searches for people who are not renowned, but just happen to be mechanical engineers or nurses or architects. But once the entries begin to include more than directory information, as in the *American architects directory* or the *Directory of British scientists,* we find the directory beginning to merge with the who's who type discussed earlier (page 183).

Probably most directories are confined to current names, but examples are encountered of retrospective listings that contain no more than the merest directory information, *eg,* G H Baillie *Watchmakers and clockmakers of the world* (third edition 1951). From the librarian's point of view alumni lists fall into this category also, sparse in biographical detail, but basically non-selective.

It is perhaps worth noting in passing that there are some gaps among current professional directories. In Britain, for instance, there is no published list of teachers or of magistrates, although virtually all of the former are on the computers of the Department of Education and Science and all of the latter in the files of the Lord Chancellor's Office.

Among all the various occupational groups there is one which stands out as exceptionally favoured by the reference book compilers—authors and writers. (What the difference is between the two is difficult to say, although for nearly forty years the *Author's and writer's who's who* has so distinguished them.) Not only do they get more than their fair share of space in the general biographical dictionaries, but they have dozens of their own, both current and retrospective. If a man is a writer of any kind, not necessarily a writer of ' literature ', the searcher's chances of finding an entry for him somewhere are distinctly better than average. But then in many libraries, enquiries about writers are very common. The observant reader may notice that of the close on fifty cases in this chapter over a dozen are about people who are primarily known as writers, and perhaps a dozen more are about people who are writers incidentally. This is a not inaccurate reflection of the proportions of such enquiries put to librarians, at least in public and academic libraries.

Case 127: The search for information on John D MacDonald, an American writer, seemed no sooner begun than ended, for the librarian immediately encountered a sixteen-line entry in *Who's who in America* for John D(ennis) MacDonald, described as ' writer and editor '. But then after a few moments of perusal of the volume, the puzzled reader returned: ' I don't think this can be the man I want '. It emerged in the succeeding discussion that his man was a popular writer of thrillers, whereas the man in *Who's who in America* wrote about angling and poker.

Having made sure that there was no other likely candidate in the volume, the librarian checked some of the more recent cumulations of the *National union catalogue*. John Dennis MacDonald (1906-) was indeed there, but he was immediately preceded by the much more prolific John Dann MacDonald, author of novels with titles like *Death trap, Beach girls,* and *A ballet for Cinderella*.

This second John D MacDonald was obviously the wanted man.

The librarian found his name in the cumulated index to the first twenty volumes of *Contemporary authors,* and followed up the reference to volume 2, though when he came to the actual volume he found it in the *revised* edition of volumes 1-4. There in the formatted entry he found ample information under the standard headings: personal, career, writings, work in progress, side-lights (*ie,* comment), and biographical sources. The creator of Travis McGee, described as a 'knight in slightly tarnished armour . . . a thinking man's Robin Hood', MacDonald was credited with thirty million copies of his novels sold, six films, and twenty-seven TV features.

Case 128: The reference librarian asked for some background information on Alan Hackney recalled the name only in the context of the authorship of a very funny novel about army life entitled *Private's progress,* published some years earlier. He confirmed with the enquirer that this was indeed the man he wanted, and then began his search. The first discovery he made was that the author did not figure in the general sources like *Who's who* and *Biography index* and *Chambers'* at all.

Without further ado, the librarian turned therefore to the specific biographical dictionaries of authors. *Twentieth century authors* (1942) and its *First supplement* (1955) he thought would be too early for a writer who had swum into the public ken so comparatively recently, so he made for the exceptionally wide-ranging American series *Contemporary authors.* He was able to check in the most recent cumulation of volumes 25 to 28 (1971) and the cumulated index to the previous 24 volumes, and in the latter he found a reference to an entry in volume 7/8. This proved to be a reasonably adequate summary of the career of Hackney, 'writer of books and films', born in 1924, and perhaps best known for his film (and book) *I'm alright, Jack,* starring Peter Sellers as a trade union official.

As a British writer, he would perhaps also be found in the newly-published edition of *Author's and writers who's who,* the librarian guessed. The seven-line self-compiled entry was very brief, offering no more than the bare minimum of facts, but did add one or two details to the earlier *Contemporary authors* account.

(*See also* case 110).

Standing in a class by themselves as biographical reference sources are the lists of the titled. Although the venerable European works like the *Almanach de Gotha* and its successors are perhaps currently consulted less than they used to be, the retrospective value of such compilations remains, for the history of many of the families they treat is inextricably intertwined with national history. To assume that entry to such works is by birth whereas entry to *Who's who* or DNB is by merit is to draw too sharp a distinction. In Britain in particular, while it can not be said that the institution which is the peerage is flourishing, the House of Lords remains an integral part of the legislature, and the summit of the judicial system, as well as invariably providing a handful of cabinet ministers for each successive government. New creations continue (now mostly life peerages rather than hereditary titles), and at a humbler level the twice-yearly honours list adds hundreds to the roles of the baronetage, the knightage, and the many other orders of chivalry. What this means for the librarian is that he should not omit to include in his searches in appropriate cases works like *Burke's peerage, Debrett's peerage,* and *Kelly's handbook to the titled, landed and official classes.*

Case 129: In a search for information on George Philips, a Lancashire cotton manufacturer and friend of the famous Sydney Smith, the first two problems encountered were the determination of the approximate period when he flourished and of the precise spelling of his surname. As the reader had no information to add on either, the librarian looked up Sydney Smith's dates in the *Concise DNB*—1771-1845. As for the name, he was left with no alternative but to check under each of the four possible spellings (Philipps, Philips, Phillips, Phillipps) in all the works he consulted. But he had no luck at all with British lists like DNB, Boase *Modern English biography,* Musgrave's *Obituary,* or with indexes like Phillips *Dictionary of biographical reference,* Hyamson, and Riches. The universal lists like *Chambers'* and *Webster's* and *Lippincott's* were also checked without success.

The first gleam of light appeared when an approach was made through the biographies of Sydney Smith. The first consulted, Hesketh Pearson's *Smith of Smiths,* gave a clue right away by referring to him as *Sir* George. In the hope that this might indicate baronet, rather than merely knight, *Burke's peerage* was tried. As he had discovered, Sydney Smith died in 1845, and on the assumption that Philips was roughly contemporary, the eighth edition, for 1846, was tried first—with success! The entry gave the usual *Peerage* information, short biography, armorial bearings, motto, lineage, *etc,* and the name of his heir, George Richard Philips. A check under this name in a later edition gave the date of Sir George's death as 3rd October 1847, and straightaway *Palmer's index to the Times* was searched (under 'deaths') in the hope of an obituary notice. The *Times* did not seem to have one, but with the date of death established it was a simple matter to find the short obituary in the *Annual register* for the year and in the *Gentleman's magazine* for December. In view of his Lancashire connections, the *Manchester Guardian* was also searched, and a most useful obituary found in the issue for 9th October. The topographical approach was then tried, but the Lancashire Victoria county history volumes brought little more to light apart from a note on Sedgeley Hall, his house near Manchester, where Sydney Smith was a frequent visitor. To round off the story, the British Museum *Catalogue of printed books* (always worth checking if there is the slightest possibility of your man being literary) brought to light the fact that in Manchester in 1793 was published his pamphlet *The necessity of a speedy and effectual reform in Parliament.*

(*See also* cases 109, 134, 152.)

The really difficult enquiries about people are those where the usual biographical reference sources have proved fruitless. And yet in the literature there are descriptions and discussions and portraits and profiles and thumb-nail sketches of thousands of significant and interesting people who fall into this category. The challenge to the librarian is that this material is buried in non-biographical sources, and he sometimes has to unearth it without benefit of aid from indexes.

Perhaps the most outstanding single type of source in this category is the obituary notice, as the previous case illustrates. Almost invariably found in a newspaper or periodical, for many people their obituary notice may be the only occasion when an extended biographical account appears in print. Countless thousands of them, particularly in local newspapers, may never be read again, becoming submerged in the flood of unindexed trivia that such a newspaper file so often becomes. But the librarian usually has one thread which may lead him back through the maze—the date of death. For an obscure figure, this is the most important single fact to determine at the outset of the search, suggesting as it does the point to enter likely files in search of an obituary notice.

In the offices of the world's great newspapers very considerable care is taken with such obituaries, the common practice being to prepare them in great secrecy well in advance of their subject's death. This veil of secrecy is sometimes pierced, however. Somerset Maugham, for instance, claimed to have read his *Times* obituary, for the editor sent it to him to check for accuracy. The next day when Maugham complained that although accurate it was not half warm enough he was invited to ' tidge it up '. Which he did. Some newspapers employ staff obituary writers, who often make it their business to visit and talk to those they judge to be prospective subjects, but distinguished outside contributors are often used, and it is not unknown for a pair of elderly professors, or generals, or statesmen, or judges, to be commissioned by a paper to write mutual obituaries, each in blissful ignorance of the other's macabre task.

Case 130: An obituary query slightly out of the ordinary came to a large research library by letter. It asked simply for the author of the *Times* obituary of Rupert Brooke. The librarian's first step was to pinpoint the date of the young poet's death. The *Concise DNB* for 1901 to 1950 gave 1915, which permitted him then to check the appropriate volumes of the *Index to the Times* for the precise location. Under ' Brooke, Sub-lieut R ' was indexed firstly his death (in the issue for 26th April) and secondly ' an appreciation by our Cambridge University correspondent ' (7th May). Unable to question the enquirer, the librarian had to assume that what he was interested in was the former, comprising a strictly factual summary of the poet's life (anonymous) and a moving obituary tribute beginning ' " WSC " writes : " Rupert Brooke is dead . . ." '.

So who was this ' WSC '? In England in the first half of the 20th century the best known holder of those initials was of course Winston Churchill. Could it indeed be he? As the librarian knew, Churchill was at that time First Lord of the Admiralty, and Brooke was a serving naval officer, and so *prima facie* the supposition would bear investigation. The three-column entry for Brooke in DNB for

189

1912-21 made no mention of Churchill, but the librarian was intrigued to note its author, ' EM '. He guessed who this was, and the
key to contributors confirmed that it was indeed Edward (later Sir
Edward) Howard Marsh, who according to *Who was who, 1951-60*
was not only a patron and connoisseur of art and letters but a civil
servant and private secretary to Winston Churchill for many years.

Trying another tack, the librarian sought out a bibliography of
Churchill. The most substantial (1,000 items) listed by Besterman
A world bibliography of bibliographies was Frederick Woods *A
bibliography of the works of Sir Winston Churchill* (1963). This
immediately confirmed Churchill as the author.

[Even more striking testimony is furnished by Michael Hastings'
biography of Brooke, *The handsomest man in England* (1967),
which reproduces in facsimile the first page of Churchill's own
manuscript, written on headed Admiralty stationery, beginning
' Rupert Brooke is dead . . .'.]

(See also cases 102, 110, 116, 117, 133.)

Where such newspapers are indexed, as in the *Index to the Times*
and the *New York Times index,* the obituaries will naturally be
indexed also, but for many years libraries and others have made
special efforts to index obituaries from local newspapers or specialist journals, and some of these indexes have been published, *eg,*
Quaker necrology (1961) from Haverford College (Pennsylvania)
which gives references to death notices of Quakers in the Middle
Atlantic region from 1828, and the *Index of obituaries in Boston
newspapers, 1704-1800* (1967) compiled by Boston Atheneum. Many
years ago the British Record Society brought out *An index to the
biographical and obituary notices in the Gentleman's magazine,*
(1886-91), and in recent years we have seen the remarkable *New
York Times obituaries index* (1969) with 350,000 entries from 1858
to date.

Obituaries are the most striking example of the vast amount of
biographical information hidden in periodicals. But access here is
even more difficult than it is to obituaries, where the date of death
can normally provide a starting point. Of course some periodicals
produce indexes, and the more important are covered by indexing
and abstracting services (see chapter 1), but these are primarily
concerned with the major subject and not with the biographical

data which is usually peripheral. Since 1946 we have one of the H W Wilson indexes devoted to biographical information. Covering some 1,600 of the periodicals indexed by the other Wilson publications as well as separately published biographies, obituary notices from the *New York times, etc,* the quarterly *Biography index* with its annual and three-yearly cumulations has eased the searcher's task.

But *Biography index* lists comparatively few names in total, and of course ignores the pre-1946 literature. For this the research worker has to utilise any bibliographical help he can. Medieval names are very well covered by C U Chevalier *Répertoire des sources historiques du moyen âge: bio-bibliographie* (new edition 1905-7), and some help is afforded by the 90,000 entries in Max Arnim *Internationale Personalbibliographie* (second edition 1944-63). Strictly speaking this latter work is an index to bibliographies of individuals, but as Walford points out ' Because these bibliographies are often appended to biographical material, this work serves as a key of sorts to biographical data '.

Case 131: A reader in a large research library was seeking any information at all about a man called Bodmer, reputed inventor of the conveyor belt, thought to be Swiss in origin. Hyamson, as the single list with the most names, was the obvious source to check, but proved fruitless. So in turn did *Webster's, Chambers',* Riches, Arnim *Internationale Personalbibliographie,* and *Biography index* from its commencement in 1946 to date. The librarian noticed, however, that where the surname Bodmer did appear its holder was invariably Swiss. Finally, a likely candidate was suggested by a very brief entry in *Lippincott's universal pronouncing dictionary of biography* which read in full: ' Bodmer (Georg) a Swiss mechanician, born at Zurich in 1786, invented numerous machines, and an improved method of spinning cotton. Died in 1864.'

This at least was a start, but clearly the enquirer wanted much more. In checking Hyamson, the librarian had noted among the couple of dozen works analysed the great national biographical dictionaries of not only Britain and the United States but also Austria, Belgium, Italy, and the Netherlands. Conspicuous by its absence was a Swiss DNB. Walford confirmed that there was such a compilation: the nine-volumed *Dictionnaire historique et biogra-*

phique de la Suisse (1921-34). Although the enquirer admitted he could not read French, the librarian decided to try this work. After some initial difficulty amid the dozens of Bodmers (arranged not alphabetically by Christian name but firstly by canton and then by family) he eventually ran down Hans Georg, 1786-1864, ' mécanicien et inventeur '. His French was adequate to translate the very brief entry indicating Bodmer's activities in foundries in Germany and railways in Austria, but he could trace no mention of conveyor belts. Neither were there any bibliographical references, but the entry did set the librarian to thinking of *Allgemeine Deutsche Biographie*, the great 56-volume German equivalent to DNB, which was published between 1875-1912. Hospitable to many notabilities not strictly German, it might well include Bodmer. And so it proved, with a 29-line entry for Johann Georg Bodmer, as he was here called. Unfortunately, the enquirer could not read German either, and the *fraktur* type made it difficult for the librarian also. Nevertheless, he managed to gather the important fact that Bodmer had spent some years in England, particularly in Bolton. Even more important, the sole bibliographical reference (in roman type) was to an English source the 'Annual report of the London Institution of Civil Engineers 1868-69 '.

This information transformed the whole enquiry, for there was now a possibility of tracing further references in English primary sources, particularly periodicals and patents. His absence from Hyamson implied his omission from DNB, which Hyamson analyses completely. (In passing, the librarian noted the Hyamson claims to analyse *Allgemeine Deutsche Biographie* also, but obviously only selectively!) But he could well figure in Frederick Boase *Modern English biography*, whose 30,000 entries for persons who died after 1850 include very many names not in other works. And indeed the librarian did find a fifteen-line entry, relating that John George Bodmer ' lived in England 1824-48, established a factory for machine and machine tools at Manchester . . . invented what is now called the travelling crane about 1826; took out 13 patents in England for his inventions '. Reference was made to ' *Min. of Proc. of Instit. of C.E.* xxviii, 573-608 (1869) '. Before turning to the primary sources the librarian decided to check *Neue Deutsche Biographie*, which although still incomplete had certainly reached the letter B. Based on *Allgemeine Deutsche Biographie*, though not replacing it, this also included many Swiss and others who have

192

influenced German history. The entry for Bodmer was briefer than that in the earlier work, but contained many more bibliographical references, two of which were in English. The first, J W Roe *English and American tool builders,* published in New Haven in 1916, the library did not possess, but the second in the Newcomen Society *Transactions* for 1925-6 comprised a 25-page article by D Brownlie ' John George Bodmer: his life and work particularly in relation to the evolution of mechanical stoking '. A most detailed study, this account described two possible applications of the conveyor belt principle introduced by Bodmer, in the opinion of the author ' one of the greatest engineers of all time '. The first, in minor key, was in the canteen of a firearms factory in the Black Forest during the Napoleonic Wars: ' he designed a highly ingenious model railway arrangement whereby all the plates and the dishes were caused to travel mechanically round the tables to and from the kitchens '. The second, major invention grew out of his work in and around the foundries of Bolton, and was described in his 1834 British patent for mechanical stokers as ' a travelling grate . . . constructed by a series of firebars attached to an endless chain passed over conducting rollers '. The article concluded with a list of 18 of his British patents, a bibliography, a reproduction of drawings from his patents, and a full-page engraved portrait with facsimile signature.
    (*See also* case 136.)

As we have noted above, the entries in a who's who are usually strictly functional, presented in outline form, and confined to the bare facts. For evaluation, comment, background, a portrait even, and general ' human interest ', the investigator needs to turn else-where. A minority of the more newsworthy figures will be found in works like *Current biography,* but the best sources by far for this kind of information are the periodicals (and newspapers), as case 7 (page 18) illustrates.

    In perhaps no other category of enquiry is it more profitable to ask the reader for any further information he may have. Cases where he has literally nothing more than a name are rare. And, from the librarian's point of view, as soon as the slightest piece of background information is furnished by the enquirer, a door may open on sources of information other than strictly biographical.

Case 132: When approached during a very busy afternoon by a middle-aged lady reader asking for something about the Earl of Cardigan the readers' adviser made a dash for the shelf carrying the peerages. In *Burke's* he could at first find no entry in the main sequence, or in the list of extinct titles, but in the index he learned that this was one of the subsidiary titles of the Marquess of Ailesbury. He therefore produced for his enquirer the volume open at the entry for Sir Chandos Sydney Cedric Brudenell-Bruce, 7th Marquess of Ailesbury, possessor of seven other titles, including Earl of Cardigan.

She was plainly taken aback to have this 3,400 page tome thrust into her lap, but fortunately the librarian, even in his haste, could see that something was wrong. It was only when he took time out to ask her about her precise needs that he discovered, firstly, that she was looking for 'a book to read' rather than simply information, and secondly, that she was interested not in the current earl but an earlier holder of the title, the man who had led the famous 'Charge of the Light Brigade' in the Crimean War.

Before abandoning *Burke's* altogether, the librarian in the long Ailesbury lineage spotted the most likely contender, James Thomas, 7th Earl of Cardigan, Lieutenant-General in the Army, who had died without issue in 1868, when his titles passed to the 2nd Marquess of Ailesbury. Neither the library catalogue nor the bibliographies (British Museum *General catalogue of printed books* and BNB) could provide a biography, so the librarian checked the DNB entry. Entered under his family name of Brudenell (with a reference from his title), he was found to have had a life filled with incident, including a duel, followed by a trial by his peers in the House of Lords, and when over seventy a fatal fall from his horse. But in the biographical note at the end of the three-column entry, the librarian read 'There is no life published of Lord Cardigan, and for a general sketch of his life reference must be made to the *Times* obituary notice, &c.' Though written of course in 1886, it might well be that this was still true.

Hyamson referred only to the DNB entry, to *Encyclopaedia Britannica,* and his obituary in the *Annual register.* In the hope of a reasonably extended treatment in chapter-form the librarian next consulted Riches *An analytical bibliography of universal collected biography.* Amazingly, the only reference for this remarkable man was to his entry in *Men of the time,* the predecessor of *Who's who.*

194

By now the librarian was convinced he must alter his approach completely by turning to the books on the Crimean War, and, if possible, specifically on the famous charge. Among the general studies of the war listed in John Roach *A bibliography of modern history* (1968) the latest was Cecil Woodham-Smith *The reason why* (1953). As luck would have it a copy was found on the library shelves. Taking its title from the famous poem by Tennyson about the charge (' Theirs not to reason why, Theirs but to do and die: Into the valley of death Rode the six hundred ') this work featured as its frontispiece a portrait of the earl. Prefacing the text was a note beginning: ' This curious story has never been told before—no biography of Lord Lucan, Lord Cardigan or Lord Raglan having, as yet, been written. It has emerged piece by piece from private letters and diaries, from dispatches and War Office correspondence, from law reports from files of newspapers and privately printed pamphlets preserved in country houses.'

It took no more than a few moments' examination of the text to reassure the librarian that he could with confidence recommend the book to his enquirer as the nearest approach available to a life of the Earl of Cardigan.

(*See also* case 133.)

It is amazing to contemplate the number of people who write books. As was noted above, even authors of moderate renown have a much better than average chance of inclusion in the reference books of the day. But even for the rest, as noted in *Case studies in reference work* (pages 132-4), bibliographies are an unexpected but useful key to biographical information. The number of names listed in the British Museum *General catalogue of printed books* or the *National Union catalog: pre-1956 imprints* is greater by far than the most comprehensive biographical dictionary, and while the actual biographical information with each entry will be confined to full names, dates of birth and death, and possibly a brief identifying tag such as 'Actuary ', ' Baptist Minister ', ' Historical Writer ', ' MD Heidelberg ', ' of Liverpool ', ' Poet ' (all different David Joneses from the BM *General catalogue*), at least the appearance of the name you are seeking does reassure you of your man's existence, and may (by examination of the works listed) lead on to further bio-

graphical information, on a dust jacket, or in an introduction, for
instance.

Case 133: When asked 'Have you anything on Francis Kilvert?' the
librarian spotted this at once as a question that could not be tackled
satisfactorily without further information. Even by taking a chance
in assuming that the man was British, the librarian would still be
faced with an initial choice between the mutually exclusive *Who's
who* and DNB. Clearly his first step was to find out if the enquirer
could tell him any more. 'Francis Kilvert? Do you know when he
was active, or what sort of thing he is known for?' was his initial
response to the question. The reader was only too anxious to
help: 'Oh, he was a clergyman, wrote a famous diary, lived about
a hundred years ago'.

DNB was now the obvious source, and together they instantly
found the one-and-a-half-column entry for Francis Kilvert, 1793-
1863, noted antiquary of the city of Bath, where he had been born
and where he seemed to have spent all of his life after he was
ordained priest in 1817. Leaving his enquirer with DNB—the librarian returned to his desk, only to be interrupted almost immediately: 'Are you sure this is the right man? It doesn't mention his
diary'. And no more it did, as the librarian discovered when he
read through the entry and the carefully enumerated list of religious
and antiquarian publications at the end. Pausing only to check
(without success) in *Corrections and additions to the Dictionary of
national biography cumulated from the Bulletin of the Institute of
Historical Research, 1923-1963* (1966), he made straight for the
entries under Kilvert in the British Museum *General catalogue of
printed books* to see if the elusive diary was included there. He
learned that it was not, but he also noticed that in addition to
'Kilvert (Francis) Rev., of Claverton, Bath', there was also listed
a 'Kilvert (Francis) Vicar of Bredwardine', with a 'see' reference to
Kilvert (Robert Francis). When followed up, the five entries for
this second Kilvert showed clearly that the quarry had been run to
earth, for they all related to his diary, first published in three
volumes in 1938-40. Birth and death dates are not appended to the
BM *General catalogue* headings, but one of the entries indicated that
the diary covered the years 1870 to 1879. The obvious source of
biographical information on a late nineteenth century vicar was the

196

annual *Crockford's clerical directory*, which Walford told him had started in 1858, but the librarian soon found that the library's set did not go back anything like far enough.

Casting around the biographical shelves in the hope of some gleam of light he checked without success in Hyamson, Boase, and *Webster's*, before finding in *Chambers'* the first scrap of biographical information on the man together with the one significant fact that explained all the bother he had had. The entry read: ' Kilvert, Francis (1840-79), English clergyman, whose *Diary* (*1870-79*) (discovered 1937 . .) describing his life as curate and vicar, is an important social document of his period '. Clearly, here was a genuine example of posthumous fame. Obscure and unknown until the publication of his *Diary* sixty years after his death, he would obviously not appear in any of the reference books compiled before that date.

[The three-volume edition of the *Diary* by William Plomer (new edition 1969) contains in the introduction to each volume some details about the author, including a long obituary from an unnamed local newspaper. The dust jacket quotes the opinion of the *Times literary supplement* on the work as ' one of the most interesting and entertaining diaries ever written and an addition to English literature '.]

Bibliographies are particularly apt at unveiling the man behind his pseudonym, and there are of course bibliographies specialising in this field, the best known of which in English is the nine-volumed Samuel Halkett and John Laing *Dictionary of anonymous and pseudonymous English literature* (new edition 1926-62). But all these works cover only authors, and not every pseudonym is a penname. In such cases the searcher can turn to specialised sources like Julian Franklyn *A dictionary of nicknames* (1962), G E Shankle *American nicknames* (second edition 1955), or to some of the biographical dictionaries like *White's conspectus of American biography,* which functions as an index to the earlier volumes of the *National cyclopaedia of American biography* and includes a twenty-page index of pseudonyms, nicknames, sobriquets and the like.

Case 134: An assumed name that had at first led the library assistant astray was Lord George Sanger. When asked for 'anything about' him, instead of enquiring further she consulted the various peerages at her disposal (*Burke's, Debrett's,* and even the fourteen-volumed *Complete peerage* (' Cokayne '), which unfortunately still lacks an index). In none of them did ' Sanger ' appear, either as a current title, an extinct title, or a family name. Already nonplussed, she asked the enquirer still waiting at the desk, 'Are you sure it's a British title?', only to learn that it was not a proper title at all : ' It's one he gave himself '.

It was not until she consulted *Webster's* and *Chambers'* that all became clear : George Sanger (1825-1911) and his brother John were English circus proprietors, both calling themselves ' Lord '. *Chambers'* added its usual bibliographical reference ' See George Sanger's *Seventy years a showman*'. The library catalogue had no copy listed, so the assistant turned again to the biographical reference works. Hyamson directed her to the second supplement to DNB, where was conveniently summarised Sanger's very long and active life, culminating when he was shot dead by one of his own employees, who afterwards committed suicide. As for his title, it seemed that he was in later life hampered by the rivalry of American travelling circus proprietors, and so ' In 1887 he took the title of " Lord " George Sanger by way of challenge to " the Hon " William Cody (" Buffalo Bill "), who was touring England with his " Wild West " show '.

The value of the biographical information in the great general encyclopedias was also illustrated in *Case studies in reference work* (pages 61-65); outstanding in this regard is the eleventh edition of *Encyclopaedia Britannica* (1911), which is indeed analysed in Hyamson *Dictionary of universal biography*. Their particular usefulness lies not only in the overtly biographical entries they contain, which in some works may amount to a quarter of the total, but in the information about people that can be extracted *via* the subject index from the non-biographical articles. The encyclopedia yearbooks, too, should not be forgotten as convenient sources of information on those newcomers to renown discussed earlier (page 176).

Case 135: In a small university library the assistant was approached by a student asking for a short account of the Dreyfus case, mention of which he kept encountering in his reading. The assistant recalled that the case involved a French army officer in the 1890's wrongly convicted and imprisoned on Devil's Island for passing secrets to the Germans.

'Have you looked in the catalogue?' was the first question he asked, but the student shook his head, 'No, I don't want a book. Just a short summary'. The librarian's suggestion that he should try the *Encyclopaedia Britannica* was not received with enthusiasm. Nevertheless, the librarian led his reader to the appropriate volume where he discovered a very clear and interesting account, extending over two columns and concluding with a three-item bibliography. The librarian pointed out that the author of the article (represented of course only by his initials) was in fact David Thomson, Master of Sidney Sussex College, Cambridge, and one of the most distinguished of modern historians. He could see that the student was impressed, so he left him with the words 'Let me know if this isn't satisfactory'.

Many figures of interest have a fame (or a notoriety) that is purely local, and where the usual biographical reference sources have proved useless, any clues as to location is worth pursuing (see *Case studies in reference work*, page 41).

Case 136: The assistant in a large research library was approached by a reader seeking information on John Ayliffe, executed for forgery in the 18th century. Neither *Chambers'* nor *Webster's* seemed to know him, but Hyamson directed the assistant to the DNB entry for John Ayliffe (1676-1732), a jurist, born in Hampshire, whose 'chief titles to fame are his two treatises on the canon law and the civil law, into which he threw the whole learning of his life' As the mode of his death was not even hinted at, the assistant felt confident in distinguishing this obvious pillar of the English legal establishment from his contemporary and namesake, the forger.

In pointing this out to his enquirer, the assistant was interested to hear the response. 'No, this isn't the man at all. I think the one I want came from Wiltshire'. Without more ado, he went over to the nine volumes of the still incomplete Victoria County History of Wiltshire. Checking through the indexes (one to each volume) he came upon two John Ayliffes: the first ' fl. 1562 ', and so could be dismissed; the second ' d. 1759 ', and was obviously worth pursuing. Following up the reference he read in volume nine that this later John Ayliffe had been born at Tockenham, 1718-19, and educated at Harrow, returning to become a local schoolmaster. ' Subsequently, in his attempts to secure the Grittenham estate, Ayliffe was guilty of many frauds, and was executed for forgery in 1759.' A footnote referred to volume 21 of the *Wiltshire archaeological and natural history magazine,* pages 199-204.

Upon examination this particular volume was found to be for the year 1888, with a 17-page paper on ' The Ayliffes of Grittenham ' by the Rev Canon J E Jackson. Including an actual mounted photograph, much faded, of a portrait painting of John Ayliffe in fancy dress, the paper told a fascinating tale of this extravagant young adventurer, constrained by schoolmastering, whose ideas ' expanded much too magnificently for his means ' and who ended his life in Newgate.

[The *General index to the Gentleman's Magazine, 1731-1786* directs the searcher to ' Some account of John Ayliffe, Esq, lately executed for forgery ' in the issue for December 1759.]

But quite apart from these usual local non-biographical sources, many workers have been both surprised and pleased to learn of the existence of purely local biographical reference sources such as *Dorset who's who* (1911), *Suffolk celebrities* (1893), *Norfolk notabilities* (1893), *Lancashire leaders* (1895-7). In Britain works of this kind are an obscure and dwindling group: much better known are the regional who's whos in the United States, *eg, Who's who in the midwest.*

It is worth remarking, in parenthesis, that the reverse is sometimes true: the compilers of *Who's who in the world* remind us that some of the distinguished figures they treat ' may be scarcely known in the local community but may be widely recognised in some special field of endeavour '.

As with many other enquiries (see pages 117, 196, and *Case studies in reference work,* page 40), a hint as to even an approximate date when your man flourished can often lead towards the information you require. The date of death is particularly crucial here, suggesting as we have seen the point at which to start looking for obituary notices.

In trying non-biographical sources in search of information about people, the librarian often benefits from one feature that many of them share—a name index. No doubt because this interest in people is so universal, when the thoughts of editors or compilers turn to providing keys to their works, an index of names is one of the first that springs to mind. This is true also of the huge quantities of biographical material that remain in the form of unpublished manuscripts: wherever calendars are made of such collections still in private hands or deposited in libraries almost invariably is a name index produced as well. An outstanding example is the three-volume ' Index of persons ' issued as part of the *Guide to the reports of the Royal Commission on Historical Manuscripts, 1911-1957* (1966), and its predecessor covering 1870-1911. An attempt is currently being made to compile a location register of biographical manuscripts.

It is perhaps an inevitable consequence of the pervasive nature of biography that virtually any resource within the library may be called upon in the course of a query about a person. Patent specifications, for example, are technical documents of a very specialised kind, yet they are always provided with name indexes, and for many thousands of obscure inventors they may represent the only occasion when their names appeared in print. Apart from the oblique light that the specification itself may throw on the life and work of the inventor, the legal preamble often contains his full name and address. In many cases this has furnished a point of departure for a successful search for further biographical details in, for instance, specifically local sources.

Case 137: With one particular enquiry about an inventor or an originator it was not feasible to turn to the name indexes or to the patents. For one thing, the name of the inventor was not known to the reader; and for another, it seemed likely that this unknown pioneer had made his contribution to progress in the days before the patent system had got under way. The specific enquiry was: ' Is it true that the length of a yard measure was determined by the length of some king's arm?'

For a moment the librarian found himself absolutely bereft of ideas. More as a gesture of hope than of faith he reached for *Whitaker's almanack,* where he read that the yard measures 0·9144 metre, based on the ' " United Kingdom primary standard " in the custody of the Standards Department of the Board of Trade '. But there was no mention of any king's arm.

By now the librarian's faculties appeared to be functioning normally and on the shelves devoted to books on inventions he spotted E F Carter *Dictionary of inventions and discoveries* (1966). Under ' yard ' he read as follows: ' 1305. Standardized by King Henry I of England as, the length of his arm ' [sic]. Apart from the unusual punctuation, there was obviously something wrong here, for the king in 1305 was Edward I not Henry I. Alternatively, if the king was right the date was incorrect, for Henry reigned two hundred years earlier. Unfortunately no references were given, but now the librarian had a name (or possibly two names) he was able to consult the standard biographical sources. DNB soon confirmed that Carter had got the name right (' he is said to have made the length of his own arm the standard of measure throughout the kingdom '), and provided a reference (*Gesta regum,* v, 411).

The other side of the coin, however, is the one that shines particularly brightly for the librarian, for the pervasive nature of biography means that an enquiry on any subject can turn into a biographical problem if there is a person connected with it (see *Case studies in reference work,* page 39). Indeed, where a biographical approach does lie open, the investigator should bless his good fortune: in *The modern researcher* by Jacques Barzun and H F Graff (revised edition 1970), one of the most highly regarded works of its kind, we are told that ' The researcher who can make biography the starting point of his labors has a head start '.

Case 138: A newspaper rang the local public library one day asking the librarian to recommend some good books on seals. After a couple of minutes at the card catalogue and another moment at the shelves, while the enquirer waited, the librarian felt confident in suggesting R M Lockley *Grey seal, common seal: an account of the life histories of British seals* (1966) and Louis Darling *Seals and* *walruses* (1961). Then followed a slight pause on the line. ' No, those are not the kind of seals I want ', was the terse reply. The librarian realised immediately he had fallen into an elementary error: this was obviously an engineering query and he should have suggested something like Erhard Mayer *Mechanical seals* (1969) or W L Morse *Seals handbook* (1969). Had he done so he would still have been way off target, for as the caller went on to explain, the seals he was interested in were those used on documents as a means of authentication. 'As a matter of fact,' he continued, ' I am trying to confirm the story that the Great Seal of England was once thrown into the Thames.' The library card catalogue straightaway drew the librarian's attention to A B Wyon *The Great Seals of England,* which turned out to be a magnificent folio volume, plentifully illustrated, published in 1887. Nothing could be traced in the index about the loss of a seal, and the entries under ' Thames ' all referred to instances of views of the river appearing in the design of seals. And yet the alternative prospect of a page-by-page check through the text was not appealing.

It struck the librarian that this was just the sort of query to have figured in the pages of *Notes and queries,* so he instituted a search through the dozen or so *General indexes.* Though he found entries under ' Great Seal ' and ' Seal, Great ', none of them when followed up led to anything pertinent.

One of his colleagues was a historian and an archivist, so it seemed natural to consult him with this particular problem. He was not able to suggest a specific source but he did recall the story; according to his recollection it was the king himself who had thus relieved himself of his seal, whilst fleeing from London. He was sure it was not one of the medieval monarchs, which limited the field somewhat. What Kings of England had been forced to flee their capital? They could only think of two possible candidates—Charles I and James II—and of these only the latter got away. And indeed, the DNB entry for James did briefly refer to the supposed incident, without going into detail.

Back with the indexes to *Notes and queries,* this time the librarian looked under ' James II '. He had only to go back as far as 1944 to find an entry for James II and the Great Seal. This led to a note in the issue for 29th January referring in its turn to an article in the *Antiquarian journal* for January-April 1943, where ' Hilary Jenkinson enquires into the supposed disappearance of the Great

Seal of James II, and demonstrates with the aid of plates that it was merely altered for the use of William and Mary'.

This seemed to put paid to the tale of its loss, but when the librarian turned up the original thirteen-page article, 'What happened to the Great Seal of James II', he soon perceived that Jenkinson did not in fact rule out a dip in the Thames: 'The story most generally accepted has been that the king threw it into the Thames during the first stage of his flight on 11 December [1688] . . . Whatever may have been its adventures *en route,* the Great Seal of James II apparently did find its way to his successors.'

An earlier correspondent in *Notes and queries* for 5th October 1861, referring to Hume *History of England* as his authority for the story, asked 'Has the Great Seal ever been fished up again?' The editor replied by quoting Lord Macaulay *History of England*: 'after many months it was accidentally caught by a fishing net and was dragged up'. Two weeks later another correspondent gave a more precise reference from *Luttrell's Diary,* which states that in May 1689 the Great Seal was taken out of the Thames by some waterman near Lambeth.

[This story does in fact appear in Wyon, but can only be traced *via* the index under the entry 'James II, Great Seal of: dropped by him into the Thames'.]

Particularly where the head-on approach has produced no result should the librarian seek a biographical angle if he can, especially as the field of biography is so well signposted. In the words of an American professor of library science 'biographical sources are an oblique key to almost every area of human knowledge'.

An interesting feature of a number of biographical dictionaries is a subject index. This may take one of two forms: commonly an index of the biographees arranged under professions or occupations, *eg, Biography index, Current biography,* P M Riches *An analytical bibliography of universal collected biography,* or, less frequently, an index of topics dealt with in the articles on the biographies, *eg, Appleton's cyclopaedia of American biography, Concise dictionary of national biography, Chambers' biographical dictionary.* Each of the six volumes of Frederick Boase *Modern English biography* sports an index which 'contains references to the most important, curious and interesting facts, to be found in the pages of this work'.

One particularly well-furnished example is the *Dictionary of American biography* which has both forms of subject index, together with indexes by birth place of biographees, and by school and college attended. Occasionally an instance will be encountered of a biographical reference work where the main sequence is in some kind of subject order, *eg, India who's who* where the entries are arranged under profession, with nine broad headings subdivided in 125 specific professions. Probably the most ambitious example is the American *Who knows—and what* (revised edition 1954) which lists twelve selected ' knowers ' to each of 35,000 subjects.

Case 139: A group of children had spent several minutes examining books on the shelves of the reference room of a small public library before they approached the librarian's desk in a body. Each of them had been given the task of choosing one Arctic explorer to write about for their teacher, but the snag was they all wanted to write about Scott, the only one whose name they knew. The librarian had learned to be wary of doing children's school tasks for them, but felt there could be no harm in locating the names of half-a-dozen Arctic explorers for them. Right away she turned to the subject index at the end of *Chambers' biographical dictionary,* where in the ' Exploration and geography ' section she immediately found under 'Arctic ' 26 names. Surprisingly, Scott's name did *not* appear —but then she found it under 'Antarctic '. Checking the entry in the body of the work, she surmised from the absence of any mention of it that Scott of the Antarctic (*ie,* South Pole) had never explored the Arctic (North Pole) at all.

Showing the children how to look up the individual entries for Byrd, Nansen, Peary and the rest, she left them excitedly whispering.

[An identically similar approach *via* the ' Select subject index ' to the *Concise DNB, 1901-1950* would have produced 20 names, but all British, deceased during the 50-year period.]

The value of such subject access to the stores of *general* information in the biographical reference tools is easy to see. Just as with subject enquiries the biographical approach may provide the key to the problem (pages 202-4 above), cases do occur with queries about people where an attack *via* the subject can be the most profitable.

Case 140: 'Can you find me something on lightning calculators?' was a query posed in a busy public scientific and technical library. The librarian thought he knew what the enquirer meant, but took the precaution of exchanging a few words to confirm this before beginning the search. The subject of his interest of course was those few gifted individuals who can perform complicated mathematical calculations in their heads with incredible speed.

In this instance, the librarian's first problem was the choice of heading under which to look in the library catalogue and in the bibliographies. After more than a little thought, the best he could come up with was ' calculations/-ors/-ing ', *etc,* and ' mathematics/ -ians ', *etc.* Of course he found lots of items under these headings in his catalogue and in BNB, CBI, the BM *Subject index,* and the LC *Catalog of books: subjects,* but no more specific heading, and only one book remotely near the subject. This was Karl Meninger *Calculator's cunning: the art of quick reckoning* (tenth edition 1964), a 130-page work translated from the German. Disappointingly it turned out to be a mere textbook of arithmetic tricks, with no mention at all of famous practitioners of the skill.

A quick ten-year search through the general periodical indexes (*Readers' guide, International index/Social sciences and humanities index,* Library Association *Subject index/British humanities index*) was no more fruitful. And then a colleague suggested that he consult the staff information index. Immediately an entry was found under the heading ' mathematical prodigies ' referring to a four-page article of the same title in *Chambers's journal* for December 1948. Apparently missed by the LA *Subject index,* it was subtitled ' Some human calculating machines ', and was obviously bang on target. A note at the bottom of the index card directed the enquirer to see also a work indicated merely by its call number and a page reference. This turned out to be the very well-known work by W W Rouse Ball *Mathematical recreations and essays* (eleventh edition 1939), where the librarian found the whole 29 pages of chapter 13 devoted to ' Calculating prodigies ', such as Zerah Colburn, a seven-year-old Vermont boy, who could multiply large numbers together so quickly that the spectators taking down the answers had to ask him to repeat them more slowly. Among those whose feats were similarly recounted were Johann Dase of Hamburg who was able after a single glance to state the number of volumes in a bookcase, and George Bidder of Devonshire, who at a performance in 1816 immediately gave in its correct form a 43-digit number that had been read to him backwards, and then, *an hour later,* when asked if he still remembered it, repeated it absolutely correctly.

Account was given of a dozen or more of these prodigies, and reference was made to two basic articles in the *American journal of psychology* for 1891 and 1907: the first by E W Scripture on 'Arithmetical prodigies' was 59 pages in length, the second, by F W Mitchell, entitled 'Mathematical prodigies' was even longer, with 83 pages. Both of these contained further bibliographical notes on original authorities.

Once thus supplied with names, of course, the librarian could then turn to the overtly biographical sources, each of the three prodigies mentioned above, for instance, having entries in their respective national biographies: *Dictionary of American biography, Allgemeine Deutsche Biographie,* and DNB).

This possibility of approach by subject can be most effective with enquiries of the 'who was it that . . .?' type which the alphabetical arrangement by name common to the majority of biographical reference tools effectively unfits them to answer. *Webster's biographical dictionary* will tell you, for instance, who the first man was to win two full Nobel prizes, but only if you look in the entry for Linus Pauling, the American chemist. DNB informs us of the first Jew to become a fellow of an Oxford or Cambridge college, provided we look for the information under 'Alexander, Samuel', the renowned philosopher. Such biographical queries in reverse can leave the librarian feeling almost as helpless as he is when faced with the similar conundrum of finding the word to match a given definition (see *Case studies in reference work,* pages 140-2). Merely to tell the enquirer that all the reference books are arranged the other way round is to be of no more assistance than the Irishman who advised the traveller seeking direction 'If I were you, I wouldn't start from here'.

Case 141: When asked by a young reader for something about the first woman Member of Parliament, the librarian knew that she would certainly have an entry in *Who's who* (and in due course *Who was who*), and even in DNB. But first he had to find her name. An obvious source suggested itself at once: Norman Wilding and Philip Laundy *An encyclopaedia of Parliament* (third edition 1968). In the entry 'Women in Parliament' he read: 'The election of women to the British Parliament, was made possible by the passing of the Parliament (Qualification of Women) Act in 1918, and the first woman to be elected was the Countess Markiewicz (1868-1927) for a Dublin constituency in the same year. An Irishwoman who married a Pole, she was an uncompromising Republican, and like the other Sinn Feiners elected at the same time, she did not take her seat in the House of Commons. The first woman to do so was Viscountess Astor, who sat for the Sutton Division of Plymouth from 1919 to 1945.'

This information put the librarian in a bit of a quandary as to who was indeed 'the first woman MP' that his young enquirer was interested in. Eventually he plumped for Lady Astor, who he was surprised to learn (from *Chambers'*) was an American. *Chambers'* gave the date of her death as 1964 (*ie,* too recent for a DNB entry) and referred to a 'Life by Collis (1960)'. The library's own catalogue revealed this as Maurice Collis *Nancy Astor: an informal biography,* which he was lucky enough to find available on the shelves for his enquirer to borrow.

One fact about biographical enquiries there is no avoiding: their high rate of failure. The reason is not far to seek. In theory, the librarian may be asked for information about anyone who has ever lived, yet he knows, for instance, that even in Britain, with its unrivalled public and private records, those who are treated in the basic volumes of DNB amount to no more than one in every 5,000 of those who reached adult life throughout the period covered, and that *Who's who in America* lists only one in every 3,300 of its potential 200 millions and more. The truth is that the vast majority of us will never attain the biographical reference tools.

But, as we also know, nearly every person is listed somewhere, and in published sources. Here the approach by place as suggested above (pages 199-200) will often produce results: voting lists, 'phone books, town directories, are examples of general listings, covering in total the bulk of the adult population, but which are essentially local in character. Librarians have noted in recent years an increase in the number of such enquiries about ordinary people, for one of the prices we are paying for our increasingly complicated society is the regrettable need for personal checks on such matters as credit-worthiness or loyalty.

The librarian will often surprise himself with what he can piece together about the life of a seemingly obscure individual by using scattered facts derived from a variety of such sources. His problem then is when to stop, for reference searches of this kind tend to turn into research investigations (see pages 158-60 above).

In enquiries where the subject is the reverse of obscure the libra-rarian has his problems too, for there is much duplication of coverage in the biographical reference sources. The wealth of detail, much of it repetitive, can be an embarrassment, and inexperienced readers can be spoiled for choice.

Case 142: When asked about Axel Munthe, the Swedish writer, the librarian immediately found a 217-page biography in the catalogue: G L Munthe *The story of Axel Munthe* (1953). But this was too much for his enquirer, a young student. 'No, I want only a summary', was her reaction. Entries for him were found in both *Webster's biographical dictionary* and *Chambers' biographical dictionary,* but these (three lines and eight lines) were too brief. The 19-line entry in *Encyclopedia Americana* was a little better, but still not precisely what was wanted. A DNB entry would have been just perfect, but as a Swedish writer he was of course ineligible, although he did figure in *Who was who* for the decade of his death in 1949. But again this entry, though useful, gave the same basic facts as the others, and little else. Comment there was in plenty around the time of his death, much of it indexed in *Biography index,* but it was not until *Twentieth century authors* (1942) was consulted that the librarian arrived at the right mixture to suit his reader: one and a half columns (including a small portrait), with a lot of references. The *First supplement* (1955) added 'Axel Munthe died at ninety-one, in the Royal Palace at Stockholm, where for ten years he had been the house guest of King Gustav V. San Michele, his home in Capri, which gave its title to his best known book, was converted into a museum, with the proceedings going to charity.'

Biographical enquiries are particularly prone to failure for what may be described as mechanical reasons. The great majority of the search tools are arranged alphabetically by the subjects' surnames, but as every cataloguer knows, what is and what is not the correct surname in a certain instance can be a difficult matter to decide. Robert W Murphey has pointed out that reference-book makers are still arguing over such fine points as whether Leonardo da Vinci should be listed under 'Leonardo' (as in *Chambers'*), or 'Vinci' (as in *Webster's*), or even 'da Vinci'.

Apart from such obvious problems as change of name on marriage or elevation to the peerage, there are variations in form from one country to another, as well as divergences arising from alternative systems of transliteration from, for instance, the cyrillic alphabet, and the lack of any standardised spelling especially before the 18th century. A good biographical dictionary (like a good library catalogue) will endeavour to provide for every possible approach with its apparatus of 'see' and 'see also' references, but the searcher must be prepared to meet the compiler half-way. But even the most far-sighted cataloguers cannot provide for the enquirer who has simply got the name wrong. The alphabetical arrangement adopted by the biographical reference tools is one of their great strengths, offering virtually instant one-place reference, but the penalty to be paid if you have not got the name right can be total failure.

Case 143: An enquiry over the 'phone for background details on H MacDonald Seward, described as an important man in the Conservative Party, sounded like a prospective chairman preparing a few words of introduction about his speaker (*see also* case 107). *Who's who* was immediately to hand, but he could not be found among the Sewards listed there (or among the MacDonalds). The enquirer's reaction was 'But you must have something about him. He was a Member of Parliament a few years ago'. Aware that not all ex-MP's could expect to retain their *Who's who* entry indefinitely, the librarian enquired 'Do you know anything else about him?' 'Well, I think he is a Liverpool alderman', was the reply. The *Municipal year book* was also close by the 'phone, so the librarian was able to check immediately under Liverpool in the county boroughs section. While no Seward appeared, there was listed an Alderman H M Steward. Back with *Who's who* his fifteen-line entry soon confirmed that here was the man the caller really wanted. (*See also* case 112.)

An interesting slant is given to biographical queries when the enquirer wishes to see a portrait of his subject. Leaving aside the commercial and other services outside the library that make a business of providing pictures of people, the librarian will find portraits in some of the sources already discussed. For some 45,000 figures of the past he has available a monumental guide in the *ALA portrait index: index to portraits contained in books and periodicals* (1906), but for twentieth century people he will usually have to hunt. It helps to recall which biographical reference works include portraits with their entries (*eg, Current biography, National cyclopaedia of American biography*) or at least those which make a special point of noting the location of portraits in the bibliographical references given (*eg, Biography index*, Boase *Modern English biography*, Ireland *Index to scientists*, DNB).

Case 144: A clear and precise request for a portrait of William Paterson came from a most helpful reader who explained that the subject of his attention had been a seventeenth century Scottish businessman closely involved with the abortive Darien Scheme to settle the Isthmus of Panama. *Chambers' biographical dictionary* (which looks with special favour on famous Scots) helped the librarian fill in some of the background—and confirm the spelling—and listed two lives (by S Bannister, published in 1858 and by J S Barbour in 1907) as well as an edition of his works (1859). He was, it seemed, even more renowned as founder of the Bank of England in 1694.

Hyamson indicated a DNB entry which the librarian decided to check before examining the biographies and collected works. He looked immediately for the note at the end of the six-column entry where he read: 'The only known portrait of Paterson is the pen-and-ink wash-drawing in the British Museum [MS] executed in 1708'. The question then was, 'Has this portrait ever been reproduced?'.

Paterson's name was found in the *ALA portrait index*, with two references. The first was to James L Caw *Scottish portraits*, a two-volumed compilation published in Edinburgh in 1903. Tantalisingly, no copy could be traced in the library so it was not possible to discover whether the portrait there indexed was one unknown to the DNB contributor. The second reference read: 'drawing* (Brit.

Mus.) ILN (1894), 105: 115'. The asterisk indicated that it was some form of photographic reproduction, and the abbreviated bibliographical citation was of course to the *Illustrated London news*. When pursued, this was found to be a line block of a fairly amateurish drawing used to illustrate an article celebrating the bicentenary of the Bank of England. No source was given for the original, but it was clear that this was in fact a reproduction of the BM drawing described by DNB.

Case 145: A portrait request with a nice twist was the 'phone call to a large city library from the local TV station wanting a photo of Karsh of Ottawa, perhaps the most famous portrait photographer in the world. Without hesitation the librarian made straight for the latest *Biography index* and began to work his way back. The first entry (under 'Karsh, Yousuf... Armenian-Canadian photographer') he found was in the 1961-64 cumulation; it referred to an autobiography *In search of greatness* (1962), which unfortunately the library did not possess. Continuing his search, he soon ran across further references, but the most useful was to the December 1952 issue of *Current biography* (and of course the 1952 yearbook). As is its practice, *Biography index* clearly indicated that the articles were accompanied by a portrait.

[By chance shortly afterwards the librarian encountered an excellent portrait photograph of Karsh in a totally unexpected source, the *Lincoln library of essential information*.]

Raising similar problems are the requests for a person's signature, usually needed for purposes of comparison in the course of authenticating a document or a painting. Fortunate are readers in those libraries with large collections of autograph letters, indexed by name. Only slightly less favoured are those with access to collections of autographs alone. Probably most enquirers have to be content with facsimile signatures, such as those in Ray Rawlins *Four hundred years of British autographs* (1970), or in the appendix of over six hundred monograms and signatures in *Who's who in art*.

Case 146: Help was required in a busy reference library one day by a reader with a manuscript letter on notepaper with the printed

212

heading ' 10, Downing Street, Whitehall '. It was undated, but what made it interesting was the signature, which appeared to be that of W E Gladstone. The reader wanted to know two things: Was it genuine? How much was it worth?

First of all the librarian felt obliged to explain that it would not be possible for him to pronounce with absolute certainty on either of these questions, for the authentication of an ALS (autograph letter signed) is a highly specialised task, beyond the competence of most librarians; and the value of such an item in hard cash depends on so many factors that even in the trade it is not always possible to give a quick answer. Nevertheless, he offered to help in any way he could.

Several possible sources came to mind, but he decided to try the recent guide for autograph collectors by Ray Rawlins *Four hundred years of British autographs* (1970). As expected this did produce a good clear facsimile of Gladstone's signature, which the librarian encouraged the enquirer to compare with his version. It also contained the information that ' Wellington, Gladstone, and Palmerston were all prolific writers who lived into their eighties and are thus very common autographically . . . letters of . . . Gladstone . . . were once very valuable but are now worth only a few pounds '.

The trouble with collections of this kind is that inevitably they are confined to the famous. Usefully supplementing them are the handful of biographical dictionaries that feature facsimile signatures with their entries, *eg, National cyclopaedia of American biography*.

It was Disraeli who advised ' Read no history: nothing but biography. For that is life without theory '. That biography does reflect the many-hued pattern of human life is clear, and this is why, as Louis Shores writes, ' there is perhaps no phase of reference work that will challenge the ingenuity of a reference worker more than biographical enquiries '.

4

books about places

MAPS (AND ATLASES, which are no more than volumes of maps, and charts, which are maps of water) are of course the sources *par excellence* of information about places. They are, moreover, non-textual sources, conveying their message not by the written word but by pictorial means. Indeed, much of their information content could not be communicated in any practical manner by textual methods. To that very large category of queries about places asking 'Where is it?' they provide the solutions in the simplest way possible—by demonstrating the required location on a stylised facsimile of the surface of our globe.

Case 147: The enquirer from the local newspaper office asking for a map of Berlin had one special proviso: it must show the location of the notorious wall between east and west. The library was only a modest-sized town library, without a special collection of city maps, but the librarian was fairly certain he could find at least a small map of Berlin in one of the atlases. But would it show the wall? A glance at the *Statesman's year-book* gave him his *terminus a quo*: 'The East German Government tried to stop the outflow [of migrants] by erecting a brick wall along the border in Berlin on 13 Aug. 1961'. Clearly the plan of Berlin that he was sure he could find in the five-volumed *Times atlas of the world* would be useless, for the relevant third volume, Northern Europe, had been published in 1955. It so happened that his library had also purchased the one-volume ' com-

214

prehensive' edition of 1967. The useful key to the map plates printed on the endpapers indicated at once that there was a city map of Berlin inset on plate 63. Upon examination this turned out to be the usual double-page spread covering Germany north-west, with the Berlin plan in the top left-hand corner. Though small, it was adequate, for it did indeed have the Berlin wall clearly marked.

Unfortunately for the purposes of this book, however, this particular virtue of maps and atlases makes it both difficult and unsatisfactory to illustrate their use by purely textual and narrative case histories. Indeed one recent textbook for librarians regards them as 'outside of the mainstream of reference works'. Whilst not conceding this, the studies which follow, however, can only demonstrate certain limited aspects of the use of such works, so invaluable to the reference librarian and his readers.

Case 148: When a colleague passed on to her during a busy lunch hour a phone message asking for the local authority for Great Cheverell the assistant in a commercial library in the north of England knew she had first to find out where the place was. Making the assumption that it was somewhere in England, she went over to the atlases, but she could find no entry in the gazetteer to the great *Atlas of Britain* or in the 'Short general index to the towns and villages' at the end of the Bartholomew *Survey atlas of England and Wales*, which in spite of its age (second edition 1939) is still the most useful reference atlas for England and Wales. She had taken the precaution of checking under 'Cheverell' as well as under 'Great', and therefore felt she could go no further at this stage with the atlases.

Turning to the gazetteers, she first of all checked the one she had been told was not only the most recent (1965), but also had the most entries (345,000): the *Times index-gazetteer of the world*. Here, under 'Cheverell, Great' she found an entry locating the place in Wiltshire. There was no plate or map reference, thus indicating that the place was not marked on any of the maps of the *Times atlas of the world,* but the entry did give geographical co-ordinates of latitude and longitude (51.17N 2.01W), enabling it to be located on any suitable map showing Wiltshire. But apart from details such as these the *Times index-gazetteer* is not very informative, and so the assistant examined some of the other volumes on the shelves. She drew a blank with *Webster's geographical dictionary, Chambers's world gazetteer,* and the *Columbia Lippincott gazetteer of the world,* which seemed to suggest that it must be a very small place, but in Bartholomew *Gazetteer of the British Isles,* under 'Cheverell, Great' she read ' par. and vil., N Wilts, 5m. SW of Devizes; 1846 ac., pop. 281; P.O.' She now was in a position to return to the Bartholomew *Survey atlas,* where she soon located the village on one of the excellent half-inch to the mile maps that comprise the volume. As she discovered, however, these maps do not indicate local authorities or their boundaries, the only map in the volume to do so being a single plate for the whole of England and Wales, obviously at a much smaller scale, showing the administrative counties only. The *Atlas of Britain* at first sight seemed much more likely, with two full page maps showing the 1958 administrative boundaries at a scale of 1 : 2,000,000, but even with a reading glass it proved too difficult to match up the estimated location of Great Cheverell with the very fine detail on the maps.

At this stage, seeing her peering at the huge volume on the map table, the colleague who had given her the query came over and exclaimed 'Why don't you try the Ordnance Survey county administrative areas maps?' When she admitted she did not know what these were he produced the sheet for Wiltshire, explaining that all the counties in England and Wales were covered by a separate map (at either the half-inch or 1 : 100,000 scale) ' showing the administrative county, municipal boroughs, urban and rural districts, and civil parishes '. The Wiltshire sheet, revised to 1st July 1966, clearly showed on a half-inch base map the village of Great Cheverell, situated within the boundaries (overprinted in red) of the civil parish of Cheverell Magna, itself part of the Devizes rural district, one of the areas making up the administrative county of Wiltshire.

[It is worthy of note, however, that this particular enquiry could have been just as well answered from textual sources. The General Register Office *Census 1961 England and Wales: index of place names* (1965) lists Cheverell Magna (the 1951 edition called it Cheverell, Great) as a civil parish, population 319, indicating in the column headed 'Administrative county in which situated ' that it is in Wiltshire, and in the column headed ' Borough, urban district or rural district in which situated ', that it is in Devizes rural district.]

The atlas is one of the oldest types of reference work we have, said to derive its name from the illustration of Atlas, the famous figure from Greek mythology, bearing the weight of the heavens on his shoulders, placed as a frontispiece to early works of this kind. Something approaching 10,000 are listed in the Library of Congress *List of geographical atlases* (1909-), and yet, irreplaceable as they are for indicating locations, showing contours and boundaries, *etc,* the great atlases are less useful in solving some of the other enquiries that people have about places, as the previous case suggests. It is amazing what information on a host of subjects that a map can be used to convey in the hands of a skilful cartographer, as the *Atlas of Britain* demonstrates, but there still remains much data on places better communicated by conventional textual means. This is why many popular atlases can be found with text pages of encyclopedia-type information.

Case 149: A pair of teenagers called at the local public reference library on the way home from school one day to ask which were the main areas of Britain suffering from depopulation. Further discussion revealed that they had been assigned the topic of depopulation as a ' project' and each intended to choose a different area to concentrate on. Clearly, the raw data on the topic would be available in the long series of decennial census reports; there would be articles and probably books on the subject to be traced in the indexes and bibliographies and in the library catalogue.

The thought struck the librarian that the *Atlas of Britain* might help: 'planned as a cross-section through the middle of the twentieth century' it would obviously have population maps. Since the introduction claimed that 'to a large extent each map in this atlas has been an experiment', perhaps it would have depopulation maps also! And so it proved. Following the page showing the 1951 population came a beautifully drawn and printed map of Britain in very many colours, 'Persistent population change', covering the years 1931 to 1961. Using the figures extracted from the decennial censuses (and the Registrar General's estimates for the war years when there was no census), the maps showed with great skill by means of colours whether the total population of each local authority had increased or decreased in each of the three decades of the years 1931 to 1961. In particular, the names of places showing a persistent de-

217

crease, *ie,* a drop in numbers in each of the three decades, were printed in blue. The two young investigators were thus able to pick out by the concentration of blue names those areas of depopulation deserving of further study.

Particularly useful, however, for the many quick-reference queries about places that are posed in libraries are the gazetteers, which are dictionaries (or more accurately encyclopedias) of places. It is relevant to recall the origin of the term: the earliest works with such titles were designed as companions for 17th century newspapermen (or 'gazetteers') needing to check geographical facts in a hurry. The true role of the gazetteer is complementary to the atlas, furnishing information that a map cannot provide, or cannot provide so conveniently or speedily.

Case 150: When asked over the phone what Yasnaya Polyana was famous for the assistant in a technical college library suspected that she was being used to help complete a crossword, but as she had no idea whether it was animal, vegetable, or mineral, she decided it might be useful for her to probe a little deeper. 'What is it? it sounds like a drink', she replied. Her caller said he thought it was a place.

Checking the *Times atlas* she discovered from the index that it was indeed two places, both quite separate, but both in Russia. The *Chambers's world gazetteer* provided the solution: 'Vill. 7m. from Tula, birthplace and home of Tolstoy. His house (a museum) was sacked by the Germans in the 2nd World War, but re-opened in 1946'.

In her classic text *Introduction to reference work* Margaret Hutchins reminds us that 'In many ways the problems and techniques of finding information about places resemble those concerned with persons. There are the problems of identification: the same name applied to more than one place and the several names or forms of names for the same place . . . the problems of obscurity, the disputed facts and the unknown details about famous places'. On the other hand, the number of places in the world is obviously very much smaller than the number of people, and each, by definition, does at least have a local habitation and a name. It might seem, therefore, to the newcomer to reference work, that the many enquiries about the location of particular places should be fairly easy to satisfy. Experience soon teaches him otherwise.

Case 151: It did not take the reference librarian in a large city commercial library very long to realise that there was something unusual about the phone query for the location of Membris, thought to be a village ' somewhere in England '. The place was not mentioned at all in the two most obvious sources, John Bartholomew *Gazetteer of the British Isles* (ninth edition 1943) with over 90,000 entries, and the Ordnance Survey *Gazetteer of Great Britain*, with over 40,000 names, *ie, all* those marked on the quarter-inch maps. Neither could it be found in the ' Short general index to towns and villages ' in John Bartholomew *Survey atlas of England and Wales* (second edition 1939). The possibility of an entry in one of the world gazetteers was therefore remote, but the librarian felt he had to check, just in case, in *Columbia Lippincott* (130,000 entries), the *Times index-gazetteer* (345,000), *Webster's* (40,000), *Chambers's* (12,000), and in the separately published indexes to the great Italian (250,000) and Russian (200,000) world atlases—all without success.

He was obliged, therefore, to fall back on his second-line sources, lists of names he had employed on occasion in the past, but less informative than the regular atlases and gazetteers. There was no entry in Eilert Ekwall *The concise Oxford dictionary of English place-names,* and he drew a blank too with the list of *Post offices in the United Kingdom and the Irish Republic* (over 20,000 names) and the supplementary *London post offices,* but made his first strike with the *Railway and commercial gazetteer of England, Scotland, and Wales* (46,000 names), designed primarily as a guide to the rail network but claiming to include ' every railway station, town, village, hamlet, parish, and place in Great Britain '. Under the heading ' Membris, Northamp.' appeared the direction ' see Woodford-c-Membris '; and under this heading the librarian learned that Woodford-cum-Membris was 69 miles by rail from London, the nearest station was Woodford Halse, and the population was 1,764, according to the 1951 census. Mention of this last reminded him of the very comprehensive two-volumed General Register Office *Census*

219

1961 England and Wales: index of place names (65,000 entries); here too he found an entry for Membris referring him to Woodford-cum-Membris, described as a civil parish in Daventry rural district with a population (by 1961) of 1775.

Back once more with the Bartholomew *Gazetteer* he found himself now able to locate the entry for Woodford-cum-Membris, giving the population (presumably the 1943 estimate) as 1,611 and the area 2,797 acres. A note added the words ' Contains W. Halse: which see '. The entry for Woodford Halse read ' eccl. dist. and vil. (ry. sta. W. and Hinton, L.N.E.), Northants, 7½m. S. of Daventry; pop. 1,611; P.O., T.O.' The next stage was to locate it on a map, and the Bartholomew *Survey atlas* was again consulted. Woodford-cum-Membris was not mentioned in the index, but Woodford Halse was, and the spot was easily found on the appropriate half-inch map. There was, however, no sign of the word ' Membris ' on the map, either alone or with Woodford, and thus no location that he could point to as Membris, the place he had been asked about; curious, the librarian thought he would probe deeper.

In the main reference library he looked up the *Victoria history of the county of Northamptonshire,* in four volumes from 1902 but still incomplete. There was no index but his familiarity with the standard arrangement adopted by the VCH soon enabled him to locate a well-illustrated eight-page chapter on Woodford—only to discover that it was all about another Northamptonshire village of the same name, known in full as Woodford near Thrapston. It soon became clear that the volume dealing with the other Woodford had yet to be published, but on one of the topographical maps showing the names and boundaries of parishes he did find Woodford-cum-Membris clearly delineated in red.

It was not until he consulted Samuel Lewis *A topographical dictionary of England* (seventh edition 1849) in four volumes that he came upon the clue he was looking for: in the course of the 34-line entry on Woodford he read that it is ' sometimes called Woodford Halse, from the Manor of Halse, of which it is a member, and Woodford-cum-Membris from the two attached hamlets '. George Baker *The history and antiquities of the county of Northampton* (1822-41) gave the names of these two hamlets as Farndon and Hinton. Could it possibly be that ' Membris ' was not a place at all, but simply the ablative plural of ' membrum ', and ' cum-membris '

220

no more than Latin for 'with members'? This would explain why Membris was not to be found on the map, but (as he quickly confirmed) Farndon and Hinton were.

The librarian is of course aware that a place enquired about may be artificial, *ie*, man-made (a village, a bridge, a city square, a diocese) or natural, *ie*, geographical (a mountain pass, a coral reef, a river, a volcano), but he must also remember that proper names are sometimes given to phenomena as diverse as railway tunnels, colleges, missile launching sites, battlegrounds, country 'seats', grouse moors, zoos, and archaeological sites, and that their nature is not always evident from their names.

Case 152: The tutor librarian of a college of education found a note from one of the academic staff in her mail one morning asking for ' a list of references on Maiden Castle '. The name, as it happened, meant nothing to her, but when she tried Bartholomew *Gazetteer of England and Wales,* however, she found no fewer than three Maiden Castles : an ancient fortification two miles east of Durham on a cliff a hundred feet above the River Wear; an ancient camp in the North Riding of Yorkshire, near Reeth; and in Dorset, two miles to the south-west of Dorchester, ' One of the largest earthworks in England, covering an area about 160 ac.' This last sounded the most promising, but she felt she should telephone her enquirer first to make sure. While she was about it she also tried to obtain an indication of what was wanted more precise than ' a list of references '. It emerged in the course of the conversation that what the enquirer had meant to imply was that he wanted some real solid archaeological information and not just ' snippets ', as he called them.

Back with the atlases and gazetteers, the librarian could not find the site mentioned in the index to Bartholomew *Survey atlas of England and Wales,* though she had no trouble in discovering its contours standing out clearly on the appropriate map within the volume, with its height given as 432 feet and its (presumably) Latin name as Dunium. It was apparently unknown to *Webster's geographical dictionary,* but the *Penguin encyclopedia of places* and the *Columbia Lippincott gazetteer of the world* furnished helpful background, the latter describing it as the ' finest earthworks in Great

Britain: c.115 acres. Evidences of neolithic village dating from c.2000 B.C. were found during excavations, 1934-47. An Iron Age fortified village, established here c.300 B.C., is believed to have been taken by the Romans and occupied until about A.D. 70'. Gazetteers never give bibliographical references, but it was a safe bet that the excavations mentioned here would be amply documented somewhere or other.

As so often, a quick and easy lead was provided by one of the great general encyclopedias. *Chambers's* was found to have a main article 'Maiden Castle', a full column in length, complete with map, and most important, a full bibliographical citation for the excavation report: R E M Wheeler *Maiden Castle* (Society of Antiquaries Research Committee, Report no. 12, 1943).

Identification cases such as this where it emerges that there are several places with the same name are normally not too difficult to solve, because the enquirer can usually provide sufficient supplementary details to eliminate the unwanted places. Sometimes the librarian is not so fortunate: a reader enquiring about Newtown simply *must* have more than the name to start with, for there are over 170 places called Newtown or New Town in England and Wales alone, all listed in the General Register Office *Census 1961: index of place names*.

Case 153: ' Where does the River Ouse start?' seemed like a perfectly straightforward query until the librarian found that the index to Bartholomew *Survey atlas of England and Wales* does not include rivers. The second blow fell when he discovered from the index to the *Times atlas* that there are three English rivers of that name. As the meagre information given with the entries was insufficient to distinguish them the librarian was obliged to try the gazetteers. *Chambers's world gazetteer and geographical dictionary* revealed a fourth River Ouse, but furnished data adequate for task in hand. The enquirer had no hesitation in dismissing the Great Ouse (160 miles), the Little Ouse (24 miles), and the Sussex Ouse (30 miles). The one that interested him was the Yorkshire Ouse, about which *Chambers's* had this to say: ' the main stream (c.60m.) formed by the junct. or influx of numerous feeders, most of which drain the eastern valleys of the Pennines. The most important of these are the Swale and Ure (whose junct. nr Boroughbridge constitutes the beginning of the Ouse) '.

Boroughbridge had an entry in the index to Bartholomew *Survey atlas* and the librarian in a matter of seconds was able to pinpoint on the relevant half-inch map the very spot his enquirer was seeking.

Often more troublesome are those instances from the other end of the spectrum where a single place is known by more than one name. A place may indeed have two or more names of equivalent status, *eg*, Wales/Cymru, Dublin/Baile atha Cliath, but more common is the case where one only is official and all the rest are unofficial, although there is in some countries such as Belgium an intermediate form known as ' recognised unofficial '.

Case 154: The search for the Celtic Sea initially proved so fruitless that the librarian rang back the number his enquirer had left, reporting lack of progress and asking where he had come across the name. He had been unable to find it in either the ' big three ' atlas indexes (the *Times index-gazetteer*, the *Indice dei nomi* of the *Atlante internazionale*, and the *Index-gazetteer* of the *Atlas mira*) or in the four gazetteers he checked (*Columbia Lippincott, Chambers's, Webster's*, or the Bartholomew *British Isles*).

' I'm not surprised you can't find it, I don't think it exists!' was the enquirer's surprising response. Sensing perhaps from the pause which followed that an explanation was awaited, he hastened to add: ' There is a map in today's *Guardian* showing the sea between Ireland and England marked as the Celtic Sea; I've never heard it called that before—is it correct?' Promising to call back once more, the librarian checked the library's copy of the newspaper, where sure enough he found the map exactly as the enquirer had said, used to illustrate a report on oil and gas resources in the seas around Britain. One by one he checked the atlases, including the most comprehensive British work, the *Atlas of Britain*, and the official Ordnance Survey maps : without exception that particular stretch of water was shown as the Irish Sea, leading north and south into the broad Atlantic *via* the North Channel and the St George's Channel respectively. And perhaps even more conclusively, the Irish Sea was how it appeared in the *Catalogue of Admiralty charts,* ' published by the Hydrographer of the Navy ', no less.

And the Irish Sea was how it was known to all the gazetteers as well, including those that make a speciality of giving alternative names and spellings. The only other name by which it had ever been known was given to it by the Romans : Oceanus Hibernicus.

This was confirmed by *Shepherd's historical atlas,* but R L Poole *Historical atlas of modern Europe* added one more ingredient to the puzzle : on a map of ' England and Wales before the Norman Conquest ' the stretch of sea between the Isle of Man and the mainland was shown as Mare Fresicum.

The librarian realised he had been landed with one of the most difficult of all problems—proving a negative. For even after all his searching he was still unable to say with certainty that the area was *not* the Celtic Sea. The most he could claim, as he explained to his enquirer over the phone, was that all the evidence he had unearthed showed that it was the Irish Sea.

(*See also* case 160.)

Commonly the reasons for such variations are historical, with a place having different names at various periods, some of them overlapping, *eg,* Siam/Thailand, Palestine/Israel.

Case 155: ' Can you tell me where Lutetia is?' was the enquiry received from a clergyman one evening in a busy public library. The librarian's first reaction was to ask ' It is a place? ' and his second to enquire ' Do you know how you spell it?' The reader's response was affirmative and helpful in both instances, and the librarian therefore led the way to the stand containing the atlases. He could not find the place in the *Times atlas,* or in the very comprehensive separately-published *Indice dei nomi* for the *Atlante internazionale del Touring Club Italiano,* or in the similar *Index-gazetteer* for the *Atlas Mira*: these he knew to be the three major world atlases.

Unfortunately, the enquirer had no suggestions to make as to the country of origin, so the librarian, turning to the gazetteers, first tried the one he knew to have the largest number of entries, the *Times index-gazetteer,* next the one that he had previously found the most handy, *Chambers's world gazetteer*, and then the one that was the most recently published, the *Penguin encyclopedia of places*. When he had drawn a blank with all of these too the suspicion began to form in his mind that Lutetia might be a historical name, no longer in current use, so he asked his enquirer where he had come across it. ' In an old theological book, printed in Latin ', was the reply, ' I think Lutetia is the place where it was published '. The librarian knew that a feature of *Webster's geographical dictionary*, blazoned indeed on its dust-jacket, is the attention paid to the names of ' Biblical times, ancient Greece and Rome, medieval Europe, and World Wars I and II '. And sure enough, he found an entry for Lutetia, saying simply ' See Paris '. The entry for Paris soon made clear that Lutetia was the ancient (Latin) name for the city.

[Had the librarian persisted with the atlases he would have seen in the gazetteer in the *Oxford atlas* that Lutetia was the ' Roman name of Gallic centre on island at Paris, France '. The index to *Shepherd's historical atlas* would also have guided him to the 'Reference map of the European provinces of the Roman Empire ' which clearly shows Lutetia (Paris).]

With many names the differences are merely linguistic (though none the less important for that). One large group of such multiple names are simply translated versions, common in bilingual communities, *eg*, Capetown/Kaapstad (in South Africa), Three Rivers/Trois-Rivières (in Canada), Strata Florida/Ystrad-fflur (in Wales). In another group the variations are due to the different languages within a country actually having different names for a place, *eg*, Bratislava/Pressburg/Pozsony (Czech, German, Hungarian), Dubrovnik/Ragusa (Serbo-croat, Italian), Swansea/Abertawe (English, Welsh).

But it is the third group in this linguistic category that causes most confusion: there are many place names that are known to visitors from other countries by names that would be unrecognisable to their own natives: Moscow, for instance, is not what the Russians call their capital city; the Danube is known to those whose countries it flows through as the Donau, or the Duna, or the Dunarea; there is probably not one Englishman in a thousand aware that to his neighbours across the Welsh border England is known as Lloegr. So far as the names of countries are concerned, this is a phenomenon familiar to the amateur philatelist, who soon learns that the places he knows as Finland, Hungary, Austria, and Japan are really called Suomi, Magyarorszag, Österreich, and Nippon.

Case 156: When asked what country was officially known as Shqiperia the library assistant thought at first she was in for a long search, for the place seemed unknown to the two largest gazetteers the library possessed, the *Columbia Lippincott* and the *Times index-gazetteer*. Fortunately, *Chambers's world gazetteer* and *Webster's geographical dictionary* both came to the rescue, for both directed her to the entry for Albania. There she learned that Shqiperia (or Shqipri) is the name for the country in the Tosk language and Shqipenia (or Shqipni) is the name in the Gheg language.

A glance at the relevant map in the *Atlante internazionale del Touring Club Italiano*, which always uses the local place names, showed the country clearly marked as Shqiperi.

[*Columbia Lippincott* does in fact confirm this in the entry under Albania, but omits to provide references from the official forms Shqipri, Shqipriya, Shqipni, Shqipnija. And as Stanley Gibbons Ltd *Stamps of the world* shows, Shqiperia is the form used on postage stamps.]

For historical reasons such ' exonyms ', as they are called, bulk large in English, comprising two types: firstly, names taken into the language from abroad and anglicised, or more often garbled, *eg,* Leghorn (Italian Livorno), Cairo (which came to England *via* Venice from the Arabic al Qahira), Letterkenny (Irish Leitir Ceannainn); and secondly, English names given to places abroad by explorers, travellers, or administrators, *eg,* Rhodesia (named after Cecil Rhodes; and which, so far as Northern Rhodesia is concerned is now Zambia, and so far as Southern Rhodesia is concerned, now known simply as Rhodesia, is increasingly referred to by its African leaders as Zimbabwe); Sandwich Islands (the name given by Captain Cook to what we know as Hawaii).

Case 157: Until he was asked over the phone one day for the ' real ' name for Mount Everest, it had not dawned upon the young reference librarian that such a unique geographical feature could be known by any other name. A moment's reflection told him that his naive assumption was unwarranted, for such a prominent peak could scarcely have escaped the attention of the local inhabitants in Nepal and Tibet, who would naturally have given it a name.

Columbia Lippincott provided the starting point: 'named (c. 1855) for a former surveyor-general [of India] (1830-43), Sir George Everest . . . Tibetan name Chomolungma is sometimes attributed'. The *Times index-gazetteer* incidentally revealed the existence of two Mount Everests, the second in South Africa; the *Times atlas* confirmed *Columbia Lippincott* by printing the local name in parentheses below the English name on the relevant map.

Double-checking, just to be sure, in the two other major world atlases, the librarian found that both the map and the index of the *Atlas mira* acknowledge only the Tibetan name (spelt Chomo Lungma). The *Indice dei nomi* of the *Atlante internazionale del Touring Club Italiano,* however, referred from the English name to Saragmatha, and this was the name actually printed on the map referred to. This apparent conflict was not resolved until the librarian thought to check the index for Chomolungma also: the entry referred him to quite a different map, where the name appeared as Chomolungma. The explanation seemed to be that there were two local names, depending on which side of the Himalayas you were sitting: on the map headed 'Bharat' (the official name for India) the mountain was Saragmatha; on the map with the heading 'Chung Kuo' (the official name for China) the mountain was Chomolungma.

Many countries, including Britain and the United States, have been forced to grasp this particular bull by the horns and compile lists of agreed and standard forms of names, *eg,* the *Lists* (1921 to date) produced by the Royal Geographical Society Permanent committee on geographical names for British official use (established in 1919); and the *Gazetteers* (1955 to date) of the United States Board on geographical names (founded in 1890). More recently the international organisations too have been drawn into the ring: the International Civil Aviation Organisation has its own list, in French and English, of approved names of countries and international airports. Perhaps the most lucid treatment of the whole knotty problem is *The rendering of geographical names* (1957) by Marcel Aurousseau, who for twenty years was Secretary of the PCGN. Among other matters he discusses, for instance, names which have inflected forms: when the Irish balladeer pleads ' Come back to Erin, mavourneen, mavourneen' he is employing the dative case of Eire. The difference between the name of a country and the title of a state is also explained: the United Kingdom of Great Britain and Northern Ireland, for instance, is not a country but a political entity.

The makers of atlases have tackled this problem of alternative names in a variety of ways. The *Times atlas* adopts the ' local official' form, with the English form in brackets 'in the case of important places where English practice has familiarized an alternative form '. By way of contrast, the *Oxford atlas* uses English forms for all country names, and for provinces and regions where they are well known; English is also used for the names of towns, when these are in common use, followed by the local name in brackets. The *Atlante internazionale del Touring Club Italiano* and the *Atlas international Larousse* both give place names their own national spellings on the maps.

A special difficulty arises where the local form of a name would normally be in a non-roman alphabet such as greek or cyrillic or arabic. Transliteration is the obvious solution here, although the librarian should be aware that there are a number of differing systems in use. A glimpse at how it seems to those sitting on the other side of the fence can be seen in the first edition (1954) of the *Atlas mira* where *all* the place-names are either translated into Russian or transliterated phonetically into cyrillic. In the second edition (1967) the editors did admit ' the foreign reader was badly handicapped by the Russian alphabet used in it. So suggestions coming from various parts of the globe have been taken into account, and the second edition of the Atlas is issued in two parallel versions, one using the Russian and the other the Roman alphabet. In the latter version all place names referring to countries where the Roman alphabet is used are given in the authentic national spellings, the place names for the countries with other alphabet are given in Roman alphabet, official or the most spread in the country and international editions ' [sic].

As a general rule most atlases take care to provide for alternative approaches by including variant forms in their indexes. Many atlas indexes are just that and nothing more, listing the place names (or a selection of them) that appear on their maps and locating them precisely by page and grid reference, *eg*, Bartholomew *Survey atlas of England and Wales*. Some go further, like the *Times atlas of the world*, by adding co-ordinates of latitude and longitude, and examples are encountered where further information of a gazetteer nature also appears. Such indexes indeed can often serve to supplement the regular gazetteers, particularly as they are often more up-to-date. Although neither give more than map references the separately published index to the *Atlante internazionale del Touring Club Italiano* (1968) and the *Atlas mira* (1968) are outstanding not only in this respect but also for their comprehensiveness, with perhaps 250,000 and 200,000 entries respectively.

Case 158: A question posed one evening in a busy country branch library asked simply for the new name for Benares. The assistant knew little more than that it was a town in India, but the library had quite a respectable small reference collection, and she was able to consult both *Chambers's world gazetteer* and (perhaps surprisingly) the *Columbia Lippincott gazetteer of the world*. From the former she learned that Benares is 'the most sacred city of the Hindus, on the N bank of the Ganges, 420m. from Calcutta', that it is also spelt Banaras, and was known in ancient times as Varanasi. *Columbia Lippincott* was more positive about the name, stating that since 1948 (*ie*, the year after India achieved independence from the British Raj) the city had been known officially as Banaras.

However, in the atlas, the gazetteer, the index, and the main sequence of the newly acquired 1970 printing of *Encyclopaedia Britannica* the name was unequivocally shown as Varanasi.

[This resurrection of the city's ancient name is confirmed by Hebe Spaull *New place names of the world* (1970).]

Several writers on reference work have commented upon the marked increase over the last generation of enquiries about places, the result no doubt of the successive influences of the global struggle of the second world war, television, and cheap air travel. And of course enquiries about places have never been confined simply to questions as to their location: readers also ask about population, climate, height above sea level, area, local industry, products, *etc,* as well as a host of questions more historical than geographical. The first line of defence with many of these queries too are the gazetteers.

Case 159: A visitor to the reference library one afternoon in the course of his studies into the history of English education in the years before the first world war had come across a mention in a contemporary newspaper of Brownsea Island, which, it would appear, had a significance for the newspaper's 1910 readers that escaped the readers of the 1970's.

The first step was to find out where it was. It was not mentioned in the *Times index-gazetteer* or *Chambers's world gazetteer,* but the Ordnance Survey listed it in the *Gazetteer of Great Britain* (giving, of course only the National Grid reference: SZ 0187). Once assured that it was indeed in Britain, the librarian turned to Bartholomew *Gazetteer of the British Isles* where the entry read: 'isl., with vil., Poole harb., 2m. S. of Poole, SE Dorset. The isl. is $3\frac{1}{2}$m. in circumference. On E. coast is B. Castle, modern mansion replacing one built in the reign of Elizabeth, for defence of harbour.' None of this suggested any link with education, but did allow the island to be easily found in the Bartholomew *Survey atlas* (despite its absence from the index). At a scale of half-inch to the mile the map showed it up very clearly, with the castle, two lakes, a road, and a pier.

Before leaving the atlases and gazetteers to search the general book collection the librarian thought he might as well just check in the two gazetteers he had not consulted at the outset because they were published in the United States. *Webster's geographical dictionary* had no entry for Brownsea Island, but to his surprise in the *Columbia Lippincott* entry he found what the enquirer had been seeking: ' Scene of 1st camp (1907) of Br. Boy-Scout movement '.

One particular problem with facts about places is that the enquirer will often find discrepancies between one source and another. This is partly because many parts of the world have not yet been fully explored, and others have been declared out of bounds for political or security reasons, but it is also because the geographers themselves are not agreed about the way to count or measure things. The gazetteer compilers have discovered in Swiss, French, German,

Austrian, and Italian sources, for example, different but equally authoritative figures of heights for the same Swiss mountains; and as was demonstrated some years ago in the *Library Association record,* the major encyclopedias almost all disagree as to which is the world's longest river, the Amazon, the Nile, or the Mississippi-Missouri.

Poulation figures need treating with even more care, for as *Columbia Lippincott* warns us: ' Recent population figures for many areas of the world are often difficult to obtain. Some countries have never taken a census; some take only partial censuses; some which do take censuses publish them completely only many years after the census is taken; some publish only part of the results of a census and some have been known to suppress all results of a census '.

For the librarian, when asked to furnish factual data about places it is always a good plan to check and double-check, preferably in up-to-date non-geographical sources such as directories and yearbooks.

Case 160: A request for the population of Abyssinia ran into difficulties right away. *Webster's geographical dictionary* referred the librarian to Ethiopia, ' the official name in English '. In the entry for Ethiopia he learned that there are two of them: the ancient country in north-east Africa, whose vague and shifting boundaries once enclosed part of Egypt, the Sudan, and Eritrea; and the modern state, also known as Abyssinia. But even this was somewhat confused, for he read further that modern usage establishes no clear-cut distinction between Ethiopia and the kingdom of Abyssinia, although Abyssinia would appear to refer strictly to the Amharic nucleus of the Ethiopian empire. The only population given (in the 1967 printing) was a 1939 estimate of 9,450,000.

Chambers's world gazetteer, on the other hand, had no entry under Ethiopia at all (not even in the ' Supplementary index ' where all the cross-references are gathered together), but the entry for Abyssinia did add ' in English now often Ethiopia '. 8 millions was the figure given as 'An approx. estimate of the total pop.'

Columbia Lippincott gazetteer of the world (1952) referred like *Webster's* from Abyssinia to Ethiopia: ' The name Abyssinia (derived from Arabic *El Habesha*), although never official, has been widely used '. Population estimates, however, ' range from 8,000,000 to 15,500,000 '.

The librarian by this time had realised his mistake in turning first to such geographical sources for an up-to-date population figure. Trying therefore the 1971-2 *Statesman's year-book,* he found the ' official estimate . . . in 1967 ' to be 22,667,400. Checking with the 1972 *Whitaker's almanack* he found a figure of 24,769,000, but with no source. *World almanac* for 1971 confirmed this latter figure, giving the source as a 1969 United Nations estimate.

Finally, he remembered to check in the library's own vertical files where he knew that most countries of the world had a folder in which the library staff filed fugitive material. There he was comforted to find a clipping from the *Times* for 30th Jan 1969, where he read : ' No census [of the country] exists, so that it is rash to be categorical about the numbers of the population. This is said to comprise eight million Christians, eight million Muslims, and six million pagans '.

Even in countries like Britain, which has been collecting and freely publishing census data since 1801, certain population figures are still very hard to come by. The *Census 1961 England and Wales: index of place names* tells the reader that it includes ' the names of some 25,000 places such as villages, hamlets and localities, without legally defined boundaries, for which the populations have not been, and in most cases, could not be ascertained '. It is sometimes necessary to explain such facts of statistical life to enquirers who cannot understand why the librarian appears to make such heavy weather of simple enquiries about the population of, say, the Potteries, or the Rhondda Valley or the Highlands of Scotland.

Just as encyclopedias and dictionaries are used in many enquiries merely as jumping off points (see *Case studies in reference work,* pages 50-3, 137), so gazetteers, as encyclopedias or dictionaries of place names, often serve as the first stage of a more extended search.

Case 161: When asked ' Where are the Hanging Walls of Mark Anthony? and what are they?' the librarian found that the general gazetteers failed to provide any clues at all: *Chambers's, Webster's,* the *Times* and even the *Columbia Lippincott.* Atlases too, and several dictionaries of classical antiquities were consulted in vain. In the ensuing conversation with the enquirer an unexpected ray of light was shed upon the problem when it came out that these Hanging Walls were somewhere in England! It had been assumed (quite unwarrantably, of course) that they were in some exotic Mediterranean clime. The Bartholomew *Gazetteer of the British Isles* immediately described them as a 'pl., 9m. ENE. Penrith, E. Cumberland.' They were found quite easily just south of the village of Kirkland in the Bartholomew *Survey atlas of England and Wales,* and at a much larger scale on the six-inch Ordnance Survey map, printed in the type conventionally indicating Roman antiquities. The problem seemed almost solved: the obvious next step was to consult the invaluable Victoria County History. As luck would have it, the projected four-volume set for Cumberland was found to be only half-completed; neither of the two volumes had an index; furthermore, they were general volumes, not the historical and topographical volumes, and so would not be likely to contain the required information in any case. It was recalled, however, that the VCH was designed specifically to replace the eighteenth and nineteenth century standard county histories, and so the library catalogue was consulted to see what was the standard work on Cumberland. This seemed to be the two-volumed work by William Hutchinson, published at Carlisle in 1794, but there was no mention of the Hanging Walls in the index. A fresh approach was then tried from the place-name angle. Neither J B Johnston *Place names of England and Wales* nor Eilert Ekwall *Concise Oxford dictionary of English place-names* were any help: the more detailed three-volumed work on the place-names of Cumberland by the English Place-name Society had a mention, but all it said was that the place was so named in 1794, with a reference to the work by Hutchinson, already consulted without success. It was therefore examined again; it was confirmed that the place was not in the index, but the work was this time combed page by page—not such an arduous job as it sounds since the general arrangement is by parishes. On page 258 of volume one, under 'The Parish of Kirkland: Antiquities', was found a description of the place called the Hanging Walls of Mark Anthony 'without any possible reason to be assigned for the name. They consist of three terraces, the manifest work of art, immediately rising one above the other, and each elevated between 4 and 5 yards, they are 200 yards in length, and the plain at the top of each ten in breadth.' From experience of similar queries it was thought likely that a paper on these earthworks would have been read sometime or other to the local antiquarian society. Accordingly, the *Transactions of the Cumberland and Westmorland Antiquarian and Archaeological Society* were searched, and in the volume for 1886 was found a detailed description, with map and sectional diagrams. The paper said that no one knew exactly what the earthworks were, or where they got their name, but suggested that they might be vestiges of an old system of cultivation, and that Mark Anthony was a corruption of Saint Anthony, ' a saint much venerated by rustics.'

[An alternative approach to the question, once it had been safely established from the map that the Hanging Walls were antiquities, would have been to consult A L Humphreys *Handbook to county bibliography* (1919), where the Cumberland section has a reference to an archaeological survey of the county in the journal *Archaeologia*. This is a list arranged alphabetically by place, and under Kirkland the Hanging Walls are included, with references both to Hutchinson and the paper in the *Transactions*. There is also a further reference to Samuel Jefferson *History and antiquities of Leath ward in the county of Cumberland* (1840), but this proves to be a direct quotation from Hutchinson.]

Mention has been made earlier (see pages 207-8 above, and *Case studies in reference work,* pages 140-2) of the particular difficulties of queries in reverse. Although enquiries as to the location of the abbey founded in 1066 by William the Conqueror as a thankoffering for his victory at Hastings, or the whereabouts of the grave of Robert Louis Stevenson, are clearly about places (and the answers are to be found in Bartholomew *Gazetteer* and *Webster's geographical dictionary* respectively) the gazetteers and atlases are rendered useless by their method of arrangement, which assumes that you already know the name of the place you are looking for, *ie,* Battle and Vailima. Once again the librarian has to seek what he wants from non-geographical sources.

Case 162: In search of the burial place of Oscar Wilde the librarian turned to the *Dictionary of national biography,* checking first in the

main set and then in the 'Cumulative index to the biographies contained in the supplements . . . 1901-1960' that is to be found in the
latest ten-year DNB volume covering 1951-60. But Wilde's name
was missing. Suspecting the reason, the librarian turned to the
separately published lives of Wilde, where in the latest of these,
Philippe Jullian *Oscar Wilde* (1969) he read: 'The funeral took
place on the 3rd September [1900] at Saint-Germain-des-Prés [Paris]
. . . About fifty people were at the funeral; an icy rain was falling,
and the intimate friends crowded into four carriages, to go to Bagneux cemetery.'

The *Times atlas* quickly located Bagneux on the map of Paris,
some five miles due south of the Place de la Concorde. To the librarian this seemed like the end of the enquiry, but something told
him to check DNB once again, just to make sure that they had indeed omitted Wilde. It was only on this second time round that he
noticed volume 22, a supplement to the main set, *but covering the
same period, ie,* 'from the earliest times to 1900'. He had no excuse
for missing this, for readers are warned in a note prefixed to all the
volumes of the set 'In using the main Dictionary (to 1900) it is
necessary to remember that it is in *two* alphabetical series'. He was
pleased to see that Oscar Wilde had not been forgotten, but he was
startled by what he read: 'He was buried in the Bagneux cemetery
on 3 Dec., but his remains were removed to the cemetery of Père-
Lachaise, Paris, on 20 July 1909.'

The pronunciation of place-names troubles some people; a number of the gazetteers and atlas indexes do indicate pronunciations,
and W C Greet *World words: recommended pronunciations* (1948)
is a useful guide, originally compiled for the radio broadcasters of
CBS. Problems arise not only with names in foreign languages, but
with British and American names also. Paradoxically, English
names are often found to be the most troublesome of all, for English
spelling is anything but regular, and on occasion is downright misleading. And of course while those who care for these things might
be prepared to excuse mispronunciations of foreign names they
take a sterner line with an English speaker making a hash of an
English name. Welsh place-names on the other hand, so often
thought of as fearsomely difficult, do have the virtue of a perfectly
phonetic spelling. There do exist specialist reference tools to turn to

for assistance here: one of the most authoritative (also originally compiled for broadcasters) is G M Miller *BBC pronouncing dictionary of British names* (1971).

Case 163: In checking on the pronunciation of Strathaven in re-response to an urgent telephone call the librarian was able to report a comforting unanimity among the reference books. Right away, Bartholomew *Gazetteer of the British Isles* (which she had consulted merely to find out where the place was, aware that it did not normally include pronunciations), besides characterising it as a town in Lanarkshire, population 4,207, added that it was 'locally pronounced Stravn' (*ie,* a two-syllable word, rhyming with 'haven'). *Chambers's* agreed, but its version of the pronunciation was spelt 'Strayven'. *Columbia Lippincott* indicated the pronunciation as 'Stravun', but did admit the possibility of 'Strathavun'.

The obvious problems of precisely indicating speech sounds by means of the conventional alphabet were thus neatly illustrated: though all three sources agreed on the pronunciation, they each indicated it in a different way (and the versions quoted above omit the various stress and diacritical marks also used). When she consulted G M Miller *BBC pronouncing dictionary of British names,* however, the librarian noticed that each pronunciation (including that for Strathaven) was shown in two ways, not only (like the other sources consulted) using an English modified spelling system, but also according to the much more precise system of the International Phonetic Association.

Many place-names can be pronounced more than one way but it is a sensible rule to follow the local version, *ie,* the way it is pronounced by the people who actually live there. But there are occasional exceptions even to this method: by their inhabitants Carlisle and Newcastle are stressed on the first and second syllables respectively; everyone else puts the emphasis on the other syllable, and this has become the accepted national pronunciation.

A large minority of the enquiries received are about the names themselves rather than the places. Readers frequently ask about the meaning or the derivation or the earlier forms of names: such questions are etymological rather than geographical. Place-name study of this linguistic and historical character is a discipline in its own right, with a vast literature: R B Sealock and P A Seely *Bibliography of place name literature* (second edition 1967) extends to 362 pages, though it covers only the United States and Canada.

Case 164: When asked where Buckfastleigh in Devon got its name from the librarian guessed he would not have far to look, for we are fortunate enough to have for just this purpose Eilert Ekwall *The Concise Oxford dictionary of English place-names,* now in its fourth edition (1960) and 'a remarkable piece of work', according to the *Times literary supplement.* Firmly based on the principle that the explanation of place-names cannot proceed on the strength of the modern name-form alone, the work always seeks out earlier forms before attempting an etymology. Buckfastleigh is derived from the three Old English words *bucc,* a male deer, *faesten,* a stronghold, and *leah,* forest. Buckfast, therefore, is the stronghold of the male deer, and Buckfastleigh is the forest of Buckfast.

Of course not all places about which readers may be curious are terrestrial: from the days when man first lifted up his eyes to the heavens he has assigned names to the objects that can be observed there by day and by night. The 1967 revision of the *Times atlas* devotes five pages to the moon, although the first edition of 1895 had included no more than one small map taking up half a page. And as in our generation space exploration has become a reality we may expect a continual stream of celestial maps and new-coined place names.

The librarian should also remain on the alert for enquiries about places that exist neither in the heavens above nor on the earth beneath; for fictional places conjured up in the minds of writers may be just as real as an object of interest and attention as any jungle of asphalt or geological aggregate. Problems of this kind are exactly similar to those not uncommon enquiries about fictional people discussed above (pages 174-6).

Case 165: When asked for information on Yoknapatawpha County the young librarian turned confidently to the *Columbia Lippincott gazetteer of the world,* for she knew it claimed to list every US county, and the derivation of the name was obviously American Indian. Drawing a blank, she was momentarily taken aback, but by the time she had unsuccessfully consulted *Webster's geographical dictionary* (which emphasises the United States and Canada), *Chambers's world gazetteer,* and the *Times index-gazetteer* with its 345,000 entries she had come to the conclusion that there was no such place—except perhaps in the imagination.

The three-volumed *New century cyclopedia of names* includes both real and fictional names of people and places, but was no help on this occasion. From W R Benet *Reader's encyclopedia,* however, she learned that the place is 'An imaginary county in Mississippi which serves as a setting for many stories by William Faulkner. Jefferson, the county seat, is modelled in part on Oxford, Miss. The novelist gave the county realistic detail, providing a map and population figures '. The *Oxford companion to American literature,* in a 31-line article on Yoknapatawpha County gives these population figures ' according to the map that its creator printed in the 1951 edition of *Absalom, Absalom!*', and lists the 14 novels set in whole or in part in this mythical place. It adds further that it is based on Lafayette County, and that its name is presumably of Chickasaw derivation.

A major stumbling block in the path of the seeker of information about places is the tendency they have to change their names. Byzantium, for instance, became Constantinople in 330 AD, and then Istanbul in 1930; Cape Canaveral has been Cape Kennedy since 1963; St Petersburg was first changed in 1914 to Petrograd and then in 1924 to Leningrad.

Case 166: The staff of a university library was called upon as a matter of some urgency to help a local businessman trace the whereabouts of Sukarnapura. The name was not to be found in any of the gazetteers to hand—*Columbia Lippincott, Webster's,* the *Times, Chambers's,* including the most recent, the 1971 *Penguin encyclopedia of places,* but it was eventually run to earth in Hebe Spaull *New place names of the world* (1970) as ' Sukarnarpura [sic], West Irian, Indonesia. Now Djapura '. Though the index to the *Times atlas* had been found to have no entry for the place, it was felt that it would do no harm to glance at the appropriate map of West Irian (formerly Dutch New Guinea). Surprisingly, there in large letters appeared Sukarnapura—obviously the capital city of West Irian. The appearance in parentheses of what was probably the old name, Hollandia, suggested a possible explanation for this strange state of affairs: the cartographer had altered the name on his map but the indexer had not followed suit in his index. If this theory were correct, the place would be found still entered under Hollandia. But a check soon revealed that there was no index entry under Hollandia either!

The mystery seemed to deepen momentarily when *Webster's geographical dictionary* was consulted a second time, under 'Hollandia', for the entry revealed yet another change of name, to the Indonesian form Kotabaru. But back at the *Times atlas*, this name *was* found indexed. In summary then, the successive names of this capital city of West Irian over the last 25 years were Hollandia (on the *Times* map but not in the index). Kotabaru (in the index but not on the map), Sukarnapura (on the map but not in the index), Djapura (neither on the map nor in the index).

(*See also* case 158.)

It is probably true that the reasons for most changes are political: indeed at particularly turbulent times or in certain sensitive areas the causes are obviously so. The realignments in eastern Europe and the dismembering of the old colonial empires has probably produced more place-name changes for our generation to digest than any other comparable period, *eg,* Königsberg, once in East Prussia, Germany, is now called Kaliningrad and is in the Soviet Union; Batavia, former capital of the Dutch East Indies, and actually the Latin word for Holland, is now Djakarta, capital of Indonesia; Jesselton, former capital of British North Borneo and named after ' a nonentity on the court of directors ' of the North Borneo Chartered Company, has been given the Malay name Kota Kinabalu. Africa, in particular, in recent years has been described as a ' blossoming nightmare for map makers ', but what are probably the most notorious changes took place after the posthumous attack on Stalin, when dozens of Soviet and other Communist towns that had been called after him were obliged to seek other names: Stalino in

Bulgaria is now Varna, Stalin in Rumania is now Brasov, and the most famous of all, Stalingrad, is now Volgograd.

The editors of *Columbia Lippincott* point out that in some instances 'in addition to ordinary place-name changes, local usage prevents proper identification. For example, in China's Yunnan province the district of Lungchwan has a winter and a spring capital, Shanmulung, and a summer and fall capital, Changfengkai, each of which is called simply Lungchwan during the period in which it is the seat of the local government'.

And of course we must not forget that completely new places are emerging all the time. Brasilia, planned from the ground upwards as the new capital of Brazil, is perhaps the most striking recent instance.

Although not involving a place-name change strictly speaking, a phenomenon similar in its effect for geographers and librarians is the sudden leap of some obscure locale into the world's consciousness. One notably spectacular instance was Bikini (population 167), an unknown South Pacific atoll until the nuclear bomb tests of July 1946, and now a household word in a dozen languages in another derived context.

Case 167: 'Can you tell me where Abbotsinch is?' was the plea made by a visitor to a public library one morning. Is it somewhere in Britain?' the librarian enquired. By way of reply the reader produced a letter in which her correspondent had written 'I will be landing at Abbotsinch on the last Saturday in August, and I hope to see you during the following week'.

The place was clearly a port of some kind, but it was not in the index of either the *Atlas of Britain* or John Bartholomew *Survey atlas of England and Wales*. Neither was it in the *Times atlas of the world*. Furthermore, the librarian could not find it in the Ordnance Survey *Gazetteer of Great Britain,* or the General Register Office *Census 1961 England and Wales: index of place names,* or (at least at first) in John Bartholomew *Gazetteer of the British Isles*. Then in the last, where the entry would have been, he noticed in the margin the small triangular symbol indicating a new entry in the supplement. No more than a single line, it was sufficient: 'Renfrew, 1½m. N of Paisley, Glasgow aerodrome'. Checking in the most recent atlas of Scotland he had, the *Reader's digest complete atlas of the British Isles* (1965), the librarian found Abbotsinch clearly shown on the map of the west of Scotland and on the ' Transport: air travel ' map, but strangely enough not in the index.

Of course it is not only the names of places that change: it has been said that geographic data gets out of place more rapidly than perhaps any other type of reference information. The gazetteers have great difficulty keeping pace with such changes. Their limited sales (compared with dictionaries, for instance) mean that frequent revisions are impracticable. Atlases seem to cope better, some of the major world atlases adopting like the major encyclopedias a policy of continuous revision. The *Rand McNally commercial* is the only large atlas to appear annually.

To enable themselves to keep up with these and other changes geographers have developed their own specialised tools. From the United States in alternate years we have *New geography,* which tells us that ' One of the most serious drawbacks to modern knowledge is the lack of reliable *current* information about geographical matters '. *Geographical digest,* an annual first published as an experiment by the Research Department of George Philip, the famous London map firm, aims ' to provide in a concise form information on recent changes in the world of interest to geographers, and especially to provide such information as is difficult to obtain without consulting many sources '.

Case 168: The librarian had no luck at all with the atlases in trying to trace Namibia, which a reader claimed was 'another new country ', mentioned in the newspapers. In spite of being lucky enough to possess up-to-date editions of what are generally regarded as the three finest world atlases—the *Times* (1967), the *Atlas mira* (1968), and the *Atlante internazionale* (1968)—he had drawn a blank with all three. Each of them, however, had drawn his attention to the Namib desert, the arid coastal plain extending along the Atlantic coast of South-west Africa, but suspicion was not proof.

He thought next of checking the *Statesman's year-book* or the *Index to the Times* to see if they mentioned the place, but then he remembered the useful little annual *Geographical digest.* Examining the latest issue (1970), he was dismayed to find no index, so he turned to the section headed ' Recent significant political changes '. There, to his delight, on the very first page he read that ' The name " Namibia " has been officially adopted by the United Nations in place of " South-West Africa ".'

[Browsing some weeks later through the recently published *Penguin encyclopedia of places* he found an entry (in the addenda, not in the main sequence) for Namibia.]

Of course some of the geographical data in the gazetteers and atlases and elsewhere is unchanging, the height of a mountain or the latitude and longitude of a city, for instance, but some changes are very drastic and very permanent, when places in fact cease to exist. Some are simply wiped off the face of the earth, by plague, tempest, fire, or the hand of war; others are removed more considerately, but just as positively, as for example, the villages of Derwent in Derbyshire and Capelcelyn in Merioneth, submerged beneath the waters of the Ladybower and Tryweryn reservoirs. Far more commonly, if less dramatically, are places removed by a stroke of the legislator's pen. Middlesex, for example, a historic county deriving its name from the ancient kingdom of the Middle Saxons, was abolished by the London Government Act of 1963. Burgundy too, kingdom, duchy, and province of France, disappeared with the Revolution, when it was divided into three *départements*.

Case 169: The reader enquiring after Torrington-street in London claimed that he could not find it on any of the maps or in any of the directories that he had tried. The librarian confirmed this when he checked in the two obvious sources, the ' Street directory ' section of the latest annual *Kelly's Post Office London directory,* and *Bartholomew's reference atlas of Greater London.* He also tried without success the *Geographia Greater London atlas* and the new 1970 edition of William Kent *An encyclopaedia of London.*

The most authoritative source in such matters is the list issued by the London County Council *Names of streets and places in the administrative county of London* (fourth edition 1955), but Torrington-street did not appear there either. This immediately raised the suspicion in the librarian's mind that what he had embarked upon was not a problem in geography but a historical quest. This was reinforced when he tried the first edition of this work, published in 1901: Torrington-street, postal district WC, in the parish of Bloomsbury, and in the metropolitan borough of Holborn, was clearly listed, with the locality given as Keppel-street. A more precise indication was given by James Elmes *A topographical dictionary of London* (1831): ' Torrington-St., Russell-square, is the first turning on the right hand side of Keppel-street, going from the square '. Keppel-street was easily located in *Bartholomew*, but clearly did not lead from Russell-square: in between the two stood the very substantial bulk of the University of London Senate House.

Amid the 70 loose sheets making up the Pergamon Press *Atlas of London* (1968) are a number of reproductions of early maps. On the B R Davies map of 1851 the librarian found that Keppel-street did indeed extend to Russell-square: with the aid of a reading-glass he was able to make out Torrington-street, the first turning on the right, going from the square.

A commemorative booklet issued in June 1938 by the University of London, *The Senate House and library*, described the acquisition by the University in 1927 with the help of a gift of £400,000 from the Rockefeller Foundation of a site in Bloomsbury 1,190 feet by 480 feet north of the British Museum for use as its headquarters. This obviously incorporated Torrington-street, and although it was mentioned nowhere in the booklet it appeared clearly as a short but broad tree-lined avenue right in the centre of an aerial view taken in 1925. A later aerial view of the completed building left the librarian in no doubt that the site of the former Torrington-street is immediately below the main tower block which so dominates Senate House and comprises the main bookstack of the library of the University of London.

The last case reminds us too that there are specialised atlases devoted to reproducing for us the outlines of the world as it used to be, and while thematic atlases such as the *Oxford economic atlas of the world* (third edition 1965), or the *National atlas of disease mortality in the United Kingdom* (second edition 1970), being specifically subject sources, are outside the scope of this book, an exception is made for this very important category of historical atlases.

Case 170: A schoolboy visited the reference library one afternoon in search of the site of Brunanburh, 'where there was a famous battle', as he described it. The index to *Shepherd's historical atlas* provided a location immediately on a map of 'England in the ninth century', the conventional crossed swords and the date 937 indicating the place and time of the battle in Cumberland.

Double-checking, as she had been taught to do with queries of this kind, the assistant found an apparent difference of opinion in R L Poole *Historical atlas of modern Europe,* with the putative site given as '? Brunswark or Birrenswark Hill, near Ecclefechan, co. Dumfries', which of course is in Scotland, not Cumberland. *Chambers's world gazetteer* added some background on the battle in which the West Saxons under Athelstan defeated the Danes, Scots, and Welsh, but went on to say: 'Many suggestions of the possible site include Bourne (Lincs), Birrenswark (Dumfriesshire), Burnley (Lancs)'.

Turning to the most authoritative work she could think of, the Oxford history of England series, she read in the volume by Sir Frank Stenton *Anglo-Saxon England* (second edition 1947), 'The site of the battle, which appears in the poem under the name Brunanburh, has not yet been identified'. A footnote referred to A Campbell *The battle of Brunanburh* (1938). In the circumstances the best she could do for her young enquirer was to explain this uncertainty, pointing out the positive location made in *Shepherd's historical atlas* as one possibility. As she was in the process of doing this, the case took one last twist: she noticed that the 'Cumberland' of the ninth century extended far into modern Scotland, and *Shepherd's* site was obviously identical with Birrenswark in Dumfriesshire.

(See also cases 154, 155.)

A guidebook is defined by the American Library Association as 'a handbook for travelers that gives information about a city, region or country, or a similar handbook about a building, museum, etc.' As such, it is obviously designed to accompany a voyager on his travels. Nevertheless, the superb organisation and attention to detail evidenced by some of the better examples make them key reference sources on the places that they treat, not only for geographical but also historical information. So much so indeed are they valued that some older editions are sought after as collector's items.

Particularly outstanding are the great guidebook *series,* with the volumes from the German firm of Baedeker still maintaining the lead they set almost 150 years ago. In France the various Guides Michelin remain in a class by themselves, and Britain's contribution is Muirhead's famous Blue guides. Of the titles from the US in this international league the Fodor Modern guides are perhaps the best known, but America's major contribution in this field has been the justly renowned American guide series, originally compiled during the years of depression by the Federal Writers' Project of the Works Progress Administration. This series, unlike the others, is confined in coverage to its home country.

Case 171: A regular reader, well known to the reference library staff as a local school teacher asked for help in locating a copy of ' Beddgelert ', the famous poem about the faithful hound who saved his noble master's young child from a wolf. The librarian vaguely remembered the story, and turned to the obvious source, the title and first line index in *Granger's index to poetry* (and its *Supplement*). With some surprise he found he was unable to locate an entry for the poem. He tried with similar lack of success the *Oxford companion to English literature,* Benet *The reader's encyclopedia, Brewer's dictionary of phrase and fable,* and the new two-volumed *Dictionary of literature in the English language* by Robin Myers.

Recalling that the poem was probably quite lengthy and thus possibly separately published, he attempted next to trace it in such bibliographies listing works by title as he could find: *British books in print, Books in print, the Cumulative book list* back to 1924, the *Cumulative book index* back to and including the *United States catalog* of 1928, and the *English catalogue of books* right back as far as 1801, all to no avail.

By this time he was running out of bibliographical sources to check, so he consulted one of his older colleagues. She too had only a misty recollection of the poem, but did recall that the story was associated with the village in Wales with the same name as the poem, Beddgelert. This, of course, was a vital clue. The establishment of provenance in an enquiry immediately opens up the topographical sources of information. Straight away the librarian turned to his guide books and among the Ward Lock Red guides soon found the one covering Beddgelert, *North Wales (southern section)* (fifteenth edition 1964), where he read that 'The village has also become known through the story of Gelert, Llewelyn's faithful dog'. Persisting with this approach he soon lighted upon the clue he was seeking: H L V Fletcher *North Wales* (1955), after outlining the legend, mentioned 'William Spenser, who retold it in a poem familiar now to half the children in Great Britain'.

Puzzlingly, however, this William Spenser was unknown to *Granger's,* and even more surprisingly to the British Museum *General catalogue of printed books.* Slightly chastened, the librarian returned to his guidebooks, where in *Wales* (fifth edition 1969) in the Blue guides series he was gratified to find that 'Beddgelert is traditionally " the grave of Gelert ", the hero of a legend first made familiar by the verses of the Hon. Wm. Spencer in 1800'. Not only was he now provided with a date, but he had an alternative spelling of the poet's surname. Taking no chances this time he checked first in the British Museum *General catalogue.* Under 'Spencer, William Robert' he found listed not only his *Poems* (London, 1835 and London, 1811) and *Miscellaneous poems* (1812) but also *Gelert's grave; or Llewelyn's Rashness; a ballad . . . To which is added that favourite Welsh air 'Beddgelert' as sung by the ancient Britons* (Carnarvon, [1850?]). As might have been expected neither of these two works were in the library, and so the librarian turned to *Granger's* for the third time. And there, under 'Spencer', at last he found the elusive entry, in the English (as opposed to Welsh) spelling, *Beth Gelert.* In a moment he had turned to the main title sequence where the locations are to be found. Seven locations he turned up, all in anthologies, two of which he then discovered in the library catalogue, and one he was able to produce from the stacks for the patient reader.

[The recent (1970) edition of *Brewer's dictionary of phrase and fable,* unlike the earlier ones, does have an entry under 'Beddgelert', recounting the legend but making no reference either to Spencer or the poem. The earlier editions have no entry under 'Beddgelert' but summarise the story under 'Beth Gelert' adding that it is 'A ballad by the Hon. William Robert Spencer (1769-1834) based on traditional legend'.]

Guidebooks are particularly useful sources for town plans, for which librarians are frequently asked. The great atlases of course include such street plans for the world's major cities (see case 147 above), and although few libraries have troubled to build up anything like an extensive collection, most towns of any size have separately-published plans of their own area. Nevertheless, the most convenient and up-to-date source to turn to is often a good guidebook. In this particular context also come those hybrid publications, part-atlas, part-gazetteer, part-guidebook, designed especially for the motorist, *eg*, Automobile Association *Road book of England and Wales.*

Case 172: 'Do you have a street plan of Skopje?' was an enquiry passed on to a large research library from the office of a national newspaper. Somewhat tentatively, since he had his doubts about the spelling, the librarian checked first in the *Times atlas* to see where the place was. He learned that it was a town in Makedonia, Yugoslavia, and that the spelling he had used was indeed correct, although the word 'Uskub' in parentheses below did indicate an alternative name. Not surprisingly, the atlas had no street plan—the place was obviously not a major city—but the librarian thought it would be useful to have an idea of its size before proceeding further.

Webster's geographical dictionary (1967 printing) described it as a commercial and industrial centre, a cathedral and university city, and an ancient capital of Serbia. Also known as Skoplje, and in earlier days as Scupi, its population (no date) was 171,893. *Columbia Lippincott* (1961) added Justinia Prima as another former name, but gave the 1948 census figure of population as 91,557. The recent *Penguin encyclopedia of places* (1971) had a population figure (dated 1961) identical with *Webster's,* but added the vital news that ' In 1963 it was largely destroyed by an earthquake which killed more than 1,000 people '.

It was obvious that to be useful any map would have to be later than 1963. The only city plan accompanying the map of Yugoslavia in the *Atlante internazionale del Touring Club Italiano* (eighth edition 1968) was of the capital Beograd (Belgrade), so the librarian's thoughts turned to guidebooks. A convenient bibliography he had used before in similar cases was J A Neal *Reference guide for travellers* (1969). The 7,500-entry place index soon directed him to no fewer than seven guidebooks which included Skopje. A glance at the descriptions in the main sequence enabled him to select the two most likely titles: *Baedeker's touring guide to Yugoslavia* (1964), containing 14 town plans, and *Nagel's encyclopedia-guide to Yugoslavia* (1968), with street plans of at least 12 cities. One of the plans in *Baedeker* was indeed of Skopje and the accompanying text made it clear that account had been taken of the earthquake: ' It is intended to rebuild the city on the same site, but obviously the work of construction will take years. Numerous buildings still have to be pulled down, and thousands of people will have to live in provisional quarters for a long time to come '.

[Though much less generally available, another obvious source is the *Enciklopedija Jugoslavije,* (1955-) of which the latest volume to appear, volume 7, covers R-SRBIJA. Accompanying the five-page article on Skopje, illustrated with photographs showing earthquake damage, is a full-page street plan in colour.]

In a class by themselves are the Admiralty *Pilots,* also known as *Sailing directions,* designed to be used with the Admiralty charts. Now over seventy in number, and covering the seven seas, they are virtually guidebooks for the sailor, amateur as well as professional. Under constant revision, with regular cumulative supplements, they are indispensable, and as Aurousseau has pointed out their indexes collectively make up one of the most important of world gazetteers, even though it has no separate existence.

Case 173: ' Can you find me anything about Fastnet Rock?' was the enquiry received from a young reader who had been sent from the children's library into the reference library. The librarian knew nothing about the place at all, although he was familiar with the name from hearing it on the weather forecasts. They found on consulting *Chambers's world gazetteer* that it was a ' Rocky islet, with a lighthouse, 4m. SW of Cape Clear, S Ireland, giving name (for meteorological purposes) to the sea area lying between the S Irish coast and 50° N lat.' *Columbia Lippincott* added its latitude and longitude, and the height of the lighthouse (160 feet). The *Times atlas* located it easily enough, a pinhead-sized speck (with lighthouse) off the south coast of Ireland. The *Ireland* volume in Fodor's

Modern guides did not refer to it at all, and there were no more than a couple of lines in Muirhead's Blue guide to Ireland.

It seemed to the librarian at this stage that the next step was to check the appropriate *Pilot*. The index map and list in the latest annual *Catalogue of Admiralty Charts and other hydrographic publications* soon identified the volume he needed: the *Irish coast pilot* (eleventh edition 1968), a 577-page volume with illustrations. In the index were 15 references to Fastnet Rock: following them up produced an assemblage of data on the rock, its lighthouse, nearby shoals and banks, tidal streams, *etc,* including a ' view ' in the shape of a photographic illustration (original dated 1955).

The value of using place as an angle of approach in any kind of enquiry has been illustrated above (pages 199-200) and in *Case studies in reference work* (pages 20-1 and 41-2). Indeed Robert W Murphey claims that ' it is all but impossible to ignore geography in talking about any subject '.

But then the other side of the coin shows us that on occasion we may be better served with information about places from non-geographical sources. This is particularly true if up-to-the-minute data is required, for sources like directories and yearbooks are more frequently revised than many gazetteers or atlases (as case 160 above demonstrates). In particular, Murphey claims that nearly all general encyclopedias give a quarter or more of their space to entries under geographic place-names. Outstanding examples are *Americana* and *Columbia*. Specifically, as sources of maps it is worth noting two points about encyclopedias: firstly, many of the great general works like *Chambers's* or *Der grosse Brockhaus* include an atlas in one of their volumes; and secondly, within the text itself may be found many more maps. According to J P Walsh *General world atlases in print* there are no fewer than 652 maps of various kinds in *Encyclopaedia Britannica*. Particularly rich in maps (including many excellent town plans in colour) is the new *Brockhaus Enzyklopädie*: in the middle of *each* of the twenty volumes is what is in fact an atlas for that part of the alphabet treated in the volume. The MOT-OSS volume, for instance, has coloured maps of the Netherlands, North America and the North Pole, as well as town plans (with street indexes) for Munich, Naples, New York, Nuremburg, and Oslo. It will usually be found that maps in the better encyclopedias have been produced by world-famous map making firms such as Hammond (in *Americana*), Bartholomew (in *Chambers's*), and Rand McNally (in *Britannica*).

Case 174: When asked for a map of the Kiel Canal at as large a scale as possible the librarian in the university college library wasted no time in checking the atlases, for he felt sure that they would not help. His library had no large scale maps other than those for Britain, so it was more in hope than in expectation that he turned to the recently acquired volumes of the German *Brockhaus Enzyklopädie*. Under 'Kiel-Canal' he learned that this was the international designation for what in Germany is known as the Nord-Ostsee-Kanal, to which the entry referred him. Fortunately, the relevant volume had just been published, so he was able to turn quickly to the article with its seven-line bibliography and clear map showing the canal's whole length from the North Sea to the Baltic.

(*See also* case 172.)

5

'difficult' enquiries

ON THE 11.15 FROM PADDINGTON *en route* for the West of England to investigate the Boscombe Valley mystery Sherlock Holmes remarked to Watson, ' It seems, from what I gather, to be one of those simple cases which are so extremely difficult '. All experienced reference librarians have similar cases to relate, and like the great detective they are well aware that as a general rule there is nothing, *prima facie*, to signal the ' difficult ' enquiry. On the contrary, some of what turn out to be the most difficult problems can appear at first sight to be the most simple.

Case 175: What turned out to be a very long hunt for the date of the first use of the SOS distress signal was initiated by a national newspaper wishing to confirm the impression given in a film shown on television that it was by the sinking ' Titanic '. Several approaches immediately suggested themselves to the librarian: the date, 14th/15th April 1912, was easily ascertained from the nearest encyclopedia, thus opening up access to the newspaper and periodical press of the day; since such a huge disaster was almost certain to have led to an official enquiry a ' form ' approach through the parliamentary papers would be another possibility; it was known that the film was based on Walter Lord's book *A night to remember* (1956) and an approach that way seemed hopeful; even the subject approach revealed several promising aspects—radio, shipping, disasters, *etc*.

To start with, the source of the information was traced to Lord's statement: ' The clock in the wireless shack said 12.45 a.m. when

251

the *Titanic* sent the first SOS ever flashed by an ocean liner'. No references were given, but in the acknowledgements the author mentioned (among other sources) the British Court of Enquiry. Its report was traced without difficulty through the *General alphabetical index to the bills, reports, estimates, accounts and papers printed by order of the House of Commons and to the papers presented by command, 1910-1919,* and bore out the statement as to the time, but made no suggestion that it was the first SOS. More informative yet at the same time more circumspect than Lord was Geoffrey Marcus *The maiden voyage* (1969), described as 'the first full-scale, detailed, and documented survey of the great disaster': ' Phillips [senior wireless operator] bent over the table and sent out the general distress call, CQD, six times . . . " Send SOS," Bride [junior wireless operator] suggested, " It's the new call " '.

J N Kane *Famous first facts* (third edition 1964) explained that the first ' radio distress signal was the CQD signal which was established January 7, 1904, by General Order Circular 57 of the Marconi Company to become effective February 1, 1904 . . . The popular interpretation of the call was "Come quick—danger ". The SOS distress signal was adopted November 22, 1906, at the International Radio Telegraphic Convention in Berlin, Germany, and superseded the CQD call in July 1908 '. More to the point Kane went on to dispose of Lord's claim for the ' Titanic ': the first ' radio SOS from an American ship was transmitted by Theodore D. Haubner, operator of the Clyde liner "Arapahoe " . . . off Cape Hatteras, at 3.45 p.m. August 11, 1909. Both the SOS and CQD signals were sent . . . Foreign registry ships had used SOS signals earlier '. This evidence seemed positive enough, but the librarian recalled Margaret Hutchins' warning that Kane's book was ' insufficiently documented to be accepted without question by every scientifically minded seeker of facts '. More checking was obviously called for.

A quick glance in passing at four or five of the general encyclopedias was totally fruitless, but the date suggested an approach through the yearbooks. Immediate success was achieved with the *Year-book of wireless telegraphy and telephony* for 1913 (the first), where an article on ' Distress signalling' filled out the information on the history of the SOS already culled from Kane, but without mentioning any examples. The succeeding issue, however, in an article on ' Wireless and life saving' gave two instances, both in 1909: the ' Republic' wrecked in collision with the ' Florida ' on

23rd January, and the 'Slavonia' stranded off the Azores (no date). In neither case was it stated what signal was used; it could of course have been merely a general call for help without the extreme distress-call letter-code being used at all.

The time seemed ripe for a subject approach *via* the books on radio, shipping, disasters, *etc*. In the two-volumed *Dictionary of disasters at sea during the age of steam, 1824-1962* [1969], compiled by a former public librarian, Charles Hocking, there was no entry for 'Arapahoe', presumably because the ship was not lost, but both the 'Republic' and 'Slavonia' sinkings were described. The entries confirmed that both had sent radio distress signals, but only in the case of the 'Republic' did it state what the signal was: CQD! By way of contrast, G G Blake *History of radio telegraphy and telephony* (1926) affirmed categorically that the 'Slavonia' signal was SOS; though he described the 'Republic' collision of July [sic] as 'the first occasion when the importance of wireless telegraphy for life-saving at sea was brought to the notice of the public', he was careful to avoid saying exactly what distress signal was used. His suspicions aroused by the mistake about the date, the librarian checked the authority quoted by Blake, R A Gregory *Discovery* (1916). Here he found, firstly, the correct date (January); secondly, the collision described not as the 'first occasion' but merely as the 'first notable instance'; thirdly, the signal given as 'Am in distress and need assistance'; and fourthly, no categorical assertion as to the call from the 'Slavonia'. With Blake's unreliability thus demonstrated it was a disappointment to find him quoted as an authority in the OED *Supplement*.

But more frustration lay ahead. A careful check of the catalogue revealed two promising books specifically treating the topic under investigation: H E Hancock *Wireless at sea: the first fifty years* (1950) and Karl Baarslag *SOS: radio rescues at sea* (1937). The former included a dramatic account of the 'Slavonia' disaster, without revealing what signal had been sent; the latter devoted a whole chapter to the 'Republic' wreck, confirming the CQD call; but, amazingly, neither referred anywhere within their substantial bulk to the first use of SOS. Hancock, indeed, does not even mention SOS in the index: the fact that the work was published by the Marconi organisation may explain this, for, as Kane pointed out, the CQD signal superseded by the SOS was their own signal.

Recapitulating, the librarian noted that at this stage in his search

253

the only challenger to the American 'Arapahoe' was the 'Slavonia';
but the only evidence that the sos signal had in fact been used was
the statement by the unreliable Blake. With such inconclusive secondary sources, he felt it was time to turn to the primary sources in
the contemporary press. He had discovered from Hocking's careful
compilation that the disaster had occurred on 11th June 1909, just
two months before the 'Arapahoe' incident. Going by the indexes,
limited in number in 1909, the periodical press did not look too
promising: the only article in the *Engineering index* of any relevance was 'Wireless telegraphy for marine intercommunication' in
the *Electrician* for 1910, a technical account merely mentioning the
'Republic' and 'Slavonia' wrecks. It was then thought that a
search through the pages of the periodicals themselves might be
fruitful. There was no English wireless periodical at the time (at
least the *Newspaper press directory* knew of none), for *Wireless
world* did not start till 1911, so the *Electrician* was tried as the next
best thing. The issue for 29th January carried an account of the
'Republic' collision, without saying which signal had been used,
but the following week's number had an irate letter from the depart-
mental manager of Marconi's Wireless Telegraph Co (Ltd) claiming
'the operator . . . preferred to put his trust in the " C.Q.D." of the
Marconi organisation rather than employ the arbitrary, and as yet
unfamiliar, " S.O.S." of the Convention'. For the 'Republic' wreck
then, this could be regarded as conclusive evidence. Maddeningly,
the long account of the 'Slavonia' in the issue for 18th June was
found to be lacking the essential detail—the actual distress call used.

In the *Index to the Times* nothing could be found under 'Slavonia'
but eventually no fewer than 17 references were located under 'shipping casualties'. Following them up one by one the librarian read
in the issue for 18th June: 'Mr Meyer Juergens, Marconi's wireless
telegraph operator in the Batavia, reports that on June 10, about 11
a.m., he received a message from the Slavonia that she was stranded
off Flores Island at 2.30 a.m. She said " Come quick. Danger " '.

Having thus eliminated the only remaining challenger to the
'Arapahoe', the librarian decided that he had reached the time to
call a halt, and to report his sadly inconclusive findings.

The knowledge that such requests for specific items of information statistically make up the bulk of enquiries in libraries of all

types and are usually easy to understand should not obscure the fact that they occasionally lead to very extensive searches. As was illustrated in *Case studies in reference work,* pages 10-13, the term ' quick-reference ' is not always a synonym for a factual enquiry.

Case 176*:* One could scarcely ask for a more straightforward factual enquiry or one more appropriate to a bibliographically-inclined librarian than the letter received by a university library asking for the first appearance in print of Samuel Johnson. The arrangement of the fifty-odd columns devoted to Johnson in the *Cambridge bibliography of English literature* makes it difficult to determine with any ease the chronological order of his publications, so the librarian decided to try the standard bibliography of Johnson (as indicated by CBEL and Walford), W P Courtney *A bibliography of Samuel Johnson* (revised edition 1915). The library catalogue soon indicated the whereabouts of a copy, and he was encouraged to discover that the entries for his works were arranged by date of publication. At the head of the list was *A miscellany of poems by several hands* published at Oxford in 1731, containing ' the first printed composition of Johnson ', a Latin translation of Pope's *Messiah.* Certainly, this seemed to be Samuel Johnson's first venture into print, but the librarian did wonder whether it was quite what his correspondent wanted —it was not, after all, an original composition, neither was it in English. His doubts were increased when he read in the standard edition of *Boswell's Life of Johnson* (1934-50) that this was a Christmas exercise, done for his tutor at Oxford while an undergraduate of nineteen, and printed without his knowledge, and to his anger.

To be safe, the librarian thought that he should also give details in his reply of Johnson's earliest *original* printed work in English, but when he came to look at the second item listed in the Courtney bibliography he encountered another problem, for the entry referred to Johnson's stay during 1732 at the house of Thomas Warren, the bookseller. It was during this visit that ' He contributed some numbers to the periodical Essay printed in Warren's newspaper. This was the *Birmingham Journal,* and in the office of the *Birmingham Daily Post* is preserved the number (No. 28) for May 21, 1733. It is believed to be the only copy in existence '. The entry went on to quote Boswell: 'After very diligent enquiry, I have not been able to recover those early specimens '.

The librarian thought it would be wise to investigate whether any further copies had come to light in the half century since the publication of Courtney. He knew from Walford and the *Cambridge bibliography* that a supplement to Courtney had been published as an article in the Oxford Bibliographical Society *Proceedings and papers* for 1938, but it was found to add nothing to what was known. Neither the *British union-catalogue of periodicals* nor the *Union list of serials* included the *Birmingham journal*, and the newspaper of that title listed in the *Times tercentenary handlist* was obviously a different publication, appearing from 1825 to 1869. There was no entry at all in R T Milford and D M Sutherland *A catalogue of English newspapers and periodicals in the Bodleian Library, 1622-1800*, and the entry in G A Cranfield *A handlist of English provincial newspapers and periodicals, 1700-1760* (1952) was very tentative: '[14 Nov? 1732]-[Feb 1734?]'. The only location given was for the solitary copy in the *Birmingham post* office (and a facsimile of this in the Birmingham Reference Library). In K K Weed and R P Bond *Studies of British newspapers and periodicals from their beginning to 1800: a bibliography* (1947) he traced a reference to J Macray 'Dr Johnson's early contributions to a Birmingham newspaper' in *Notes and queries* for 1868. Upon examination this turned out to be an enquiry from a correspondent, quoting Boswell, about the location of these early essays. It received no reply.

With the bibliographical trail so obviously cold the librarian turned finally to the great multi-volumed *Yale edition of the works of Samuel Johnson*, where in the editorial notes to volume one (1958) it summarised the whole position, thus confirming his fears: 'Towards the end of 1732 Johnson accepted an invitation to visit his old school friend Edmund Hector, now practising as a surgeon in Birmingham. Hector lodged with Thomas Warren, the bookseller-publisher of the *Birmingham Journal*, to which Johnson soon contributed his first series of periodical essays, his first appearance in print except for his Latin translation of Pope's *Messiah* made at Oxford . . . No file of the journal is known, and Johnson's first printed essays therefore are lost'.

(*See also* case 151.)

As has been explained, the difficulties encountered with some of these seemingly simple factual enquiries are not always apparent at the outset. With certain categories of queries, however, the alert librarian can learn with experience to identify the potentially thorny problems in advance. Questions posed in a form which is the reverse of what would normally be expected are obvious candidates and have already been exemplified earlier (pages 207-8 and 234-5), and *Case studies in reference work,* pages 140-2). These may be biographical queries where the reader knows something about the man he is looking for but not his name, *eg,* ' Has anyone ever won the Victoria Cross twice?' or ' What was the name of the artist who demonstrated his skill for the Pope merely by drawing a perfect circle free-hand?' Very commonly the enquirer will have the definition of the object he is interested in, and will want to know what it is called, *eg,* ' What is the name for a spade with the blade set at right angles to the handle?' or ' What do you call the jutting-out part of a stage in a theatre?' What makes these problems so difficult is that most of the reference books are arranged the other way round, *eg,* the biographical sources under names and the dictionaries under words, and alternative paths to the solutions have to be found.

Case 177: ' What do you call the part of a knife that fits into the handle?' was the enquiry received by phone one evening in a large city reference library. In the past with similar enquiries for the names of parts of objects the librarian had found useful the diagrams in the great encyclopedic dictionaries. He could find no illustration of a knife in *Webster's third new international dictionary,* but in *Funk and Wagnalls new standard dictionary* he found no fewer than twelve different types illustrated; none of them, however, gave him the word he was seeking.

He turned to the *Duden pictorial encyclopaedia in five languages,* but the labelled illustration of the knife did not show the part he was looking for. He then tried *Roget's thesaurus of English words and phrases* under such terms as ' knife ', ' handle ', ' spike ', but without success. Turning to the American *Roget's international thesaurus* he had no luck with ' knife ' or ' handle ', but under ' spike ' among terms like ' cusp ' and ' tine ' he eventually discovered ' tang '. This was confirmed as the word he was after by the *Shorter Oxford dictionary,* which gave 1440 as the date of its earliest recorded use.

[The word does appear in the English *Roget's,* listed under ' projection '. There is also a diagram of a tang, clearly labelled as such, in both *Webster's third* and *Funk and Wagnalls;* in the former it is part of a file, in the latter it is part of a sword.]

Problems of a similar nature are raised by readers asking for the sign or symbol of this or that; or even more difficult, asking what a particular symbol signifies. Outside the fields of science and technology there is no really satisfactory reference work to turn to—problems of arrangement are of course formidable—but the encyclopedic dictionaries can again often be of assistance.

Case 178: When asked one busy evening for the symbol for Young's modulus the assistant in the small borough reference library felt at first that this was a problem beyond her. But then she thought that she could at least try to find out what it was, so she turned to *Webster's third new international dictionary*. There she learned that it was ' the ratio of the tensile stress in a material to the corresponding tensile strain ', but there was no symbol mentioned. She did not understand the definition, and was about to try one of the engineering handbooks, when she recalled that the second edition of *Webster's* had a special appendix 'Arbitrary signs and symbols '. As in many libraries, the second edition had been retained on the shelves even after the publication of the third, so she found it directly to hand. She found that one of the sections of this appendix dealt with ' physics, engineering, weights and measures '. After a moment's perusal of the list she spotted the symbol she was looking for: the upper-case letter E. Surprisingly though, the entry in the main sequence of the dictionary referred to the ' elasticity' entry where a detailed explanation with formula was found, but neither entry gave the actual symbol, or even referred to the list in the appendix.

Case 179: A commercial artist who said he was designing a menu card for a new restaurant asked the librarian if she could find some signs or symbols to represent the four seasons. In the ' astronomy ' section of the 'Arbitrary signs and symbols ' appendix to *Webster's new international dictionary* she found the twelve signs of the zodiac, divided into four groups of three each to represent the seasons. But the enquirer was not too happy with this: ' Surely there must be separate signs for the individual seasons?'

One of the reference works recommended by both Walford and Winchell, *Symbols, signs and their meanings* (1960) by Arnold Whittick, had proved helpful in the past: part III is an encyclopedic dictionary of 173 pages alphabetically arranged under the names of the symbols, *eg*, eagle, leek, phoenix, swastika. Using the accompanying index, the librarian was able to discover the almond tree, or the colour green, can be used to represent spring but she could trace no symbols for the other three seasons, apart from the signs of the zodiac already seen. The library's own subject catalogue revealed an earlier work, not listed by Walford or Winchell, *Book of signs* (1930) by Rudolf Koch. When examined this was found to lack both contents-page and index, but glancing through the text she noticed chapter 8, 'Astronomical signs'. A closer look soon produced four large, clear signs for spring, summer, autumn, and winter.

It is also possible to generalise about the higher-than-average difficulty of, for instance, statistical enquiries, or reader's advisory work; the former because of the inherent problems of statistics (see *Case studies in reference work*, pages 98-103), the latter on account of the greater degree of judgement necessary to match the right book and the right reader (see *Case studies in reference work*, pages 22-6, 121-2, 128-31).

Case 180: A request forwarded to a large county library headquarters from one of the branches asked simply for a book on ' how to make a sand table '. The reference librarian dealing with subject requests had never heard the term before so he thought he had better look it up. It was not mentioned in any of the major encyclopedias to hand (*Britannica, Chambers's, Americana, Collier's, Everyman's*), or in the British dictionaries he tried first (OED, *Shorter Oxford, Oxford illustrated, Concise Oxford*), but he did find a series of definitions to choose from in *Webster's third* and in *Funk and Wagnalls*.

The actual tracking down of the relevant entries, however, provided him with an object lesson in alternative methods of dictionary arrangement. *Funk and Wagnalls'* stated policy is that ' Derivatives, compounds, and phrases are frequently run in under the root or principal word ', and so ' sand-table ' was found amid the subsidiary entries like ' sand-bank ', ' sand-crab ', ' sand-dune ', ' sand-shoe ', all ranged under the main heading ' sand ', which in its turn was followed by the main entries for 'sandal', 'San Diego', 'sandwich', *etc.* In *Webster's third,* on the other hand, ' instead of encyclopedic treatment at one place of a group of related terms, each term is defined at its own place in the alphabet '. ' Sand table ' was therefore found as a main entry among the other entries for ' sandbank ', ' sand crab ', ' sand dune ', ' sand shoe ', *etc* (*see also* pages 130-1).

Of the five definitions offered, two the librarian rejected right away: ' part of a papermaking machine ' (*Funk and Wagnalls*), and ' an inclined table used for concentrating ores ' (*Webster's third*). After some reflection he felt able to eliminate two more: ' a table having a thin layer of sand spread upon its surface: used in schools for writing upon before the advent of blackboards ' (*Funk and Wagnalls*), and ' a usu. reinforced table with raised edges holding sand for children to mould ' (*Webster's third*).

That left only ' a table bearing a relief model of a section of terrain built to scale of hardened sand that usu. reproduces the contours, streams, trees, and buildings for the study or demonstration of military tactics ' (*Webster's third*). Armed with such a precise specification, the reference librarian felt much more confident in advancing upon the bibliographies. He decided to try CBI first, not only because it was American but because of its dictionary arrangement; he was sure that if there were anything to be found he would speedily discover it under ' sand table '. And so it proved: within minutes he had two titles, both (to his amazement) British. Furthermore, despite its age T W Sloman *Building and modelling sand tables* (1943) was still listed in *British books in print,* and so a copy was ordered. The second title, A W Valentine *Sand table exercises* (tenth edition 1949) was obtained through the regional interlending system, and ' exercise number one ' was found to be on the construction of a sand table.

We know from the philosophers of the special difficulties in proving a negative, and as soon as the reference librarian spots that the question he has been asked requires him to do just this he knows that he may be faced with a considerable challenge. Some such queries bear their character plain for all to see, *eg*, ' Is it true that Shakespeare had never met a Jew when he wrote *The merchant of Venice*?' but with others their nature may be concealed, *eg*, ' Is so-and-so still alive?' ' Did Sir Arthur Conan Doyle invent skiing?'

The hapless librarian who sees such an enquiry bearing down upon him may sometimes be deceived by its form into regarding it as a harmless fact-finding or material-finding problem. The realisation that he may have to prove a negative to conclude an investigation satisfactorily sometimes only dawns upon him when he has searched for some time without finding anything. What in fact happens in such cases is that the librarian starts out as usual in search of positive information on the topic of the enquiry, let us say the meetings between Mary Queen of Scots and Elizabeth Queen of England. When the investigation fails to reveal any evidence on the subject at all suspicions are aroused that perhaps the two queens never did meet. But suspicion is not proof, and lack of evidence in support of a proposition does not mean that the contrary is true. It is at this stage that such an enquiry turns into a search for information that would disprove the proposition, evidence that would show conclusively that Mary and Elizabeth did not meet. But by their very nature, history books relate those events that did occur, rather than those that did not; and biographers concentrate on what their subjects did with their lives, not what they omitted to do. Evidence to prove a negative is much harder to come by.

It so happens that in the illustration here given the failure of Mary and Elizabeth to meet is so notoriously one of the great tragic ' ifs ' of history that the evidence is available in the biographies (although not without a deal of searching), *eg*, in Antonia Fraser *Mary Queen of Scots* (1969) we read : ' the meeting between Elizabeth and Mary, which has been so often fabled by poets and dramatists . . . was destined never to take place '. With other queries similarly requiring proof of a negative the librarian will find it less easy to reach such a firm conclusion.

Case 181: The commercial librarian who was asked 'Are there any drive-in cinemas in Britain?' guessed right away that he was faced with proving a negative. In other words, he felt sure that the answer

261

was no, given the British climate and declining audiences for the regular cinema, but how could he demonstrate this?

A trifle uncertain how to begin, he decided first to make a quick check of the general periodical indexes, working backwards from the most recent. The appropriate subject-heading in the *Library Association subject index/British humanities index* appeared to be ‘cinemas’, but none of the references over the previous ten years related to drive-ins. Under the term ‘drive-in’ there were no entries at all. His confident assumption that there were no such cinemas in Britain was shaken when the *International index* (under ‘drive-in theaters’) directed him to a photograph and short description in the *Illustrated London news* of 22nd July 1961 of Denmark’s first drive-in cinema ‘built in an old gravel pit about 15 miles from the capital’. If the Danish climate was not too inhospitable, perhaps the British climate was not such an obstacle after all! The complementary H W Wilson index the *Readers' guide to periodical literature* used ‘moving picture theatres, open air’ as a heading, but the references were to American drive-ins. The librarian was interested to learn in passing of the advent of drive-in church services and even drive-in funeral parlors (‘Time saved for busy mourners’).

Second thoughts suggested to the librarian that the trade directories and yearbooks might be a more likely source of information. Henderson *Current British directories* listed only one, the *Kinematograph and television year book,* which gave the number of British cinemas in 1969 as 1,581, but did not indicate whether any were drive-ins. It did, however, give 4,500 as the number of US drive-ins. These figures were confirmed by the volume beside it on the shelf, the much more substantial *International motion picture almanac.* The section treating ‘The industry in Great Britain and Ireland’ gave the 1969 figure of 1,581 cinemas, but no drive-ins were mentioned. The comparable American statistics ‘as of June 1970’ showed some 4,500 drive-in theatres, ‘accounting for approximately 23 per cent of the total box office gross’. A 30-page list of drive-in theatres was also included, all in the US or Canada.

David Woodworth *Guide to current British journals* quickly enabled him to identify the most likely trade journal, the *Kine weekly,* ‘aimed at the cinema manager’. But the entry also made clear that there was no index published, neither was it covered by any of the abstracting or indexing services; in other words, it was typical of its kind (see pages 61-2). It was clear that there was no alternative to a page-by-page plod through the weekly issues. The librarian searched his conscience and decided that he could not in fairness to his other waiting readers devote to this search the time that it would obviously take. He determined to spend no more than five minutes on a rapid skimming through the pages of the last two or three years, and if nothing emerged, to ask his enquirer to call in himself to continue the search. Before this self-imposed time limit was up, as luck would have it, his eye lighted upon a paragraph on the issue for 15th June 1967: 'If plans mature, Liverpool will have the first drive-in cinema in this country'.

Encouraged by this find to explore a little further, he made straight for the *Index to the Times,* certain now that such a landmark as Britain's first drive-in cinema would not be overlooked. Searching forward this time from his *terminus a quo* of June 1967, he discovered the appropriate heading to be 'films: theatres'. His persistence was in due course rewarded with this item in the issue for 17th February 1969: 'Associated British Picture Corporation is renewing its attempts to open the first drive-in cinema in Britain. Four times in the past four years the company has had to abandon plans after objections from the Ministry of Transport and from local residents.'

However, despite a careful scanning of the *Index* for the succeeding months no further mention was traced. And there the query had to be left, with the presumption that Britain still had no drive-in cinema, but lacking conclusive proof later than February 1969.

(*See also* cases 116, 154.)

Such problems arise frequently in bibliographical search work where after a comprehensive check the librarian suspects that the title he is searching for does not exist, either because it has been wrongly described, or, even though correctly described, it has not yet been published. Perhaps more often than not the librarian is correct in his suspicions, but to convince a reader that a book he has seen advertised (and perhaps even reviewed) has not yet been published is a task of a magnitude appreciated only by those who have tried to do it. And where the enquirer has got the details wrong, and the librarian cannot discover where the error lies, to prove that such a work does not exist is often impossible. (*See* cases 28, 36, 40.)

Enquiries about anecdotes make up another category about which the librarian does well to be forewarned. They are difficult to document by their very nature, many of them being purely oral in origin. The criteria by which they are judged very often are not accuracy, scholarship, or historical significance, but simply whether they make good stories. And so frequently the conclusion of an investigation into an anecdote is simply that it is an anecdote—an amusing or revealing story, possibly true, but possibly not.

Case 182: An enquiry posed in a large university library sought chapter and verse for the story of Charles II's enquiry to the Royal Society: ' Why is it that a dead fish placed in a pail of water adds to its weight, but a live fish does not?' Checking in the 586-page *Record of the Royal Society* (fourth edition 1940) the librarian discovered that the King, the official founder of the Royal Society, was in the habit of asking such questions of the learned members, but the work nowhere referred to this particular enquiry. A similar lack of success attended his consultations of Margery Purver *The Royal Society: concept and creation* (1967), and Sir Harold Hartley *The Royal Society: its origin and founders* (1960).

The chapter devoted to Charles II in this last work concluded with a note on the authorities used, describing Osmund Airy *Charles II* (1901) as the best life, commending Sir Arthur Bryant *King Charles II* (1931) and praising the article on Charles by Sir A W Ward in the *Dictionary of national biography*. The librarian tried DNB first, as the most convenient to hand, and found a very long article indeed, but no answer to his problem. Bryant had a number of references to the Royal Society and Charles' interest in science, but did not refer to the anecdote. Airy's four hundred pages was found to lack an index, as did a number of other biographies located, such as John Hayward *Charles II* (1933). There was an index to A I Dasent *The private life of Charles the Second* (1927), on the other hand, and to Hesketh Pearson *Charles II: his life and likeness* (1960), but neither mentioned the Royal Society. By this time the librarian felt distinctly disinclined to continue searching in this desultory way through the several other lives of Charles II that he had noticed in the catalogue so he contented himself with an examination of the most recent, Maurice Ashley *Charles II: the man and the statesman* (1971), described on its dust jacket as ' the first full scale study of the king for some forty years '—but to no avail.

A treasure house of lore about anecdotes is *Notes and queries* and it was to the cumulated indexes back to 1849 that the librarian turned next. There he found, stretching back over the generations, this very problem raised again and again. In the issue for 25th February 1939 a correspondent related the story of the King's question to the Fellows as to ' why a live fish weighs more than a dead one, and that, after listening to discussion for some time with amusement, he discomfited them by asking whether any of them had begun by verifying the virtual statement in dispute '. The correspondent wanted to know ' Where does the story come from?', but he got no answer.

Similarly unanswered went two previous enquiries, one, on 15th March 1873, asking ' What is the original authority?', the other in the issue for 19th April 1902 : ' How early a record of this anecdote is known to " N. and Q.", the readers of which, taken together, are so much more learned than any individual?' Yet another correspondent asking in the number for 23rd February 1891 for the ' original authority ' for the story was more fortunate insofar as he received a reply—although it did not answer his question. According to Professor C Tomlinson, the author of a book on the Royal Society, ' It may be classed with the silly jokes which were formerly flung at the head of science '. He had not found it in the authorities on the history of the Royal Society such as Wallis, Sprat, Birch, Thomson, or Weld. Among later correspondence on this issue one writer in the issue for 25th March 1893 warned glumly : ' To trace the paternity of this story would indeed be a difficult task '.

Difficulties involving the meanings of words do arise occasionally over the problem of denotation versus connotation. The denotation of a word is its meaning, pure and simple, but many words also carry intellectual and often emotional overtones. These comprise a word's connotation, which is not only what it says but also the additional force it has for its readers or hearers. A dictionary can deal satisfactorily only with denotations. A simple but vivid illustration is provided by the handful of well-known four-letter Anglosaxon words. These have perfectly precise denotations but until comparatively recently their connotations were such that they were not even listed by the standard dictionaries. They now appear in some recent dictionaries with their denotations plain for all to see, but all that the lexicographer can do about their connotations is to affix some such label as ' (*vulg*) ', which the *Penguin English dictionary* attaches to a word as ' a warning that it is considered highly offensive by most social groups '.

Connotations which words attract for historical reasons can sometimes grow into further denotations, additional to or even separate from the basic denotation. 'Fascist ', for example, is now a term of abuse, and some dictionaries are beginning to recognise it as such, but in an older reference work such as *Funk and Wagnalls new standard dictionary* it simply denotes 'one of the Fascisti . . . a body of Italian nationalists, organised March, 1919, to oppose Bolshevism in Italy '.

Some of the most difficult questions of all to answer are those concerning usage, that is to say, the conventions of grammar and vocabulary, described by Eric Partridge as ' one of the most delicate characteristics of language '. Why, for example, should we always speak of having a tune on the *brain* (singular), yet invariably use the plural when blowing our *brains* out? What precisely is the difference between ' Due to his age he was unable to compete ' and ' Owing to his age he was unable to compete '? Is it preferable to say inadvisable or unadvisable, inessential or unessential, insupportable or unsupportable?

The truth is, of course, that all usage is relative, but the so-called ' myth of correctness ' often obscures the issue, and it is essential to remember that modern dictionaries are descriptive not prescriptive (see *Case studies in reference work,* pages 142-4). Fortunately there are available a variety of special-purpose dictionaries, chief of which is the world-famous H W Fowler *Modern English usage* (which does in fact discuss all the above conundrums).

Case 183: ' Is it correct to sound the " h " in hotel?' was the old lady's question in a small public reference library. Unfortunately, the assistant did not quite grasp the point of the question at first: to her the answer seemed obvious. *Webster's third* gave one pronunciation only, with the ' h ', and so did *Funk and Wagnalls* and the *Concise Oxford dictionary*. But then she found that both the OED and the *Shorter Oxford* gave two pronunciations, with and without the ' h '. The older *Webster's* threw some light on the scene with the note that the pronunciation without the ' h ' is an alternative British form, 'formerly the usual pron.' Finally, Fowler *Modern English usage* cleared the whole matter up: 'The old-fashioned pronunciation with the *h* silent is almost dead'.

An oft fatal affliction to which librarians, perhaps inevitably, are prone is their tendency to treat all sources as equal. This is an area of controversy, for there are those who maintain that discrimination between sources is the task of the reader, the librarian's responsibility ceasing once he has presented the alternative or conflicting sources for the reader's consideration. All would agree, however, that the librarian must be aware of varying sources, and must know when it is important to consult them.

Case 184: The request received in a university library for an impartial account of the British-Israelites was virtually two queries in one, for the librarian first had to find out what they were. It could possibly be a way of describing the Jewish community in Britain, although he had never heard the term so used before. His ignorance was apparently shared by the encyclopedias, for there was no mention in the indexes to *Britannica, Chambers's, Collier's,* or *Americana.* Of the major dictionaries he consulted OED, *Webster's third,* and *Funk and Wagnalls* before he traced in the 1955 'Addenda' to the *Shorter Oxford* an entry for British Israel: ' title of an organization that maintains that the British Commonwealth and the United States of America are the principal Israel nations of the world '. A reference was given to 'Anglo-Israel', where a fuller explanation was found in the form of an extract from the 1910 *Encyclopaedia Britannica: 'Anglo-Israelite Theory* . . . The contention that the British people . . . are the racial descendants of the " ten tribes " forming the kingdom of Israel, large numbers of whom were deported by Sargon, King of Assyria, on the fall of Samaria in 722 B.C. The theory (which is fully set forth in a book called *Philo-Israel*) rests on premises which are deemed by scholars . . . to be . . . unsound '.

Clearly then there was a literature on the topic. When a subject approach to the library's card catalogue produced no results the librarian turned to the bibliographies, consulting first the more recent volumes in the hope of a title in print that could be considered for purchase. There was no entry in *Subject guide to books in print*, nor could anything be traced under the title in *Books in print* or *British books in print*. The *British national bibliography* was searched next, in the expectation that its full cataloguing would enable some evaluation to be made of any material found. What was discovered fell into three main groups: a dozen or so small pamphlets mostly published either by the Society for Proclaiming Britain is Israel or the Covenant Publishing Company; two journals (a monthly, gratis, published by the SPBI, and a quarterly, at one shilling a number, published by the British-Israel World Federation); and a couple of more substantial works, also published by the Covenant Publishing Company, both in 1961, entitled *The drama of the lost disciples* and *Have you ever thought . . .? a young man's challenge*.

The *parti pris* nature of virtually all of this literature was evident, and when a similar crop was gathered from the British Museum *Subject index* and the *Cumulative book index,* the librarian decided it was time to try further afield.

With the *Essay and general literature* index from 1970 right back to 1900 he drew a complete blank, and a twenty-year search of the general periodical indexes produced no more than two references: nothing was found in the *Readers' guide to periodical literature;* in the *International index / Social sciences and humanities index* was a reference to C G Howie ' British-Israelism and pyramidology: the Bible and modern religions ', *Interpretation* 11 July 1957 307-23; and in both the *Library Association subject index / British humanities index* and the *International index / Social sciences and humanities index* appeared J Wilson ' British Israelism ', *Sociological review* ns 16 (March 1968) 41-57.

Before searching for these two journals he thought he would take the opportunity whilst with the periodical bibliographies to check if he could on their academic soundness and impartiality. The list of periodicals indexed at the front of the *International index* gave a Richmond, Virginia, address, but no publisher for *Interpretation*. The *Union list of serials* added its sub-title *a journal of bible and theology,* located it in over forty American libraries, and described it as the successor of the *Union Seminary review* which ran for 57 years. The *British union-catalogue of periodicals,* however, furnished no more than two locations, only one of which (Birmingham University) had the required volume. *British humanities index* gave no more than the mere title of the *Sociological review* in its list of periodicals indexed, but the corresponding list in *Social sciences and humanities index* showed it as thrice-yearly publication of the University of Keele. When a copy of the relevant issue was located in the library its academic *bona fides* was confirmed: edited by Professor W M Williams, assisted by a distinguished twelve-man editorial board, the particular number examined contained articles by contributors from five English and Scottish universities. The 17-page paper by John Wilson, lecturer in sociology at the University of East Anglia, was found to be an account of some of the results of research between 1963 and 1966 into the British Israel movement (which has claimed a membership of two million). Most significantly, the author stated ' No other objective study of the movement exists '.

There is also agreement that the librarian should attempt to double-check in many of those cases where the reader is seeking a specific factual answer. Just because a fact is so positive, so finite, and stands forth so proudly when enshrined in print, this does not always ensure that it represents the truth. What may appear as fact is often only opinion and even the very concrete and measurable facts of size and number, time and place, are occasionally matters of dispute (*see* pages 230-2).

Case 185: To dispose of a phone query asking for the height of Nelson's column, the famous monument in Trafalgar Square, London, would be the work of a moment: so thought the assistant in a busy public reference library. Almost immediately she found the answer in *Chambers's encyclopedia*: 184 feet. *Everyman's encyclopaedia,* however, gave 145 feet! Double-checking in *Britannica* produced a third figure of 170 feet 2 inches overall, including the 17 feet statue, and although *Americana* agreed with *Chambers's, Columbia* outbid them all with 185 feet! *Whitaker's almanack* gave a very precise 170 feet $1\frac{1}{2}$ inches.

Hoping that she might find specifically London sources more reliable she made first for the most authoritative source she could think of, the splendid multi-volumed *Survey of London* published by the London County Council. Trafalgar Square she found treated in volume 20, with a plate showing William Railton's original 1839 design for the monument. The text gave the height of the fluted column as 145 feet, which was a reduction on the original design, but omitted to say whether this included the square pedestal or the statue itself which was sculptured by Edward Hodges Baily. The *London* volume in the Red guide series was more explicit, averring that 'the total height of plinth, column, and statue is 170 feet 2 inches', but the *London* volume in the Blue guide series did not agree, giving 185 feet as its contribution. William Kent *Encyclopaedia of London* thought that the true figure was 184 feet 'from the pavement to the top of Nelson's hat'.

The most precise (but not necessarily thereby the most accurate!) measurements were found in David Piper *The companion guide to London* (second edition 1968) and F R Banks *London* (fifth edition 1971) in the Penguin guides, both of whom agreed on 167 feet $6\frac{1}{2}$ inches for the column plus 17 feet $4\frac{1}{2}$ inches for the statue, total 184 feet 11 inches.

Finally, in P W White and Richard Gloucester *On public view: a selection of London's open air sculpture* (1971), the librarian read: 'The total height of the original design was 203 feet high but it was reduced to 170 feet 6 inches in the interests of public safety'. With no fewer than seven variant measurements thus located in as many minutes, she decided to call it a day.

Now and then it will happen that the information the enquirer seeks is of so everyday a nature that the librarian may have to go to what can seem a ridiculous amount of trouble to run it to earth. In the words of a former editor of the *Times,* Sir William Haley, 'the matter of fact, though common, is seldom recorded'. Those who need convincing of this should choose any well-known figure from the current world of politics or entertainment or sport and then try to discover whether he (or she) wears spectacles for reading. The librarian must beware of dismissing any such enquiry as 'trivial'. To do so almost always involves a purely subjective judgement, putting the librarian's convenience before that of the reader. That is not to say that a librarian should provide the answers to all questions, any more than the physician should prescribe drugs for all symptoms. But he must treat each query seriously, explaining where necessary the reasons why he feels unable to furnish the answer. Perhaps the work has been set as a school task and the teacher expects his pupils to find the information for themselves; perhaps the search would be so time-consuming for the librarian that other enquirers would be kept waiting too long; perhaps the enquirer is wanting a specialist opinion which he should really be seeking from a professional source. To take such decisions, and particularly to justify them to the reader, is not an easy task; but it is one of the features that makes reference work a profession and not merely an answering service.

Case 186: The young assistant in a large city library was uncertain at first whether to take seriously a phone call asking for the inventor of the yo-yo, until a senior colleague reminded him that the toy industry did make a not inconsiderable contribution to the national economy. He soon learned that the yo-yo did not figure in E F Carter *Dictionary of invention and discoveries* (1966), and no mention was found in *Britannica, Chambers's, Americana, Collier's,* or several other encyclopedias. Even the *Oxford English dictionary* did not at first seem to know it, but eventually a definition was run down in the 'Addenda' to the third edition of the *Shorter* OED (1955): 'a toy resembling the old bandalore'. No derivation was given, but the date of the earliest occurence was quoted as 1932. A bandalore was defined as an obsolete term for a toy containing a coiled spring, which caused it, when thrown down, to rise again in the hand by the winding up of the string by which it was held (1790). *Webster's third new international dictionary* had a more compact definition, deriving the word from ' *yo-yo,* a trademark ', but gave no date.

Guessing that this would be just the sort of thing to interest *Notes and queries,* the librarian checked the index to the 1932 volume, thus bringing to light the very gratifying note in the number for 29th October: 'This popular string top, now selling by the million, appears by its name, to have originated in China or Japan. Some day somebody will write to " N. and Q." to know when it was first introduced, so it may be as well to note that it became common all over Great Britain in 1932.' A month later there was a much fuller note tracing the bandalore/yo-yo back to the Greeks, suggesting that the word 'spring' in the OED definition was a misprint for ' string ', and referring to a recent article in the *Illustrated London news.*

When consulted, this fully-illustrated article positively identified the yo-yo with the bandalore of antiquity which was shown quite clearly portrayed on a piece of Greek porcelain and became very popular in Britain around 1790. Some months later, however, again in *Notes and queries,* a correspondent pointed out the essential difference between the yo-yo and the bandalore. The latter has the string *fastened* to the axle or the disk, but in the yo-yo the axle *passes through a loop* in the winding and supporting string. The writer went on to say: ' It is really a very wonderful and novel invention. There is no game other than billiards that requires so delicate a touch '.

It seemed likely, then, that the yo-yo was indeed a recent invention, and a short search backwards from 1932 through the classified abridgements to the British patents in Class 132 (iii) Toys soon unearthed patent number 209,288, granted in 1924 to Charles Murray of the Philippines. The essence of his claim was the improvement in the old toy by having the string looped round rather than fastened to the stem of the spool. The accompanying illustration made it clear that here indeed was the inventor of the yo-yo, although the word itself was not used. Its probable American origin suggested that Mathews *Dictionary of Americanisms* might be helpful, and here the librarian found its origin given as ' you-you ', often used by children at play, with the earliest reference a 1932 application for registration of trade mark 300,504.

[An alternative approach, once the date of its introduction had been established from the dictionary, would have been to search the contemporary periodical indexes. This would have brought to light a number of interesting articles indexed in *International index,* although it is probable that the patents would still have required consulting for the name of the inventor. Surprisingly, the useful article from the *Illustrated London news* does not seem to be indexed anywhere, even in the Library Association *Subject index to periodicals,* which lists the journal as one of those analysed.]

Their textbooks usually warn reference librarians not to dispense medical or legal advice. This is sensible, for not only are these subject areas of a highly sensitive and often intensely personal character, but they can be exceedingly specialised. The risks, and of course the consequences, of misinformation are high. A recent report in the *Guardian* told of retribution overtaking a man who married his niece, despite his explanation to the magistrate that none of the books in the library suggested that it was illegal. And of course medicine and the law are the special preserves of two of the oldest and most articulate of the professions. For enquirers in real need, skilled advice is widely available, in some countries free of charge in appropriate cases.

That is not to say that a librarian should refuse to entertain queries in the fields of medicine or law: there are many instances where the provision of assistance is quite legitimate, and even a moderately alert librarian can usually distinguish such enquiries from those which are in fact asking for a medical or legal opinion.

Case 187: An enquiry as to the last amnesty in Britain was approached at first *via* the historical quick-reference books, such as *Steinberg's dictionary of British history* (second edition 1970), Sir Sidney Low and F S Pulling *The dictionary of English history* (new edition 1928), and *Newnes dictionary of dates* (second edition 1966). Failure to find anything at all suggested to the librarian that he might do better with constitutional or legal sources. There was no entry under 'amnesty' in either Norman Wilding and Philip Laundy *Encyclopaedia of parliament* (third edition 1968), or *Abraham and Hawtrey's parliamentary dictionary* (third edition 1970), but in Jowitt *The dictionary of English law* (1959) he read that an amnesty was ' an act of pardon or " oblivion " . . . by which crimes against the Government up to a certain date are so obliterated that they can never be brought into charge '. Three examples were quoted, the latest being given as ' 1747, 20 Geo.2, c52 '. This the librarian recognised as the lawyer's shorthand for an act of Parliament.

The *Chronological table of the statutes* gave him the short title of the act as ' General pardon ', but also made clear that it was no longer in force, having been repealed by the Statute Law Revision of 1867. Clearly this was an amnesty, but was it the latest? Perhaps the encyclopedias would help. *Chambers's* had no entry in its index for ' amnesty ', but *Britannica* had a main entry devoted to the subject in the course of which the librarian read: ' The last British amnesty was that of 1747 extending to participants in the second Jacobite rebellion '.

One of the greatest problems, and therefore one of the greatest challenges, that reference librarians face is that so often they are working against the clock. This is not simply a matter of information being called for on the instant (although this certainly happens frequently enough), but is due to the fact that in probably all libraries specialist reference staff are insufficient in numbers for the demands made upon them. There is always another enquirer waiting with his problem.

Case 188: In the course of a very busy evening with many readers waiting for help at the desk in a city reference library the telephone rang, demanding of course immediate attention. The caller was the local newspaper office, with a press deadline to meet, wanting to know as soon as possible ' What is a Lambeth degree?' Confirming first of all that it was an academic qualification, the librarian promised to call back as soon as possible. ' Can I hold on? It really is rather urgent ', pleaded his caller. The librarian looked round at his waiting readers, and decided he must be firm: ' No, I'll have to ring you back; we are very busy just now. I'll try to call you within the hour '.

Twenty minutes and five enquiries later the pace had slackened sufficiently for the librarian to get away from the desk, leaving his colleagues to cope. He was sufficiently familiar with the pattern of higher education in Britain to be aware that the London borough of Lambeth had not been favoured with a university, so he first checked the *Commonwealth universities yearbook,* the *International handbook of universities,* and the *World of learning.* Finding no Lambeth listed, he next tried *American universities and colleges,* where he discovered that Lambeth College, Tennessee, gives bachelor's degrees.

His enquirer, instead of expressing admiration at his speed and efficiency, seemed reluctant to accept this finding. In fact he was sure that it was not what he wanted. And so, after confirming that he could still be spared, the librarian resumed his search. In some perplexity where to turn, he tried the major encyclopedias (*Britannica, Chambers's, Americana, Collier's*) and the great unabridged dictionaries (OED and *Supplement, Webster's third, Funk and Wagnalls*), but without finding a mention. Moving to the lesser encyclopedias (*Columbia, Everyman's*) and more dictionaries, he at last found in the ever-valuable earlier edition of *Webster's* his first clue: 'An Oxford or Cambridge degree, conferred honoris causa by the Archbishop of Canterbury'. This was confirmed by the *Concise Oxford dictionary* (but not the *Shorter Oxford*).

The logical next step was to consult the appropriate yearbooks: the *Oxford university calendar,* the *Annual register* of the University of Cambridge, and the *Church of England year book.* He was quite taken aback to discover no trace of a Lambeth degree in their indexes, and a careful search through the text was equally fruitless.

When a check of the *British humanities index* and its forerunner the *Subject index to periodicals* produced nothing at all, one of his colleagues suggested that this was just the sort of enquiry to get into *Notes and queries.* And so it proved: a glance through the indexes commencing in 1849 produced at least forty references in the 19th century alone. Changing his tack and working backwards from the present day, the librarian found in the issue for 24th November 1942, apropos of another query, a quotation from *Halsbury's laws of England* (1910), where the right to confer degrees was listed as one of the special privileges of the Archbishop of Canterbury, a remnant of the Papal authority reserved to him by a 1533 statute of Henry VIII. As a final check he consulted the library's current (1955) edition of *Halsbury,* where in the ecclesiastical law volume he read: 'The Archbishop may confer all the usual degrees, with or without examination and on the laity as well as the clergy . . . These degrees (which are known as Lambeth degrees) confer no right to membership of any university. The recipient is entitled to wear the academic costume of the university of which the Archbishop is himself a member . . . The Lambeth degree in medicine does not entitle the holder to registration as a medical practitioner'.

(*See also* case 181.)

All librarians have problems put to them from time to time that they are unable to solve. Sometimes, as with medical and legal queries, the librarian is the wrong person to ask, and the enquirer who wants a painting valued, or wishes to know whether his invention has already been patented, or needs a letter translated from Chinese, merely has to be directed to an antique dealer, or to a patent agent, or to a professional translator. Now and then, however, even with enquiries legitimately addressed to him, the librarian has to admit that the problem is too difficult (*see* case 146).

More commonly, perhaps, the enquiry fails through no fault of the librarian himself, but simply because he exhausts all the available resources without finding what he wants (*see* cases 68, 75, 94).

With a long-drawn out enquiry it may well be that *force majeure* obliges the librarian to relinquish his search before all the possible resources, physical and human, within and without the library, have been tried. In such circumstances he will naturally explain to his enquirer exactly how matters stand, but it must be remembered that with some enquiries there genuinely is no answer, either because the question is intrinsically unanswerable, such as ' What will our diet be like in the year 2000?', or because the information is incomplete or disputed or lost. Children seem especially talented at thinking up such problems, and the solutions can be particularly difficult to explain to enquirers.

Case 189: A group of children came to the public library one day with a task set them by their teacher: to find how the spinning-jenny got its name. It was defined (as a mechanism for spinning more than one strand at a time) in the *Concise Oxford dictionary* and also in the *Shorter Oxford,* but in neither case was an explanation given of its origin. In the big OED the earliest recorded use was given as 1783, but a note warned : ' The reason for this use of the personal name is uncertain '.

In the circumstances the librarian wondered if he could find anything else to add to this dry, academic note. Surprisingly, *Brewer's dictionary of phrase and fable* had nothing to offer, neither Eric Partridge *Origins* nor *The Oxford dictionary of English etymology* had an entry, *Webster's third new international dictionary* laboured the obvious point that the expression was a nickname from the name Jane, and the older *Webster's* had no etymology at all. Then in *Funk and Wagnalls new standard dictionary* was found a quotation from G M Towle *Heroes of invention* (1890): ' James Hargreaves . . . made a spinning frame, with eight spindles and a horizontal wheel. This machine he called after his wife (Jenny) '. This confident assertion seemed so at variance with the scholarly hesitation of the OED that the librarian decided to pursue the matter further.

He knew that *Notes and queries* made a speciality of enquiries such as this, so he checked through the cumulated indexes. In the issue for April 1865 he discovered that this very problem had been a bone of contention for generations. In his *Compendious history of the cotton manufacture* Guest claimed that the machine was named after Jane, the daughter of Highs, a rival inventor. Most other writers maintained that Hargreaves called it after his own daughter Jane, but as the article pointed out, Hargreaves had no daughter! A dictionary of 1853, Pulleyn *Etymological compendium,* derived the name from Hargreave's [sic] wife Jane, but according to Baines *History of the cotton manufacture* the name of his wife was Elizabeth.

By now the librarian's sleuthing instincts were really roused. He recalled that he had not consulted the encyclopedias. He found that according to *Britannica* the machine ' is said to have been conceived when Hargreaves (in about 1764) observed the actions of a spinning wheel that had been accidentally overturned by his young daughter, Jenny . . . Several jennies, which he named after his daughter, were built and sold to help support his large family '. Finally, as a counter to his claim, he found that the author of the article on Hargreaves in the *Dictionary of national biography* referred to Thomas Highs, a rival claimant for the invention, who had a daughter Jane, while Hargreaves 'undeniably had not', but was nevertheless forced to conclude that the spinning-jenny was ' so called for unknown reasons '.

With DNB and OED thus concurring, the librarian had little choice but to agree. He explained this to the children, but suggested they copy out as a possible derivation the charming anecdote from *Britannica.*

(*See also* case 170.)

Explanations to the enquirer are also called for when he asks the wrong question: where he assumes, for instance, that there is a list of all the inventions in the world, or a book that can teach him how to lip-read; or where he expects a simple answer to a problem that admits of none, such as a summary of the effect of drinking on crime in the United States, or statistics on the number of cats in Scotland.

One final lesson it is hoped that the reader of this work and its predecessor will have learned : that the various categories of reference materials are not mutually exclusive. Actual experience as reflected in the case histories shows clearly that in practice the librarian may use encyclopedias for a bibliographical enquiry, may consult periodical indexes to help him find the meaning of a word, may use bibliographies to locate data about people, or may look in a dictionary for the history of a subject. The reader will also have noticed that many enquiries for their solution require the hunt to be pursued in and out of the various categories of reference materials, as the twisting course taken by the problem requires. The determination of a search strategy to guide the librarian through the various information sources, and its continual modification to take account of what the search reveals, is the very essence of the reference process.

further reading

SINCE THE PUBLICATION of the suggestions for further reading in *Case studies in reference work,* pages 157-8, the most important book on reference work to appear has been William A Katz *Introduction to reference work* (McGraw Hill, 1969), of which the second volume deals with reference services. A novel approach to the subject was taken by Donald J Sager *Reference: a programmed instruction* (Columbus, Ohio Library Foundation, 1968), the first such textbook in the field. *The present status and future prospects of reference/information service* (Chicago, ALA, 1967) contains the proceedings of a stimulating conference at Columbia University.

Thomas J Galvin has produced a second collection of thirty-five case studies, *Current problems in reference service* (Bowker, 1971), and Kenneth F Kister, his colleague at the School of Library Science, Simmons College, Boston, has compiled *Social issues and problems: case studies in the social sciences* (Bowker, 1968). Thomas P Slavens has also joined the ranks of the compilers of reference work case studies with his *Library case studies in the social sciences* (Ann Arbor, Campus Publishers, 1967).

index

OF ALL THE WORKS referred to in the text, only those that have major significance as reference or bibliographical sources are indexed here. The individual case histories are entered under a single descriptive phrase, *eg*, Nelson's column (case 185).

Author indexes *see* Indexes
Authors 185-6, 195-7; of quotations 90-8, 116-7, 134-5
Authors' and writers' who's who 185, 186
Autobiography 151, 152, 179-80, 180, 181, 211
Autographs 193, 212-3
Automobile Association *Road book of England and Wales* 247
Ayer's *Directory of newspapers and periodicals* 65, 69
Ayliffe, John, the forger (case 136) 199-200

Baedeker's guides 245, 248
'Bagford the biblioclast' (case 115) 168-9
Baillie, G H *Watchmakers and clockmakers of the world* 184
Bartholomew, J *Survey atlas of England and Wales* 215, 216, 219, 220, 221, 222, 223, 228, 230, 233, 240
Bartholomew, J G *Gazetteer of the British Isles* 81, 216, 219, 220, 230, 233, 234, 240
Bartholomew's reference atlas of Greater London 242
Bartlett, J *Familiar quotations* 88-100 passim, 102, 103, 105, 106, 107, 108, 109, 110, 111, 113, 115, 117, 119, 120, 121, 124, 125, 126, 128, 129, 130, 131, 133, 136, 138, 139, 140, 143, 144, 147
Basic English, Against (case 24) 43-5
'Beauty in the eye of the beholder' (case 61) 99
'Beddgelert' (case 171) 245-6
Belgium, Language conflicts in (case 50) 85
Bells, Manufacture of (case 9) 20
Benares (case 158) 229
Benét, W R *Reader's encyclopedia* 53-4, 238, 245
Bénézit, E *Dictionnaire critique et documentaire des peintres* . . . 157
Benham's book of quotations, proverbs and household words 88, 89, 91, 92, 93, 94, 95, 106, 108, 111, 112, 113, 115, 119, 121-2, 123, 124, 125, 126, 128, 129, 130, 131, 138, 139, 140, 146, 147
Berlin wall (case 147) 214-5

Berrey, L V and M van den Bark *The American thesaurus of slang* 131, 142
Besterman, T *World bibliography of bibliographies* 181, 190
Bibliographies 8, 21, 34, 53, 57, 62, 68-9, 74, 127, 128, 195-7, 278; of periodicals and newspapers 55, 62-75, 81-3. *See also* Bio-bibliographies; Indexes; titles of individual bibliographies, *eg, Cumulative book index, British union-catalogue of periodicals*
Bio-bibliographies 168. *See also* titles of individual bio-bibliographies, *eg,* M Arnim *Internationale Personalbibliographie*
Biographic approach to enquiries 95-7, 113-4, 124, 128, 134-5, 136, 139, 140-1, 202-4
Biographical dictionaries 7, 114, 157, 163-8, 169-75, 182-4, 191, 193, 197, 200, 204-5, 209, 209-10, 257. *See also* titles of individual biographical dictionaries, *eg, Dictionary of national biography*
Biographical directory of the American Congress 182
Biographical indexes *see* Indexes, Biographical
Biography 114, 116, 149-213, 218-9, 235, 261, 264, 278
Biography index 158, 159, 163, 165, 173, 186, 191, 204, 209, 211, 212
Birbeck College calendar 170
Birmingham, Bishop of (case 112) 164
'Black bottom' (case 91) 135-6
Bliss, A J *A dictionary of foreign words and phrases in current English* 148
Blue guides (Muirhead) 245, 246, 249, 270
Boase, F *Modern English biography* 159-60, 187, 192, 197, 204, 211
Bodmer, John George (case 131) 191-3
Book review digest 49-50, 115
Book review index, 49, 50
Book reviews 47, 49, 115
Book titles 127-30, 143
Books and memory (case 58) 94-5
Books in English 51
Books in print 77, 128, 245, 268

Chartists (case 125) 180-2
Charts 214, 224, 248, 249
Chevalier, C U *Répertoire des sources historiques du moyen age: biobibliographie* 191
Chi é 163
China's space programme (case 49) 84-5
Chronological table of the statutes 273
Church of England year book 275
Classification 10, 11, 35
Cokayne, G E *The complete peerage* 198
Collected biography 182
Collier's encyclopedia 46-7, 55, 56, 259, 267, 271, 274
Colour television (case 44) 77-8
Columbia encyclopaedia 249, 269, 274
Columbia Lippincott gazetteer of the world 216, 219, 221, 223, 226, 227, 229, 230, 231, 232, 237-8, 238, 240, 247, 248
Colvin, H M *Biographical dictionary of English architects* 182
Commonwealth universities yearbook 170, 274
Complete peerage, The 198
Computer classification of finger prints (case 16) 30-1
Computers *see* Mechanisation
Concise dictionary of national biography 139, 187, 189, 204, 205
Concise Oxford dictionary 56, 76, 147, 154, 168, 259, 266, 275, 276
Concise Oxford dictionary of quotations 126
Concordances 92-3
Concrete ships (case 20) 36-8
Conference proceedings 59
Conrad, B *Famous last words* 97
Contemporary authors 186
Continuous welded rails (case 34) 57
Courtney, W P *A bibliography of Samuel Johnson* 255
Craig, William (case 104) 154-5
Crane, R S and Kaye, F B *A census of British newspapers and periodicals, 1620-1800* 83
Cranfield, G A *A handlist of English newspapers and periodicals, 1700-1760* 256

Crockford's clerical directory 159, 160, 171, 182, 197
Crone, J S *A concise dictionary of Irish biography* 162
Cumulated fiction index 50
Cumulative book index 11, 20, 32, 33, 34, 38, 45, 47, 51, 68, 77, 115, 128, 206, 245, 260, 268. *See also United States catalog*
Cumulative book list 17, 45, 245
Current biography 177, 177-8, 193, 204, 210, 212

'Dark day' (case 32) 55
Date approach to enquiries 43-5, 171, 188, 189, 190, 200-1, 251, 252
Davidoff, D *A world treasury of proverbs from twenty-five languages* 145
Davidson, John (case 124) 178-9
Debrett's peerage, baronetage, knightage, and companionage 73, 150, 186, 198
Depopulation (case 149) 217-8
Derelict land reclamation (case 15) 29
Diaries 180, 195, 196-7
Dictionaries 12, 42, 54-6, 87, 104, 125, 126, 130, 132, 135-6, 144, 232, 233, 257, 265-6, 274, 278; of biography *see* Biographical dictionaries; of places *see* Gazetteers; of proverbs *see* Proverbs, Book of; of quotations *see* Quotations, Book of. *See also* titles of individual dictionaries, *eg, Oxford English dictionary*
Dictionary of American biography 134, 166, 168, 205, 207
Dictionary of American English 131, 135
Dictionary of national biography 98, 124, 150, 151, 152, 156, 159, 160, 161, 166, 167, 168, 169, 170, 171, 176, 183, 187, 189-90, 192, 194, 196, 198, 199, 202, 203, 207, 208, 209, 211, 212, 234-5, 264, 277. *See also* Institute of Historical Research *Corrections and additions to the Dictionary of national biography*
Dictionary of New Zealand biography 166
Dictionary of Welsh biography 166

284

287

Stevenson, B *Book of Shakespeare quotations* 92
Stevenson, B *Home book of bible quotations* 92
Stoker, Bram (case 110) 162-3
Strathaven (case 163) 236
Street directories *see* Local directories
Subject enquiries 78, 155-8, 261
Subject guide to books in print 11, 20, 34, 47, 56, 268
Subject headings *see* Indexes
Subject index to New serial titles 74
Subject index to periodicals see Library Association *Subject index to periodicals*
Subject indexes *see* Indexes
Suffolk celebrities 200
Sukarnapura (case 166) 238-9
Survey of London 269-70
Symbols 258-9

Tang (case 177) 257-8
'Teach your grandmother to suck eggs' (case 81) 122-3
Teachers of history in the universities of the United Kingdom 184
Technical reports *see* Research reports
Telephone directories 12, 208
'Tennis, anyone?' (case 92) 136-7
'There'll always be an England' (case 69) 108-9
Thieme-Becker *Allgemeines Lexikon der bildenden Künstler* 183
'Thin end of the wedge' (case 80) 121-2
'Thin red line' (case 62) 100-1
Thomas, Dylan, Last words of (case 60) 97-8
Times see Index to the Times, Palmer's index to the Times
Times atlas of the world 214, 215, 218, 222, 224, 227, 228, 229, 235, 237, 238-9, 240, 241, 247, 248
Times index-gazetteer of the world 215, 219, 223, 224, 226, 227, 230, 232, 238
Times tercentenary handlist of English and Welsh newspapers 73, 82, 83, 256
Titles of books 127-30, 143
Titles of periodicals 44-5, 55, 68

Torrington-street (case 169) 242-3
Town directories *see* Local directories
Trade directories 262
Trade journals 20, 61, 66, 262-3
Trade marks 272
Translated phrases, proverbs, and quotations 89, 99, 101-2, 107, 130, 144-6
Translated place-names 225, 228
Transliterated place-names 228
Trelawny of the 'Wells' (case 31) 53-4
Twentieth century authors 151, 163, 186, 209
'Twenty-six soldiers of lead' (case 75) 115-6

Ulrich's international periodicals directory 64, 65, 66, 68, 69, 70, 74
Ultrasonic guidance aids for the blind (case 17) 31-2
Union list of serials 65, 67, 69, 70, 72, 73-4, 83, 84, 256, 268
Union lists *see* Location lists
United States catalog 245. *See also Cumulative book index*
'Uptight' (case 96) 141-2

Van Buren, M *Quotations for special occasions* 118
Vertical files 232
Victoria County History 188, 200, 220, 233
Voting lists *see* Electoral registers

Walford, A J *Guide to reference material* 35, 36, 46, 54, 60, 79, 83, 93, 112, 120, 144, 147, 197, 255, 259
War games magazines (case 37) 64-5
Ward, W S *Index and finding list of serials published in the British Isles, 1789-1832* 84
Waugh, Evelyn (case 102) 151-2
Weather forecasting (case 23) 41-2
Webster's biographical dictionary 150, 156, 157, 159, 162, 168, 172, 173, 174, 175, 183, 187, 191, 197, 199, 207, 209
Webster's geographical dictionary 216, 219, 221, 223, 225, 226, 230, 231, 232, 234, 238, 239, 247

Webster's new international dictionary (second edition) 55, 258, 258-9, 266-7, 275, 276

Webster's third new international dictionary 34, 55, 56, 76, 126, 128, 132, 135, 136, 141, 143, 148, 257, 258, 259-60, 266, 267, 271, 274, 276

Weed, K K and R P Bond *Studies of British newspapers and periodicals from their beginning to 1800* 256

Wentworth, H and S B Flexner *Dictionary of American slang* 131-2, 141, 142, 143

Wer ist wer 163, 165, 176

'What Manchester thinks today . . .' (case 93) 138-9

Whitaker's almanack 84, 202, 232, 269

Whitaker's cumulative book list see Cumulative book list

White's conspectus of American biography 197

Whittick, A *Symbols, signs and their meanings* 259

Who knows—and what 205

Who really is who 164

Who's who 17, 24, 73, 150, 151, 152, 153, 154, 155, 157, 163, 164, 164-5, 169, 170, 176, 186, 187, 194, 196, 207, 210

Who's who in America 150-1, 163, 164, 165, 177, 185, 208

Who's who in art 157, 212

Who's who in Germany 165, 176

Who's who in the midwest 200

Who's who in the theatre 134-5

Who's who in the world 152-3, 155, 157, 165, 172, 200,

Who was who 151, 163, 169, 169-70, 170, 171, 190, 207, 209

Who was who in America 134

Wie ist dat 163

Wilde, Oscar (case 162) 234-5

Wilding, N and P Laundy *An encyclopaedia of Parliament* 208, 273

Willing's press guide 63, 64, 65, 66, 67, 69, 70, 74, 81

Wimborne newspaper (case 47) 81-2

Winchell, C M *Guide to reference works* 35, 54, 93, 144, 147, 259

Woman Member of Parliament, First (case 141) 207-8

Woodworth, D *Guide to current British journals* 48, 63, 64, 65, 66, 67, 69, 74, 262

Words 275-7, 278

Words and phrases index 111, 115, 121, 127, 128, 142-3, 148

World almanac 79, 232

World list of scientific periodicals 69, 70

World of learning 274

World who's who in commerce and industry 183

World who's who in science 184

Writers *see* Authors

Writings on British history 181

Yard measure (case 137) 201-2

Yasnaya Polyana (case 150) 218

Year-book of wireless telegraphy and telephony 252

Yearbooks 12, 78, 79, 198, 231, 249, 252, 262, 275. *See also* titles of individual yearbooks, *eg, Statesman's year-book*

Yoknapatawpha County (case 165) 237-8

Young's modulus (case 178) 258

Yo-yo (case 186) 271-2